ROSA'S SONG

The Life and Ministry of Rosa Page Welch

ROSA'S SONG

THE LIFE AND MINISTRY

OF

ROSA PAGE WELCH

Compiled and Written

by

Oma Lou Myers

Edited by Guin Tuckett

ISBN: 0-8272-3210-1

Myers, Oma Lou. *Rosa's Song*

Library of Congress Catalog Card Number 84-1882 1. Welch, Rosa Page. 2. Afro-American Christians (Disciples of Christ)—Biography. 3. Afro-American missionaries—Biography. 4. Gospel musicians—United States—Biography. I. Tuckett, Guin Ream. II. Title. BX7343.W44M94 1984 286.6'092'4 (B)

Cover design by Mel Lovings

Printed in the United States of America

CONTENTS

DEDICATION

In deep gratitude, I should like to dedicate this book in loving memory to my beloved Mother, Elizabeth Heath Page for her spiritual guidance; to my delightful father, Robert Page for whom I credit most of my musical talent, and in honor of my dear sister Lesly Page Smith and my supportive family—my husband Ewing C. Welch, and our children Lenne Welch Freeman and Gale Page Welch.

Foreword

What began as an urgent request for Rosa Page Welch to write her own story has become my task. It had long been my desire to tell Rosa's story. I often joked that if I could get her on a slow boat to China, I might be able to hang on to her coattails long enough to get the necessary information. It had taken over seven years of taping during the infrequent intervals when she was available. Even in her so-called retirement she is still serving humanity.

So, here I am, a northern white, writing the story of a close friend, a southern black. There is no color line, just the problem of expression. After attempting other approaches, I decided to try to step into her shoes—an almost impossible task. Yet this makes it more alive and meaningful, for it enables me to incorporate her own experiences and feelings as she related them to me. Much of the story is taken directly from the taped interviews. Additional information was obtained from letters and tributes written by relatives and friends from across the nation and around the world. Other sources were numerous newspaper clippings, magazine articles, church bulletins, and concert programs.

The information regarding her paternal background came to her primarily through her great-uncle Joshua Page, who had served as deputy county sheriff of Claiborne County in Mississippi during reconstruction days after the Civil War. Her maternal background was communicated to her by her mother, the oldest daughter in a sharecropper family.

A cousin, Mr. H. B. Dotson, of Vicksburg, Mississippi, shared on tape the following data regarding the unique characteristics of the Page family. It sheds light and insight upon her life.

"The beginning stream of the Page family had some of the noble and outstanding characteristics you find in those who are still living. You find they are people who stand out above the ordinary. In whatever they have done, they are people of high achievement. They had been hard workers and persistent people all though the years. They have been productive and valiant people . . . the type of people who didn't have to be coaxed but people who moved out into the front. They are people who sought excellence, and they have achieved it in the face of many kinds of odds or hardships. There is no stopping them; nothing seems to hinder them. They were outstanding in both music and drama."

Thus, Rosa Page Welch comes from an ethnic minority. The experiences, hardships, and mistreatment of her grandparents during and following a devastating Civil War left their mark on her life. Her childhood memories linger and enrich her character. It was during those years that a deep Christian faith was formed as she grew up in Port Gibson, Mississippi, under the influence of a deeply devoted Christian mother and under constant involvement in the life of the church. Rosa Page has been one of those persistent American Negroes who, in spite of many obstacles, grasped every opportunity to become and achieve what she believed to be God's will and purpose for her life. As her life drama unfolds, we come to know her as a true servant of God, ministering to people of all races, nations, and creeds.

As in all biographies, it is impossible to write a complete life history, but what has been recorded is caught up under the title, *Rosa's Song*.

Oma Lou Myers

INTRODUCTION

I have been asked to introduce Rosa Page Welch and, according to *Webster's College Edition*, introduction means "prepare the way for." I can do this because I have "prepared the way for" Rosa many times, and our friendship has spanned most of our adult years.

I am delighted to add my words to those of Oma Lou Myers' Foreword. She had given an unbelievable demonstration of Christian love as she put herself in the background and "stepped into Rosa's shoes," recording what Rosa and others have said. No one can estimate the hours of dedicated labor she has invested in order that we may have a record of Rosa's beautiful life.

How does one "introduce" a person who is so well known—this amazing Christian singer and ambassador of goodwill?

I knew Rosa first when I was a young minister's wife in Ohio. She captivated young and old alike as she spoke and sang her way into the hearts of all who heard her. When we heard Rosa sing and speak we wanted others to hear her. As doors of leadership opened to me, state and nationally, I felt it was my privilege to tell others about her. We had her come for programs in state and national board meetings, in conferences, and in our national assemblies. Leaders in other denominations heard her sing, and she was invited to sing and speak for them. She became a Disciple ambassador-at-large and Rosa Page Welch became a household name. She was beloved, admired, and respected for her beautiful spirit and courage. I have often said that she did more for bettering race relations and understanding than almost anyone I have known.

Rosa and I shared many experiences together—board meetings, assemblies—representing our denominations at the World Council of Churches Assembly in Evanston, traveling as a team across western Kentucky with a Japanese Christian, Mrs. Munakata. Rich were the times we spent in my home—sharing and planning together.

Rosa Page Welch with Mossie Wyker

Introduce Rosa Page Welch? I am convinced I can do it only one way:

At the National Assembly of United Church Women, Atlantic City, 1953, I presided as national president. It was my responsibility to introduce President Dwight Eisenhower. It was the easiest introduction I ever made. From the podium, and after a short prayer, I simply said, "Ladies and gentlemen, the President of the United States."

Now, 1984, to the hundreds of friends and loved ones across the nation and around the world, and to all who will read her book:

"Ladies and gentlemen, Rosa Page Welch, ambassador of goodwill, who through the years has promoted Christian unity as her theme song and torn away walls of prejudice."

May God continue to bless and use her.

Mossie Allman Wyker

1

Born to Be Free

EVERY human being's life begins in the quarry from which it is mined. For me, Port Gibson in Claiborne County, Mississippi, was that quarry. My ancestors were among those who learned of their freedom when President Lincoln issued his Emancipation Proclamation in 1865. Slaves were given their freedom; my great-grandparents were suddenly free persons. Yet they were left without the kind of assurance or financial means to get them started in a life of their own. It had been a devastating war that had torn families apart, laid waste great plantations, and buried homes and cities in their own smoldering ashes. The assassination of President Lincoln left the South insecure and vulnerable to the carpet-baggers.

Black people, like all of God's children, were born to be free. Those pursuing a better life moved out into what appeared to be new opportunities, new ventures of faith. Others, hesitating and fearful, chose to remain, to help pick up the pieces of a broken and bleeding South. A new nation was being born, and black people had to do their part in the rebuilding. Those days and months and years were known as the Reconstruction Period. Some blacks chose to claim the names of their white masters and landlords and move out on their own journey of faith, establishing new ways of living, building homes, churches, and schools for their families' education.

It was during those reconstruction days that churches and schools were built for the children of the former slaves, and it was during this time that my great-uncle Joshua Page—Uncle Josh—served the town of Port

Gibson as deputy sheriff. He was a tough and fearless person who didn't "take anything off nobody!" Yet, to all of us he was kindhearted. He was a source of information regarding our family heritage and history. Many times, as a child, I sat on his knee and listened eagerly to his reminiscing. It was here that I learned the almost unbelievable tale of the Page Place Riot.

I shiver as I try to recapture it now. The Pages, four brothers and a number of sisters and other relatives who had moved out of Virginia, owned and operated a plantation of several hundred acres a few miles outside Port Gibson. It was the envy of white people who lived there. An evil plot grew out of that jealousy and desire to get rid of the Pages, who, in their affluence, were tilling their cotton fields and educating their children by private tutors, all of whom lived on the plantation. I remember Uncle Josh telling what a great marksman his brother, Harrison Page, proved to be as he was able to save most of the family members during the riot. Somehow, by the grace of God, the Page family got word that white men had dug a huge hole in the ground and intended to attack the plantation, kill off the Pages, and use the hole as their grave.

In the meantime, my great-uncle Harrison and the other men barricaded the big plantation home and waited for the planned riot to take place. Great-uncle Harrison was able to kill the offenders. It was the treacherous whites who later were buried in the huge hole.

During the siege a little lad by the name of Robert Page was hiding with his grandfather in the hayloft of a barn on their plantation. Realizing it was going to be destroyed, the grandfather managed to get the young lad to safety, but lost his own life in the burning barn. Robert Page, later to be my papa, grew up in the town of Port Gibson while most of the other Pages left and moved to Louisiana.

Now we turn to my Mama's ancestry. Grandpa Wesley and Grandma Jo (Josephine) Heath lived and worked as sharecroppers at the edge of the big cotton fields some eight or ten miles outside Port Gibson. It was there that the Heaths lived in a two-room shack with cotton growing almost up to the front door. They had a small piece of land in the back for a garden, some chickens, and a hog to butcher.

Wesley Heath was a tall, handsome, light-skinned man with straight black hair and blue eyes. His father had been a white slaveholder and, like many landowners, took advantage of the slave wives who nursed not only their own mulatto children, but oftentimes the babies of the white southern wives. Wesley Heath detested that part of his past, but he proudly walked and worked beside his beloved black wife, Josephine, who was part Creek Indian. They had a family of fifteen children; my mother was the oldest.

Like other sharecroppers, they eked out a bare existence. Their family was fed and held together by a strong Christian faith and love for each other. They were constantly under the overbearing scrutiny of the landowner, who also owned the commissary where they got their groceries and daily needs. Always at the end of the year they came up short and were indebted to the landowner. It was a cruel and unjustifiable existence. Wesley and Josephine and the older children were expected to be hoeing and picking the cotton from dawn until dark. Grandma Jo would work in the fields up to the last day before the next child was born.

My grandparents sent their two oldest girls, Elizabeth and Sissy, into Port Gibson to live with a friend to get some schooling.

I remember Mama telling how they, as teenagers, would gather with all the other townspeople to listen to the town band. It was here that Elizabeth Heath met a talented young musician who not only directed the town band and orchestra but who played the violin beautifully. This young man was Robert Page, the little lad who had escaped the Page Place Riot and had grown up in Port Gibson. He was also the town barber as well as an employee of a Jewish man, Mr. Herman Marx, who owned the local mortuary and furniture store.

The small Mississippi town of Port Gibson was more fortunate than most of the southern towns involved in the demonic ravages of the Civil War. It was spared by General Grant, who, after riding through the streets, was impressed by one called "Church Street" which was literally lined with church buildings of several denominations. At one end of Church Street, closest to the bridge, was one Presbyterian Church, in particular, whose lofty steeple reached high above the tree tops and surrounding buildings. At its very pinnacle was a gold-colored hand with a forefinger pointing heavenward into blue skies above. "Too beautiful to burn" were his words, thus saving the town.

The churches formed a phalanx of symbolic meaning, representing a community that weekly needed worship. These services included the singing of the great old hymns and Negro spirituals, adding their influences to the preaching and teaching to the community of Christian believers. One of these congregations was our own family's Christian Church where, in all probability, my parents, Robert Page and Elizabeth Heath, exchanged their wedding vows. This marriage and this Christian Church from that moment on determined to a great extent what was to be my own faith, my future, and my whole life!

It was shortly after the turn of the century that I was born. As was the custom in black families, I was called "Sister" since I was the oldest girl born in the family. This name stayed with me all during my childhood years. It was a term of endearment, but it also enhanced the closeness of family ties and loving relationships. A midwife assisted in my birth and two years later helped bring my sister, Lesly, into our family.

Our little house was three rooms, fastened together in a long building called a "shot gun" structure. I remember well our pretending that the upper step was a keyboard as we sat on the lower step with our feet under the porch, beating out church hymns and Negro spirituals that we learned at church and school. I remember what a hard time I had knocking that riser board off to get our feet through. I loved the old hymns and memorized them quickly. With Lesly, the neighbor kids, and my cousins we played church. Thus, we lived out, through imagination and practice, the daily experiences that were weaving the warp and woof of our growth and culture, both religious and educational.

Mama, in her quiet but firm way, saw to it that we attended Sunday school and church, not only on Sunday, both morning and evening, but Thursday night prayer meetings as well.

Papa worked hard as a barber and for the undertaker, Mr. Marx. He then spent a lot of evenings and weekends leading the band and orchestra to entertain townfolk and fun-lovers. Papa wasn't too involved in church work, but with his music he continued to influence my whole life and the lives of the whole family. He had a beautiful tenor voice, and one of the thrills of my life was when I had the opportunity of singing with him at a special program at the First Baptist Church.

One of the things I recall very vividly is that of wanting to learn to play the organ which was the instrument of the time. That childhood dream was reinforced late one afternoon when Papa backed the old pickup (from the furniture store of Mr. Marx) to the front door of our home. I couldn't believe my eyes when he began to unload an old dusty organ. Lawd, have mercy, I was so pleased. Papa chuckled and told us how Mr. Marx had sent him out to a certain delinquent client's home to bring the organ back for reselling. When Mr. Marx saw how badly damaged and uncared for it was, he would not let Papa unload it but told him to take it out to the trash pile! Conveniently, the designated trash pile was beyond our home, so Papa felt free to claim the old instrument. He was handy about fixing things, especially anything that had to do with music; so after several nights of working on it, he managed to get the organ to play. Lesly and I took turns holding the coal oil lamp by which he worked. We had to change hands often because of the weight of the lamp. The close contact with my father in this musical way gave me greater appreciation for him than perhaps any other experiences.

When the organ was finished, we girls were given music lessons by Aunt Mary Johnson. She knew our poverty, but saw in us some potential; so she didn't charge anything for the lessons.

I was a precocious child with a serious interest in school, church, and music. I sometimes didn't live up to my best intentions. I shall never forget what happened one day! Mama sewed for people, and one time

14

Mama sent me uptown to buy some thread. I knew one store which did not sell thread, but it did sell candy, and I wanted a piece of candy; so I spent the money and went back home and I took the candy in to Mama.

Mama asked, "What is this you bring me?"

I answered, "Didn't you tell me to get this?"

Mama countered, "You know I didn't I told you to go get a spool of white thread. You take this right back to that store and tell that man you got the wrong thing and you go buy me the thread."

I started to cry and I confessed, "Mama, he already gave me a free piece of candy and I've eaten it."

She said, "I don't care if you have. You'd better go back and get my money back and go buy that thread."

Mama was usually kind and loving, but this time she sent me out to get a switch (a branch of a peach tree) so that I might be properly punished. I can still feel the sting of its branches. Lawd, have mercy—she laid it on! Because of my pranks and sometimes downright disobedience, I got many more whippings than did my less rambunctious sister, Lesly. I loved Mama dearly so the feeling of guilt brought on by my behavior was more keenly felt than the sting of the branch of the peach tree.

I felt envy sometimes, too, such as the time a prominent evangelist came for a protracted meeting. He came to eat at our house as he usually did. Normally the meat of the meal was fried chicken, served with mashed potatoes and, possibly, custard pie. He required a tall glass of buttermilk, another of cold tea, and a third one of milk or water. He was a huge man with an enormous appetite. I can still feel the pangs of hunger and envy as I drew back the curtain dividing the rooms of our little home and peeked out to watch and wait, hoping at least the chicken neck would be left for the "second table." There were moments when I felt like hating him; then later when he would preach so convincingly and profoundly, I'd find myself eager to learn more from the Good Book and actually admired him.

Once during a three-week protracted meetings with the Rev. B. C. Calvert preaching, there was an ingathering of twenty to twenty-five folk who made their confessions of faith and went to the bayou immediately for baptism. This was always an exciting time for me as a child, for I didn't quite understand about all the "dippin'" under the water. The preacher and elders immersed the candidates, naming them one by one "in the name of the Father, the Son, and the Holy Ghost!" Later, I learned the symbolism of it all, and it took on a new meaning.

I shall never forget one funny episode that took place at the close of one such meeting. Following the church services, we all walked about a half mile to the river for the baptism of what seemed a great number of folk. Everybody was singing "Shall We Gather at the River?" "Lord, I Want to be a Christian," "What a Friend We Have in Jesus," and other well-known hymns. The crowd of worshipers stood on the banks of the river and listened to an elder read the favorite text, Romans, while the elders began to usher each candidate, one by one, down into the water. It was scary to see Brother Brown, our pastor, lower each one backwards beneath the surface of the water. It was a hot day, but a gentle breeze drifted across the water. As we stood on the river bank, partially in the shade of the trees, the heat seemed more endurable, and we forgot how hot it really was. Among those to be baptized were a mother and two daughters, terribly big and fat. The mother's protruding stomach surfaced above the water until the minister laid his large hand upon it and submerged it. I got tickled and nudged Lesly who stood beside me, and we began to giggle. Mama, who was standing right behind us, pressed warning fingers into our shaking shoulders, and we suddenly remembered it was a sacred occasion. Later, when we reached home, our little house shook with laughter as Mama shared the episode with Papa. He had grown up in the Methodist Church and chuckled continuously as Mama related the amusing part of the experience.

Mama was a deeply religious person and saw to it that we understood the meaning of faith, repentance, and baptism. We knew that her faith ran silent and deep.

2

Burdened Down, Lord

AMONG the highlights of my childhood were those times Lesly and I got to go to see Grandpa Wesley and Grandma Jo. It was always in the summer, and we walked those dusty roads that circled in and around the cotton fields. Eventually, after several hours of walking and occasionally resting by the roadside, we would come to the front door of the cabin. We were always welcomed and loved.

Grandma Jo was a tall, well-built woman, who somehow was always able to manage the big family. She must have planned well to have survived—keeping the home together, the children fed and clothed, and taking her place much of the time beside Grandpa Wesley as they labored in the cotton fields from dawn till dark. Lawd, have mercy! I don't know how she ever did it unless it was because she taught all the children to take responsibility for the cooking, gardening, and working in the fields. She had one baby right after the other. I remember being too small to hoe cotton, so Lesly and I would stay with the smallest children at the end of the fields. We would be attacked by gnats. Could they ever sting and bite! How we would rejoice in the late mornings and evenings when we could go to the house and help some of the older girls prepare the meals.

Grandpa Wesley not only worked hard himself but taught his children to work in the fields. He was serious, but kind and loving to his own family, Grandma Jo, and all of us grandchildren.

We'd be very tired at the end of the day, but by the time we had gone to the house and cleaned up and eaten supper, we were refreshed and ready to go to the protracted meetings every night. There was one week in the Baptist Church, then one week in the Methodist Church and, before fall, always a revival in the Christian Church. Sometimes we rode in the wagon, sometimes we walked if there was moonlight. Long, Bible-filled sermons were preached by those visiting evangelists, and our hearts beat high with the syncopation of the spirituals. I think my favorite ones were "Steal Away" and "Lord, I Want to Be a Christian."

I always looked forward to the country church dinners on Sunday when everybody filled buckets and baskets with fried chicken, homemade bread, pies and cakes. It was during these experiences that I felt the beauty of all the denominations working together.

One of the enjoyable things about going to Grandpa and Grandma's humble home was getting to sleep on pallets on the floor. All the girls slept in one-half of a room, divided by a quilt that Grandma Jo hung up to separate us from the boys. There was no time for foolishness, for after being at church till late and knowing we had to get up early—Lawd, have mercy, how we slept!

In spite of all the fun we had on Grandpa's farm, we were keenly aware that Grandpa didn't have much time to spend with us. Occasionally, his face seemed so drawn and his shoulders more stooped than would be normal for a man in his early forties. The heavy, hard, endless work and constant concern for his large family took its toll. Yet his faith and that of his loving wife and children made life bearable. Like many Negroes, he looked toward a heavenly home where life would be joyous and he would be truly free. As he hoed, he often hummed the old melody called "Heaben."

By the middle of August we had returned from Grandpa's and began to look forward to going to school. Of all the teachers I ever had, Mrs. Richardson was my favorite. She was a motherly type who made us want to learn.

I remember our next-door neighbors, Mr. Milton Quigless and his wife Mary. They were Methodists and he sang in the choir. He was such a nice neighbor, but his wife was sort of cantankerous at times. She and Papa didn't get along well. It must have been when Mrs. Richardson was my teacher that she had a program with the kids in her room. This was the first program I was ever in. I liked to try everything. I liked to whistle and Mr. Quigless used to say, "A girl should not whistle, Sister!"

He had a beautiful tenor voice and one day he said to me, "I want to teach you a little song."

He taught me this little song without an instrument.

They called me Raggedy Pat
By my clothes and my hat
Because they are all tattered and torn.

While roaming the streets
I do not look neat.
I'm struggling for Mother and I.
Chorus:
Flowers! Bouquets! Flowers!
I cry while roaming the street
I do not look neat
I'm struggling for Mother and I.

There was a second stanza which just fitted my Dad. It said something about drinking and all. Mrs. Richardson had me dressed in a kind of raggedy dress. When I first came out, all the children laughed, which embarrassed and frightened me. I became teary-eyed. Poor Mama was sitting there wondering if I was going to sing; so were the teachers and everybody else. Mrs. Richardson looked at me; I knew I couldn't let her down and I knew I couldn't let Mama down, so I just straightened up and sang that song. I looked the part, and some of the people in the audience were crying. Mr. Quigless was so proud of me because he had taught me the song. He saw me as that "Flower Girl." It was a program I'll always remember.

There were certain times when children could bring their teacher a gift, especially at Christmastime. Mama never had any money for us to buy gifts. On one occasion I wanted to have a gift, not only because other children were giving Mrs. Richardson presents, but because I just loved her so much. We didn't live very far from the creek that the rich residents used for a city dump. I went down to the dump to try to find something. I found a tall, slender vase, glinting in the sun. Oh, it was so beautiful, such gorgeous colors. However, one of the edges was chipped, which was probably why it was discarded from a well-to-do white home. Breathlessly, I rushed home to wash and polish it. When I showed it to Mama, telling her what I wanted to do with it, she was reluctant, but she finally let me take it to Mrs. Richardson.

It was sometime later, as I grew older, that I was allowed to go into her house, a far larger and better house than most of us had. I remember going into the living room and on the mantel. over the fireplace, was the tall, slender, chipped vase I had given her. I was thrilled to think that she really thought enough of my gift to put it there and keep it so long! Early summer usually brought a company of gypsies who camped at the edge of town. They loved to hear the band concerts led by Papa. In fact, he had the privilege of playing for a wedding they had. Townspeople looked on from a distance as the ceremony was conducted and a wedding feast was prepared.

Much as I loved school, I was always glad when summer came, bringing downpours of rain with sharp lightning and rolling thunder.

Mama never let us stay outdoors when a big storm came up for fear we would be struck by lightning. Summer also meant hot and humid days. We dipped old sheets and towels and stretched them across the screen doors and windows at night. It seemed as if we were busier with all kinds of things. Papa with his band had the responsibility of escorting a funeral procession out to the cemetery at the edge of Port Gibson. I can still hear the melody "Flee as a Bird to the Mountain." Funerals were always sad; yet, there was something about the way Papa directed the band that gave one a feeling of triumph and victory.

Death seemed so final. An elderly woman called Aunt Kitty, who served as sexton of the Negro Baptist Church, would loudly ring their church bell whenever someone died, tolling out the somber message. I hated the sound of that bell and was reminded of it the night my Grandpa Wesley died. It didn't seem possible. He was so young that he hadn't even grayed yet, and Grandma Jo was only forty years old. Mama and Aunt Sissy wept silently, occasionally expressing their grief with a cry of "Lawd, have mercy" as they got us kids ready to go out to the farm. Some neighbor, I think, took us out in a surrey, and we found Grandma Jo almost hysterically screaming out her grief and sorrow. Lesly and I had to stay home with some of Grandma's younger children, so we didn't get to go to the funeral.

Children will be children. Seeing the family horse tethered nearby, someone got the idea to try to ride it. After the enjoyment of that wore off, someone else said, "Let's take it into the house." Being an obedient horse, he stepped right into the living room. But when he spied his image in the mirror on the dresser in the bedroom, he almost went crazy. We had some frightening moments as we tried to calm him down and get him outside again. Just in time, too, because we could see and hear the family returning.

It was a sad day and it threw the burden of the plantation work heavier upon the stout and brave shoulders of Grandma Jo and the older sons. Somehow, additional hard work, combined with a faith in God and love for each other, made it possible. The older boys didn't get much schooling. Fall harvest and spring planting left only three or four months for formal learning. But the boys' meager knowledge of arithmetic soon made it tougher for the greedy landowners to cheat the Heath family.

Grandma Jo never remarried, and as the years wore on she grew slightly bent. Like her faithful husband, Grandpa Wesley, she was burdened down with the daily work and the "never-quite-getting-ahead," but she carried her head proudly, rearing the family the best she could.

Shortly after Grandpa's death, a letter arrived from Great-grandma Hester, announcing her intention to come and be with her daughter Jo and visit us for a short time. She had come occasionally before but never had stayed long, and I always wanted to know her better. I had learned bits about her life from time to time from Mama. Great-grandma Hester had been a slave and had married a Creek Indian. The Indians were not necessarily slaves, yet oftentimes were treated as such. Grandma Jo had the high cheek bones and tall straight stature of her Indian father. This great-grandfather had gone off to fight in the Civil War and Grandmother Hester never saw him again.

Mama always warned us not to ask a lot of questions, which I wanted so much to do, for I was not only curious but interested in any and all ancestors. Great-grandmother Hester married again later and lived several miles away from us. She always came in a surrey, driven by a member of her family. Always she dreaded crossing the bridge that spanned the Bayou Pierre that brought folk and traffic into Port Gibson at the north end of Church Street. She never would ride a train and was scared of crossing that bridge; it was said that she prayed for a mile before approaching, just for safety's sake. Like many other women, she smoked a corncob pipe. I sort of had to get used to that. Lawd, have mercy! I bet that's why Grandma Jo never spanked us when she caught us kids puffing on homemade cigarettes out behind the barn.

There was no place to go out socially except to school or to church. Young men would walk their girls to church, sit with them, and then escort them home again. Sometimes they extended the journey home by going down by the bayou and sitting on the railing of the bridge or strolling deeper into the dark woods.

My mother's sister had a house just like ours and lived right next door. Aunt Sissy had a boy and a girl. We always played together; we had good times. Aunt Sissy's son John and I became good buddies, and Lesly and Aunt Sissy's daughter, Ruby, became buddies. So we used to plot things against each other.

I remember one time, just before the holidays, when all the women in the neighborhood were baking pies and cakes and making goodies for Christmas. Mama and Aunt Sissy were making cakes, and they had to have molasses. We had one little tin bucket, so Mama sent us uptown to have it filled with a nickel's worth of molasses. The storekeeper had a big barrel; he just pulled the stopper and let a nickel's worth of molasses flow out into our bucket.

One of us would take the bucket and say, "I will take this bucket as far as this and then one of you got to take it."

We mapped out how far each was to take it. Finally, we all got stubborn, and no one would carry it.

Ruby, who had it, just set that bucket down, and all four of us went marching back home, nobody with the bucket of molasses.

When we got home Mama asked, "Where is the molasses?"

We all made excuses about taking turns, and when it was Ruby's turn, she wouldn't.

Mama and Aunt Sissy became angry; they said, "You'd better go find that molasses, then all four of you will get a whipping!"

We started back, all mad at each other. We went to the place where we had put the molasses, and there was no bucket! We didn't know who, but we were sure somebody had taken it. We went back home and by the time we got home we were crying because we knew we were going to get a whipping. Then one of us remembered and told Mama, "We think we know where it is. Miss Ada's boy was coming along behind us and we bet that he picked up the bucket and took it."

Mama made us go to the lady's house and, sure enough, the boy had picked it up. Miss Ada gave us our bucket of molasses, and we took it back home. We never fussed about such things again.

Aunt Sissy always took us kids out in the country to pick berries with which she and Mama made jams and jellies for special occasions. Aunt Sissy was a lively person; she had a terrific sense of humor. We liked her because she would take the time to play with us.

Uncle Dan was a favorite uncle on my father's side. I used to pester him a lot. One time a minstrel show came to town, and Uncle Dan took me. There was Bessie Smith, singing the blues. It was a lot of fun, and the tent was filled with people. I was fascinated by Bessie Smith singing the blues! I thought, *This is just what I want to be! I want to be on the stage. I bet I could sing the blues!*

Thereafter, every Monday or so, we had a show—my cousins, my sister, and I. I was Bessie Smith, and I think I sang those blues just about as well as Bessie Smith. I thought I did anyway! I really put in the motions and everything. I thought I knew what I wanted to do.

The little Christian Church served as the hub of the wheel around which most of the family activities and social life turned. There was always choir practice and prayer meeting on Thursday. And, of course, each week there was a Sunday school with a long church service. Brother Brown always extended his hour-long sermons to include five or six illustrations. No matter how long he extended the services, he was our pastor, and we all loved him and his family.

I was particularly fond of his daughter Rosa. She was a beautiful young girl and was an articulate speaker. She was attending Southern Christian Institute, a college for black youth, children of former slaves, in Edwards, Mississippi, established by a group of missionary women. The faculty at that time was northern white teachers.

When I reached my thirteenth birthday, I realized that my childhood days were behind me and that suddenly I was a teenager and growing up.

I found myself reminiscing and pretending that I was Bessie Smith, singing the blues, or Rosa Brown speaking before great audiences. I found myself hoping that Rosa would tell me more about Southern Christian Institute before returning there in September. I wanted to know so many things. I was struggling with the agonies of youth.

So I listened with delight and anticipation that fall as Rosa Brown told our congregation about college opportunities. I found myself musing, "Blessed Jesus, I hope that someday I can be beautiful like Rosa and able to stand up and speak like she can and perhaps even go to SCI!"

I got so I could play the organ and accompany my papa occasionally when he would agree to sing. My biggest thrill was once when we sang together! I shall never forget his beautiful tenor voice. One of the happiest memories of my youth was when Papa was asked to play his violin for a Sunday evening service at the Baptist Church. He had me accompany him on the organ. I remember that we also sang "My Old Kentucky Home" together and I thrilled at his singing.

It was during a revival service when Brother Calvert, the evangelist, was preaching that I got caught up in a powerful sermon on baptism. I had a strong urge to go forward and I did. I can still see Rev. Calvert and Pastor Brown meeting me at the front of the church and hearing my confession that Jesus is the Son of God and I sincerely accepted him as Lord and Savior of my life. Pastor Brown marched all of us two by two down to the Bayou Pierre where we were baptized.

Although Papa participated in church activities, he did not belong. I always felt that someday Papa would join the Christian Church, and Mama and Lesly and I were thrilled one Sunday when he had attended with us, and when Pastor Brown gave the invitation, Papa went down front and confessed his faith. It was decided right after the benediction that the baptism service in the Bayou Pierre would take place about sundown before the evening church service. Again, we walked to the river singing. Mama shed a few tears and murmured a prayer of thanks. I shall never forget that day!

From that time on I began to notice that Papa wasn't taking quite as many out-of-town band or orchestra engagements. He was almost fifty, and his hair was gray at the temples. His face seemed a bit drawn, but he kept on working for Mr. Marx at the furniture store and kept barbering in his downtown shop. He spent more evenings at home, and I liked that!

Sometimes Great-uncle Josh dropped by unexpectedly for a meal or drink of cold buttermilk. Occasionally, he'd bring news of Great-uncle Harrison who had written him from some Eastern state. Great-uncle Harrison even paid Uncle Josh an occasional visit at Port Gibson, disguised as a woman in mourning with a veil down over his face. I always wanted to see him, but Great-uncle Josh kept him in hiding; the townspeople would have killed him if they'd even known, because the escapade of the Page Riot still remained in their memories. In the meantime, white landowners had taken over the Page place. We never got to go up there.

Everyone in Port Gibson honored and respected Great-uncle Josh. He walked with a limp, having been shot in the knee one night while he was serving as the town's deputy sheriff during those reconstruction days following the Civil War.

Papa kept getting thinner and Mama spent more time on her knees in prayer. Then one night, not too long before he died, I overheard him telling Mama, "Lizzie, I don't know how you stayed with me," but Mama's love for Papa had never failed.

Mama continued with her washing and ironing and sewing. By some good fortune, she had saved enough to buy a beautiful piece of material and had made for herself, for the first time in a long while, a new outfit. It was a black and white checkered skirt with a white blouse. We were all getting ready to go to church, and she was putting on her new outfit when the message came that Papa had died! I was sixteen years old at the time.

In those days they didn't have undertaking parlors where they took the body to be viewed; they brought the body right to our house. I slipped in when no one was around to look at him. He didn't look like himself in the face, but when I looked at his hands, I knew it was my papa, for he had very beautiful hands.

After the funeral and we had come back from the cemetery, the minute we came back into the house I was scared; Mama was scared, too! My Grandma Jo had come down to be with us. We had just two bedrooms. Mama and Grandma slept in our room; so Lesly and I had to sleep in that front room and we were scared. This was the room where the casket had been. It took a long time to feel right in that room and I knew why my mother didn't sleep there. Mama finally negotiated with the church for us to be the janitors, and we moved into the parsonage.

The next school year I was to be in Ms. Belle Green's room. I had heard the kids say how mean she was, so I went into her classroom scared. But when I was there a while, I discovered that Ms. Belle Green was positive. She meant for you to get your lessons, and if you didn't get them you were punished. I liked Ms. Green and took pride in seeing how well I could prepare my lessons for her. I guess I learned as much under Ms. Green as under any teacher I had. Then I went on to the tenth grade. Only two years of high school were given to black children in Port Gibson; after the tenth grade we graduated.

When I graduated, we had to have two speeches. One was the Class Day speech and the other a graduation speech. For my Class Day speech, my subject was "History Repeats Itself." By this time I was the only one in my class. The only other time that had happened in our school was when Ms. Belle Green graduated. Ms. Green wrote my speech for me as was the custom. The Class Day was at the school, but the baccalaureate sermon was at my church. Graduation was always in the First Baptist Church because it was the largest church building in town. Mama had made my beautiful graduation dress and, as she sat in the audience, I knew that she felt the pride of any mother who sees her oldest accomplish that kind of education, and wondered what the future held for her daughter.

3

A Lark Leaves Loved Ones

THAT summer of 1917 brought threatening rumblings of what would be known as World War I. Those who remembered the devastating Civil War shuddered. In spite of prayers and the dread of losing loved ones, our nation once more took up arms, confident in President Wilson's affirmation that it was "the war to end all wars." Uneasiness filled the air and bands struck up the patriotic songs like "Over There."

Young men once more were drafted to serve their country. Brave yet tearful goodbyes were said as they boarded troop trains that carried them north to New York to board ships that took them to Europe.

In the midst of this upheaval, my world changed. Things brightened, especially for me, when in midsummer Rosa Brown came home announcing to our church that one of their native daughters, Rosa Page, had been accepted to enter Southern Christian Institute as a student that fall. Lawd, have mercy! One of my long cherished dreams was beginning to unfold.

Packing was easy, for all my earthly possessions, including my personal items, fitted easily into a small trunk. Tears of joy and sadness streamed down my face as I hugged and kissed Mama and Lesly and Aunt Sissy goodbye and boarded the train that took me to Edwards, Mississippi, and to Southern Christian Institute.

Leaving Mama was difficult. She had done so much to make this moment possible. I can still hear her admonishing words, "Sister, Chile, let your word be your bond. Turn the other cheek, and don't hold hatred in your heart. You are going out into a world where you may not even be treated as a human being, but remember the words of Jesus, 'Treat other folk like you wish they'd treat you,' not like they do sometimes."

In my thoughts Southern Christian Institute had seemed miles from Port Gibson, but, as the train clicked away the miles, my reminiscence kept me occupied until the conductor announced that we were approaching Edwards.

As promised, Dr. and Mrs. Lehman had a student meet me and take me temporarily to their lovely home. We went by horse and buggy two miles to the campus. The Lehmans' kind and friendly welcome made me feel at ease, and I found my false fears dissipating. I was soon to learn that faculty women sent down from the North to teach at SCI lived in some of the extra bedrooms. It was the biggest, loveliest house I'd ever seen. It had been plundered and set on fire by Yankee troops who had left during the Civil War. By the grace of God, women who had been living there had escaped into the woods but returned in time to put out the fire and save the lovely old mansion. It stood now as a sentinel at the edge of the campus near the road that connected Jackson and Vicksburg, Mississippi. I loved the beautiful wooded area of some 1265 acres, some of which had been cleared to give space for the building of a two-story classroom, an auditorium made of red brick, and a girls' dormitory. In the basement were storage places as well as music practice rooms.

I was assigned one of the dorm rooms, sharing it with others who came determined to get an education.

My coming to SCI was really my first encounter with white leaders and teachers. They were all such fine Christian people that I, along with the rest of the Negro students, soon came to love them and in turn we felt loved. President Lehman was a powerful and understanding man, dedicated to his task. During the time he was at SCI, white people were not in favor of black people getting a higher education, and when he would leave the campus they threw stones at him. In spite of this, he kept on loving them. He demonstrated to me for the first time the Christian response. Like Stephen in the Bible, silently and inwardly he said, "Lord, do not hold this sin against them."

I was soon to learn that the Christian Women's Board of Missions of the Christian Church (Disciples of Christ) had been active in founding and giving Christian leadership since 1874 to schools like SCI. They recruited students from the Christian churches and sponsored teachers, making it possible for selected blacks to continue their education beyond the tenth grade.

Miss Adeline Hunt, who was a graduate of Hiram College, was the Dean of Women. She was a great influence on my life during my five years at SCI. She helped opened many doors that later proved to be valuable in my career.

Mrs. Lola Delehoy, who at one time served four years as a teacher at SCI and lived in the old mansion during this time, described in a recent interview the beginning days of the Institute. "The vast acres of the pre-Civil War plantation were under cultivation. A lovely Negro couple, Mr. and Mrs. Jacobs, supervised the students in the gardening and farming operations and raised all the food consumed at SCI."

A few Negro parents were able to help finance their children's education at SCI, but most of us didn't have a cent. We worked our way by doing laundry, washing dishes, helping prepare and serve meals three times a day. I poured and took care of all the milk that first year. I also got 15 or 25 cents for washing some of the faculty women's hair occasionally. We lived there through the summer time, too, picking berries, working in the garden, raising vegetables to eat fresh and to can for the winter months. It meant doing a lot of ironing with heavy flat irons heated on a circular rim that held them against the hot stoves. It was hot and it was humid, but we survived. It helped to have clothes sent by the churches in missionary barrels. Most of my clothes came from them.

One day after my first year in school, I was in the hall talking and laughing. Miss Mabel McCurdy, who had just come from New Castle, Pennsylvania, to teach music, heard my voice above the others and said, "Whose voice is that I hear?"

Miss Hunt said, "It's Rosa Page."

"Oh," she said, "her voice sounds musical; she really ought to study voice."

So they discussed this. Miss Hunt knew my mother had absolutely no money, so she wrote to a Mrs. Potts, a white woman from Chattanooga and told her about me and about my needs.

Mrs. Potts had the money there for both my voice and piano lessons. The study time was fun for I enjoyed every voice lesson and kept taking piano, too. Because of Miss McCurdy's interest and motivation, I often accompanied groups as well as soloists. The humbling thought that one dear Christian lady in Chattanooga, without even seeing or hearing me sing, was investing money for four years of training, made me work harder, practice at every spare minute, and aspire more enthusiastically toward becoming a concert singer.

Just before Easter break, during my second year at SCI, Rosa Brown came by and told me the sad news that her father, Brother Brown, had died. It was such a shock. I guess I thought he'd always be there as our pastor. Rosa said, and I could hardly believe her, "Mother will pay your way home, too, if you'll go home with me for the funeral and sing for the services."

What an honor. Several of the church people met our train. It was good to see Mama and Lesly and Aunt Sissy again. The funeral was in our little Christian Church on Sunday. I don't think I ever sang any better, and everybody cried and I sang "Goin' Home, Goin' Home, I'm just goin' home," "Steal Away," and Mallotte's "Lord's Prayer." I remember the minister conducting the service spoke on the text, "I have kept the faith." Brother Brown was buried at the same little cemetery at the edge of town where Papa was laid to rest. It was good to be home with my loved ones, but somehow things had changed, and I found myself eager to get back to SCI and my life there.

It was 1919! World War I that was to end all wars, was over. Germany was defeated and the human losses were great on both sides. More white crosses appeared in the local cemeteries as bands played again the patriotic tune of "When Johnnie Comes Marching Home Again," as bodies were returned. It was a disturbing time in history, but I still found it enjoyable to be at Southern Christian Institute.

One of the highlights while I attended Southern Christian Institute was the occasional visit of missionaries. One such occasion was when Mr. and Mrs. Emory Ross and Dr. and Mrs. Pearson came through on their way to Africa as missionaries. I remember those two couples talking to the whole student body one night, and as they sat upon the stage I thought that I had never seen four more beautiful people. I was so excited because they were going to Africa, and I thought, *Oh, some day I wish I could go to Africa. I'd like to be a missionary.*

Mother Ross, as we came to know her, the mother of Emory Ross, came down to SCI about the week before Easter. Every evening after supper while we were all seated in the dining room, she would give a message on Holy Week. She was one of the most interesting "little ole women" you ever saw. Here she was in her late 70s or early 80s, and she told us that she committed to memory something new every day.

Most evenings, we would take a chair and set it out on the lawn for Mother Ross, and we would all gather around her. She would get our attention, and then all of a sudden she would have us laughing so hard with songs such as

Said the Tree to the River,
"I'll fall right across you."
Said the River to the Tree,
"I'll be dammed if you do."

Mother Ross just sat there bubbling over, seeing us laughing so. God bless her!

Her Christian witness, like that of many others, left a definite mark on each of us. I found myself hoping and praying that I could be as Christian and effective as Mother Ross and some of my outstanding teachers.

29

I needed a new dress for Class Day, and my prayers were answered again when my dear teacher friend, Miss Stiling, gave me a beautiful piece of white and yellow checked gingham material. Each of the four graduates participated in the commencement services. Lula Perkins and I sang and also played a piano duet. At one point, I glanced at Mama, sitting in the audience and saw tears of gratitude slipping down her face.

As the excitement of graduation was coming to a close, I suddenly realized anew that my days and opportunities at Southern Christian Institute were coming to an end, too. It meant going out into the world, finding a job, and earning not only my livelihood, but money that would eventually get me onto that concert stage. My mind flashed back to the image of Bessie Smith, blues singer, in the minstrel show back in Port Gibson. I chuckled a bit at the childhood memory, but praised God that she had inspired me to be a singer. I knew that the only profession open to Negro women was teaching and that my first job, at least, would be that of teaching music. Before I ever left the campus, I was given the opportunity to be the voice and piano teacher at Union County Training School at New Albany, Mississippi. Mr. Ford, president of the Institute, talked with me, and upon the recommendation of my voice teacher and President Lehman, I accepted the position.

Again, Miss Stiling was aware of my need for a piano if I were to teach piano lessons during the summertime in Port Gibson. With her help we contacted a music company in New Orleans (a company about whom my great-aunt had told me) and found that we could purchase a good instrument for the sum of $300 including transportation to Port Gibson.

I was so thrilled when Miss Stiling gave me the down payment. In fact, I think she paid for most of it. She knew I didn't have a cent and a piano was a big investment.

The lark had flown from the nest! I had left loved ones at home in Port Gibson and had done a lot of pondering and learning. Now after five long years, I had prepared myself, with God's help and the constant supportive help of so many others, to soar higher into the realm of new opportunities already promised. I was now convinced that what seemed like an impossible dream could be attained with hard work, determination, and deep faith. "With God, all things are possible."

4

Teaching Times and
Wedded Ways

AS I rode back home with Mama to Port Gibson on the train, I realized how much I wanted to teach music. I found my memory chasing back over the years and thanked God for special teachers. If I could teach like they did, I would be content.

Upon arriving at the old parsonage where we had moved after Papa's death, I found a letter from the Rev. B.C. Calvert asking me to serve as song leader and guest soloist during a two-week evangelistic meeting which he would be conducting at First Christian Church, Clarksdale, Mississippi.

This experience assured me that people enjoyed my singing and my song leading. It gave me confidence that I could teach. I knew from the look of joy in Mama's eyes when I arrived home that the piano had come. I started giving neighborhood children piano lessons for a quarter! I was thankful for that opportunity.

The experience that I had in the revival meeting with Rev. Calvert and the eagerness with which children responded to the piano lessons that summer gave me additional courage to begin teaching that fall in Union County Training School.

Adequate arrangements had been made for my living quarters, and I was soon to meet the rest of the faculty and students. They came from Negro churches surrounding that area, and they were eager to prepare for a better life than that of their parents.

I was thrilled with the response of the students at Union County Training School. After a year I was shifted to teach at Piedmont Christian Institute, another Christian college started by the Disciple churches in the Piedmont area at Martinsville, Virginia, where James H. Thomas was president.

After another year of teaching, Dr. Lehman, who helped make assignments to schools where Negro teachers were needed, asked me to take the position opening up at Kentucky Christian Institute in Shepherdville, Kentucky. It was a new school, and Jason Cowan, a former student at SCI, was serving as principal. With his profound skill and interest in the ministry of music, he organized a quartet of two students, himself, and me. We not only sang for the student body, but visited the surrounding Negro Christian Churches (Disciples of Christ) to give concerts and tell of the work of the Institute.

As some doors closed, new doors were swinging open. After three years of teaching, I was thrilled to be asked to teach both voice and piano in my hometown of Port Gibson. I approached it with joy, excitement, and some apprehension.

I saw it as a way of getting Mama moved out of the old parsonage. I started looking around the town for a house to rent. We found one right across the street from a lovely big home; later when the big house burned down, I was able to purchase the lot for $250. With Uncle Josh's help we eventually built a home on it. I shall never forget my dear mama's look and expression as she exclaimed, "Lawd, have mercy! My first new home!"

Townsfolk look at a person differently when she goes back in a professional role. I had to prove myself. As Jesus said, "No prophet is acceptable in his own country." I never had trouble with discipline, and soon won over the kids who came sauntering into the classroom, daring me to try to teach them something! I loved my pupils and was constantly delighted by their promise and potential. I never worked harder in all my life. What I experienced prepared me for my next assignment. The commencement speaker, president of Prentice Industrial Institute was so thrilled with the performance of my pupils that night that he immediately invited me to join the staff of his school as instructor of music. Gratefully, I accepted.

I had a wonderful experience teaching that year at Prentice. When summer came I accepted my Aunt Rosa's invitation to come to Chicago for the summer. Aunt Rosa was my papa's sister. Several of my SCI friends had already gone north to look for work and new adventure.

The church had been so much a part of my life that I almost immediately started attending the Christian Church. It was only a few weeks before I was asked to sing in their big church choir. My interest in participating heightened when I learned that the talented and skilled director was a masterful musician. He not only was capable and fun-loving, but attractive and single!

To my delight, one evening during choir practice a note was passed down to me. Mr. Welch, the director, was asking to take me home. It was thrilling to have such sudden attention, and my spirits soared as we rode the double-decker bus home that night. Welch, as all of his friends called him, was always pleasant and charming and. Lawd, have mercy, I found myself overwhelmed by his attention. So much so, that before I realized it, the summer was over; Welch had proposed marriage, and in my excitement, I had said yes. He realized that I had to return that fall to Prentice, Mississippi, for a second year of teaching.

So I left Chicago, anticipating my return the following June. Yet in my heart I wondered if I was ready for marriage and an entirely different life in the big, exciting city of Chicago. Well, I had a year to think about it. Occasionally, I found myself so thrilled with the response of my students to my singing and teaching that my desires vacillated between a career as a concert singer and the responsibilities of marriage and family. In April, I received a beautiful diamond ring. One chapter of my life was coming to a close, and another just beginning.

I had returned to Port Gibson for a few weeks with Mama before going to Chicago for the wedding. Lesly had gone through SCI and after graduation had begun teaching school in the upper delta of Mississippi. Mama was aging, but what bothered me most was the lonely look in her eyes. Her many hard and difficult years were beginning to tell. She didn't laugh much or visit a lot. There were so many things I wanted her to tell me, but having been reared in Victorian days. Mama didn't know what to say to her daughters about sex or marriage or babies.

Mama worked hard those few weeks to make my beautiful white wedding dress. She was an excellent seamstress! Goodness knows, she'd had plenty of practice all those years as she had sewed constantly for neighbors, friends, and family.

Papa's half-sisters in Chicago were getting beautiful lace and making the bridal veil.

The only thing that marred my joy and excitement of the wedding was that neither Mama nor Lesly was going to be able to attend. It was a sad day when I left them and boarded the train.

I stayed with Aunt Rosa as final preparations for the wedding were made. Church folk and friends, being so fond of Welch, went all out to make the Oakwood Boulevard Christian Church in South Chicago as beautiful as possible for the service. On the evening of June 30, 1927, Welch and I were married.

We were greeted and wished well by hundreds of people. Welch had gone far beyond his financial means to make it a beautiful affair, and I loved it. Yet I felt a twinge of loneliness among so many strangers with so few of my own relatives.

Finally, the wedding reception was over. A friend had promised to take us to the streetcar stop where we boarded and traveled out to my aunt's to change from our wedding attire and finish packing suitcases for the wedding trip by train to Frankford, Missouri. Naturally, I was excited but a bit apprehensive about meeting Welch's mother. When we reached her modest home, we saw her standing in the doorway with a smile on her lips and outstretched arms. She welcomed us by calling out, "Bless you, my children. Come in! Come in!"

We were there five or six days. It was during that trip that I learned more about the college in Missouri where Welch had studied music before transferring to Kentucky State. It was from these schools that Welch had received his degree in music. He was privileged to meet and study under some of the greatest professors of music. Gradually I realized more and more that good fortune had come my way in my meeting and marrying a man who, in his own right, was a great musician and lover of the art.

Much to my delight and surprise as Welch carried me over the threshold of what was to be our home, a small apartment in South Chicago, I caught sight of a beautiful concert grand piano which seemed to take possession of the whole place. I was speechless when he told me it was mine. Lawd, have mercy, what a wedding present!

We stayed in that little apartment on Michigan Avenue for a bit over a year until our daughter, Linnie, was born on August 17, 1928. Needing more room, we found a six-room flat on the third floor of an apartment on Calumet Avenue.

Welch also sold pianos for a large music company in Chicago, and knowing how difficult it would be to move the huge concert grand, he was able to make a trade for a smaller Chickering parlor grand which helped us financially. Arrangements were made so the piano people could pick up the big piano from our kitchenette apartment and deliver the smaller one to our Calumet Avenue flat.

A sweet, elderly Jewish woman, Mrs. Wolfson, was the apartment building owner. Since we had just enough furniture for two rooms, she let us have enough from her apartment to help furnish the other four rooms. I think she let us have all the furniture for $85. We were able to pay about $25 down and finished paying in monthly installments. Since there were three bedrooms and the rent was $60 a month, we were able to get two former SCI students, single fellows, to rent the rooms. That is how we were able to stay there, but the depression was getting worse all the time.

34

Finally, the two young men had to give up their rooms and find some place cheaper so they could make ends meet.

On October 15, 1930, our son, Gale Page, was born. Times were getting tough. Welch had been working for the Armour Meat Packing Company, but his wages were down to $13 a week. He didn't get much for directing the choir either, and it became very difficult to pay the rent, buy the groceries, and besides that, I wasn't well. The depression was oppressive; people were losing their jobs and, in some cases, their homes!

Poor Mrs. Wolfson was really having a difficult time. She came to talk to us and said, "I don't like to have to say this because I know you are having a hard time, but I am almost on the verge of losing the building. In order to save it, I am going to have to ask you to move so that I can try to raise the rent."

We, of course, understood the situation. She had been so nice to us, we knew what she was saying was true, and we sympathized with her.

We finally told our troubles to Mrs. Cooper, an elderly friend from our church, for whom our daughter, Linnie, had been named. She came to us a few days later and said, "If I can get the people out of my house on Giles Avenue because they are not paying me, I will let you move in there until things get better."

Well, I know it wasn't Christian, but I found myself praying that she could get those people out of that house, for it was not easy to get welfare people out. Finally they moved and, Lawd, have mercy, we didn't have to be evicted. Gale was just nine months old when we moved there.

When we moved into the house on Giles Avenue I actually cried. It was the filthiest place I had ever seen! But it was better than being set out on the street; so we went in there thanking the Lord. My poor husband would go to work, come home, and begin scrubbing floors and walls and everything. We wore ourselves out trying to make it livable. Finally, Mrs. Cooper said, "I am about to lose this house anyway, so if you can arrange a way to make payments, I'll just turn it over to you."

We had a wonderful lawyer friend who was a member of one of our white Christian Churches. We talked to him about it; I don't know how he got the taxes reduced, but he did. With what Welch was earning and with a bonus he got, we were able to make the smaller mortgage payments. It provided a home for us and also relieved Mrs. Cooper. We finally paid it off about thirty years later. That house was where our children grew up.

As the days wore on, I found myself restless and at times depressed. I felt I had to give expression to the God-given talents that so many others had helped me develop both at SCI and during the five years of teaching. I felt compelled to justify the many sacrifices my mama made by sewing, ironing, and doing without for herself, and the sacrifices others had made.

I prayed that God would have mercy and help me find a way to express his love with others through my singing and playing.

In spite of economic depression and lack of money, our meeting and knowing the right people at the right time, gave Welch and me and our two children, Linnie and Gale Page, outstanding opportunities to develop our musical skills. In fact, when Linnie was just a tiny baby, Welch's professor of music at Kentucky State, Mr. Nathaniel Dett, came to Chicago to give a concert. Welch went to hear him, of course, and later I got to meet him when he came to our home.

Welch made arrangements for Linnie to study piano with Miss Josephine Innis, who was nationally known and had her studio in southwest Chicago. Linnie had some natural ability and took to the piano like a duck to water.

The Chicago Tribune newspaper sponsored the "Chicagoland Music Festival" which was a contest in different voice ranges. Auditions were held at various sites throughout the city. My husband belonged to a group called the Deep River Quartet and they entered, singing many times as they worked their way to the top. They won first place when they sang at Soldiers Field on the night of the festival.

In the meantime, I read an ad in the local paper where a group of music teachers was giving five voice lessons for less than two dollars. I saved my pennies and started studying with a teacher. He encouraged me to sing with a group where I again met a wonderful friend, Mabel Malarcher, who had a beautiful soprano voice. She had sung in a women's quartet with my cousin in New Orleans and had come to Port Gibson on vacation with my cousin. After the group practice, I was talking with Mabel about how I only had one more voice lesson, and she suggested, "Well, Rosa, why don't you let me take you to my voice teacher, Nakutin, and he will give you an audition; that won't cost you anything. You can see what he thinks about you."

She took me to his studio. Mrs. Nakutin and I had a lot of interesting conversations. She told me a lot about Jews. "You know, Rosa," she said, "Jews and Negroes are distantly kin."

I had never heard that before. Later when I went to the Holy Land, I was so interested because I saw Jewish people who were black and had the same type hair as mine.

Mr. Alexander Nakutin was the best voice teacher I had. In his studio no one ever expressed any racial prejudice, and he had students of all races. His studio was in the Kimball Building in downtown Chicago. I took lessons for a couple years from him. I hadn't been with him very long when it was time for the big Chicagoland Music Festival. I thought that this would be good experience for me, so I entered. I didn't tell Mr. Nakutin until the last minute and he looked shocked! He certainly didn't encourage me, but I have always been adventurous.

The competition started out with sectional contests. On the south side everyone went to a small theater where our names were taken and we were given a number. My number was 14. I couldn't believe my eyes, fifty-eight were sopranos trying out! There was a very pretty light-skinned girl who was all dressed up in a formal. Negro mulattos always got further, so I was sure she would win if any Negro would. We all sang and then they called up the four finalists. I was sitting there never dreaming my number would be called; when the first three were already standing there, I suddenly realized that my number 14 was the fourth one called. I ran up so fast that I forgot my music and had to go back for it. As I joined the mulatto girl and the two whites, I was thinking what a great experience this was. I just knew that there could not be two black winners. Each of us sang again. A white girl was called first, then the beautiful mulatto girl, and then I was called. "Oh, Blessed Jesus." I prayed, "just get me through this!" I won third place—perplexed, but elated!

I could hardly wait to get home and share the good news with Welch for I was ecstatic. He rejoiced with me and, bless his unselfish heart, encouraged me to continue with my voice lessons.

A Tribune newspaper reporter interviewed us all. The story came out in the paper the next morning. I had told him about my church and my student days at SCI and the wonderful musical training I had received. I was so excited I just rambled on and on, wanting to share all the wonderful experiences the Lord had allowed me to have.

Quite by coincidence, Mr. Cahill, vice president of the United Christian Missionary Society in Indianapolis, and his daughter were spending some vacation time in Chicago, and in looking for entertainment had read in the *Chicago Tribune* a notice of the contest. They attended, and the following morning purchased a paper and learned, much to their delight, that their secret judging of the contest was identical to the judges' rating. They, too, had given me third place and were equally surprised to read that I had attended SCI. When Mr. Cahill saw my name in print, he remembered that on one of his visits to the Institute he had seen me as I led the student body in singing in the dining hall.

No doubt seeds had been sown. Seeds, like ideas, are sown only to lie dormant for a while, then germinate, and eventually grow and flourish. Completely unaware of the contact, I didn't dream that it would eventually and significantly affect my whole future.

5

"When He Calls Me . . ."

WINNING the contest was the beginning of a significant change in my thinking. I was especially grateful that Welch rejoiced with me. I continued my lessons with Alexander Nakutin who made no bones about not necessarily approving my entering the contest. Yet, I knew he was pleased that I had done so well.

New ambitions stirred within me and an air of expectancy enveloped my very being. Several days later this feeling was heightened when a letter arrived from the national office of the Christian Church in Indianapolis. The name on the return address was Miss Lura Aspinwall, completely foreign to me, yet I opened the letter with eager anticipation!

It revealed how Mr. Cahill and his daughter had attended the contest in Chicago and had read the article in the morning paper that told something about me. Lura, who was then a national campus worker with the Board of Higher Education of the Disciples of Christ, had approached Mr. Cahill regarding a song leader for a Nebraska Student Conference and he had enthusiastically suggested me. An SCI classmate, Mr. Vance Smith, who was the first black person to take a position in our national office, added his testimony on my ability in song leading. All of this had prompted her letter to me. She wanted to meet me in downtown Chicago for lunch on a certain date; so I answered by return mail that I would be glad to meet her.

I can't describe my feelings as I jolted along on the fast-moving streetcar to learn more of her request to lead singing for a student conference in Nebraska. As I ascended the elevator to the tearoom at Marshall

Field's for the appointed meeting, I was conscious of the fact that I would be looking for a white woman and she for a black and this, too, would enable us to recognize each other. As I left the elevator she was standing nearby to meet me and stepped out to say, "You must be Rosa Page Welch."

Well, I practically fell into her arms as she welcomed me. As we ate together and chatted about the forthcoming conference, she told me that Dr. Harold Fey would be the guest speaker for the event. I learned that Lura had formerly been associated with Dr. Hunt, pastor of the First Christian Church in Lincoln. She had been succeeded by a young woman named Winona Mills, a graduate of Cotner College also located in the capital city. Winona was not only serving in that capacity but was also serving part time with the state organization known as Nebraska Christian Foundation. Both positions gave her the opportunity to work with the students on the campus of the University of Nebraska. This really sounded like a tremendous opportunity! As we talked further and I saw it as a possibility, she said she would check the train schedules and confer with the local church about the finances involved. She would also clear other details about Winona Mills and would let me know when to arrive. So we parted with a feeling of cooperation and a great sense of joy.

What an opportunity! I felt God was calling me and I must answer! In the meantime I not only continued my voice lessons with Nakutin, but got involved with Gertrude Smith Jackson, a fine voice teacher who had organized a group of Negro singers and started a little opera company in South Chicago. As I sang with that group before audiences, and as I sang with our church choir, often as soloist, it gave me a new sense of worth as well as added courage.

As the time for the conference approached, it was with a mixed feeling of joy and apprehension, for it would be the first time I would be facing an all-white audience. Many of them were students attending the University of Nebraska from all over the state. My fears were softened as I recalled that whites are always willing to listen to a black singer. I took courage and boarded the Burlington train that was to take me to Lincoln. As I journeyed along I felt the presence of God with me and the strong feeling that God would be with me in whatever happened. My confidence was secure that all would be well.

In an interview, Winona Mills Gerhart relates the incident from her viewpoint:

"It was to be a first experience for the young people involved in the conference and also for the members of First Christian Church to have a close relationship with a black person, for there were very few Negros at that time in the whole city of Lincoln.

"It was a time in history, 1934, still in depression days and there was a considerable amount of racial prejudice. It was a time when Negroes would not have been accepted as members of the congregation. This made preparations a bit more difficult. Dr. Hunt was most supportive, and he preached meaningful sermons that helped pave the way for Rosa Page's arrival time.

"The church had a three-story educational building with the third floor being given over to the youth department. It had a kitchen where meals could be served for many of the youth activities. The gracious cooperation of the women of the church who offered to assist with meals and cooking gave adequate undergirding to our plans.

"There was the problem of Rosa's housing. With the lack of funds for public housing and the dorms closed for the Thanksgiving break, it became apparent she would need to stay in a private home.

"After the death of my father, my mother and I had continued to live in our big spacious home across the street from the old Cotner College campus. We were also near the Bethany Christian Church. It was quite natural for us to ask her to stay in our home, especially since Dad had built a bigger home so I could feel free to have many student activities there. Mother always welcomed students of all nations so we decided Rosa Page Welch would stay with us. I remember so well making preparations for this very special person and having all sorts of feelings about what it would be like having someone different in our home.

"The congregation as a whole was accepting of the idea, but it was a time for people to think seriously about the teachings of Jesus and what our attitudes as Christians should be on this issue.

"Everything seemed to be ready, and it was with great anticipation that my close friend, Don Gerhart, who was beginning to show me attention, and I drove through a beginning snowstorm to the station to meet Rosa Page's train. As we stood in the snow waiting for the train to come to a stop, we were filled with great emotion! Then the only black woman appeared at the door of the coach closest to us. Dressed in a bright red coat she had a smile that completely allayed any fears we may have had. The warmth and acceptance she radiated enabled us to scoop up her baggage and dash through the near blizzard to Don's car and take her to the church. The meal was about over, Rosa Page Welch was introduced, and she began to lead the group in singing 'Amen, Amen.' Her voice was so thrilling that we soon forgot that she was a black person from Chicago, and we were singing our hearts out in thanksgiving to a God and Father of us all for his wonderous love.

"As the evening moved on we realized we must get to bed and so Don took us to our home in Bethany. I could sense that he, too, had a feeling of warmth and acceptance of Rosa Page, and as we sat parked in our driveway with the snow swirling around us, we had a long intimate conversation about our relationship. We felt so free to share with her our feelings about each other and in terms of the matter of militarism, for at this time it was one of the big issues. I was very much the pacifist, having come out of Union Theological Seminary not too long before, and many people there shared my conviction. Don was in the National Guard, and of course I had many misgivings that I could ever be happy with him if he had that kind of an idea about life in these United States. Rosa Page became an arbitrator between Don and me on this issue. After we went inside the house she was able to talk to me and help me to understand that there are all kinds of people, but that we are all God's children.

"None were affected more intimately than Mother and me. Our anxious days of preparation and apprenhension about receiving Rosa Page in our home had vanished when she came."

Any apprehension or fears I may have had about coming to Lincoln had vanished. If there were any icy barriers left between us, they were soon melted away, for I could sense true acceptance.

It was good to go home. As I entered, Welch and the children were waiting with open arms. I realized at the same time, by the look on his face, that he was quite relieved to have me home. This was the first experience he had had in keeping the children while I was away. In the days that followed I found it quite difficult to share with Welch the experience I had, especially the significance and depth of the spiritual meanings and the realizations that had come to me. I was caught up in an event that had changed my thinking considerably about white people. For the first time I realized that there was such a commonality—such a revelation—that in our all being children of God we are one! We are all alike. We have the same needs, the same desires, and similar ambitions. I found it difficult to share all of this with Welch to the extent that I would have liked.

He encouraged my continuing in the Little Opera in South Chicago as well as my singing in our church choir which he still directed. But beyond that, he wanted me to continue my lessons with Alexander Nakutin. Both Welch and Mr. Nakutin shared my dream of some day being a concert singer. My recent experience had caused me to do some deep thinking regarding my future in relation to my family. I wondered what this would mean if I continued to take opportunities that came my way. Maybe Mama would come and stay and help with the children.

In the midst of that wondering just what God wanted me to do with my voice, with my life, a second letter arrived from Indianapolis. This time the name of Miss Rose Wright was on the return address. Curious, I tore the letter open and much to my delight found the first paragraph relating that Lura Aspinwall had given a glowing report of the effectiveness of my song-leading and the response of the students at the Nebraska conference.

The next paragraph was an invitation for me to come to Logansport, Indiana, to lead singing for an annual midwinter World Fellowship Youth Meet which was scheduled to be held between semesters. Miss Wright explained that these programs were a part of her responsibility as Director of Christian Education in the state of Indiana. She was soon to be succeeded by John Harms from Oklahoma. He was to share in the final planning event, and it was interesting to learn later that similar difficulties arose as they struggled with bringing a Negro leader into their midst.

Rose Wright shared in the following letter how traumatic it was to settle the housing problem; Negroes could not stay in public hotels, and it took courage for individual church members to open up their homes. But finally they did. As Rose Wright shared in a letter:

"Since we were determined that as many nationalities and races as possible should be represented at our World Fellowship Meets, and since Negroes, particularly, were not comfortable in most Indiana churches, we always had to make a special effort to persuade Negro youth to attend. Now, here, all of a sudden we were to have in our next meet a fine soloist and song leader who just happened to be a Negro.

"So it was with great enthusiasm that I reported our good fortune at the first committee meeting of the host church for our next World Fellowship Meet. I said that we would, of course, want nice homes for the two nights our Negro and other nationality groups were to be with us. It was as if some calamity hit everyone at the same time. The foreboding silence was gradually punctured by nervous, low, one-to-one conversations around the room. Finally the minister spoke for all, 'Miss Wright, I'm afraid any Negroes would have to stay overnight in some other town. Negroes have never been allowed to stay over night in our town.'

" 'Oh,' I said, 'I'm sorry, but in that case we will have to take our Youth Meet to some other town.' Again, silence as the committee members looked at each other uneasily. They had been looking forward to the meet. Their church young people wanted it. Finally, one brave Christian woman spoke, 'Miss Wright, I will keep two Negro guests overnight in my home.' Another said, 'I will too.' and they did!"

When I arrived, I sensed that I was a curiosity—a drawing card. To my amazement over three hundred young people were in attendance. The adult leaders were all fine people; one was a Dr. Nakarai, a Japanese professor at Butler Seminary in Indianapolis. I hadn't had the opportunity to know anyone from a foreign country before. I was free to go to any interest group; so I went to his on Japan and was impressed with the way he conducted his group. He talked about Japan, the customs, and the mores of the Japanese people. Then the last fifteen minutes so he said, "Now I am sure you have questions about the Japanese people; so write them out and send them up to me and I will try to answer them."

The response to that approach was tremendous and made me wonder if the same couldn't be done regarding Negroes.

I had the strong feeling, as I did in the Nebraska conference, that God was in the whole situation and that there was a purpose for my being with these precious white young people. I realized that I had the responsibility not only to help the young people sing but also to be a real witness for Jesus, to express his love no matter what happened to me. I used spirituals for the most part in song-leading because I discovered in the very beginning that white people looked upon spirituals as being kind of comedy songs. They did not get the real spiritual impact of them; so I felt it my responsibility to help them get a new appreciation of spirituals for what they are. I would tell them that there were other types of songs that were born in the hearts of black people, that along with the spirituals there were the work songs and there were some play songs, but the spirituals were the ones that I was especially interested in.

I discovered that the spiritual "Amen" was one of the best songs to begin with because of its simplicity and because the group had to remember only one word—and everybody knew that one word, A-a-men. They all liked its lively tune and it just appealed to them. By the time I got through helping them to sing "Amen" and into "It's Me, It's Me, Oh Lord," they really felt the music. By then they had gotten over the strangeness of my being a black song-leader, and I could feel the spirit of the group changing. Others I used were "Let Us Break Bread Together on Our Knees," "Were You There When They Crucified My Lord?" and "The Crucifixion." Then, "Steal Away," which most of them had heard, "Swing Low Sweet Chariot," "Lord, I Want to Be a Christian in My Heart," and "There Is a Balm in Gilead." I also used "Hand Me Down a Silver Trumpet, Gabriel," and "Tramping," "Trying to Make Heav'n My Home." "I Ain't Gonna Study War No More" and "He Is King of Kings, He Is Lord of Lords." Sometimes I started off by singing a solo. I usually chose some of my most used ones, "Sweet Little Jesus Boy," and I would do "The Lord's Prayer" by Mallotte. Often I would lead the group singing "The Lord's Prayer," which is a West Indian chant. I used "Prayer" by Guion several times. The words are so wonderful and they are so fitting that I used it quite often. I had discovered in that student conference in Lincoln and again in the Indiana youth meeting just how powerful music can be.

Near the close of that first World Fellowship Meet, the whole experience reached a high spiritual climax when in a true moment of reconciliation, the pastor of the host church invited me to sing at the morning worship service. During the communion service I was to sing "Were You There When They Crucified My Lord?" and one of my favorites through the years, "Let Us Break Bread Together on Our Knees."

It was a high moment for me and I prayed desperately, "Blessed Jesus, help me to bind together our hearts in Christian love as you speak through me this morning in the singing of these songs." My prayer was answered, for by the close of the communion service, God had sent his spirit into the midst of these wonderful precious young people and adults. His message of love for all mankind and for each of us as children of the same God and Father was evident as even the pastor, who was wiping away a tear, waited a few moments as we all sat in complete silence and knew that Christ was in our midst.

Before I left, John Harms asked if I would be available to lead a week-long youth conference in Indiana in June. I was thrilled at the invitation and in the back of my mind I was thinking how I could use the approach Dr. Nakarai had used.

I didn't tell Welch for some time about the invitation John Harms had extended, but I found myself returning time and again to the idea of writing Mama to see about the possibility of her making her home with us in Chicago. She could be helpful in the care of the children and would relieve Welch of the total responsibility, making it possible for me to accept the challenges and invitations that seemed to be coming my way.

In the meantime, the women's group of the Alden Disciple of Christ Church in Mooresville, Indiana, invited me to present a concert. This was my first appearance before an all-white adult audience. During the intermission a very fine-looking woman came up and introduced herself as Mrs. Summers. She and her husband had been missionaries in India with the Church of the Brethren. She happened to be visiting in Mooresville and came with a friend to the concert. She said to me, "I live in Chicago, too, and I wonder if sometime you would come to one of our Brethren meetings?"

"Oh," I answered quickly, "I would be glad to do that!"

It wasn't long before Mrs. Summers called and invited me to come to the home of Mr. and Mrs. Al Brightbill. Al was one of the outstanding directors of music for congregations and choirs of the Church of the Brethren and was also on the staff of a Brethren Seminary in Chicago. He taught me a great deal about leading group singing. They asked me to sing both before and after the business meeting.

I got to meet the Brightbill family, and from that time on their family and my family became very close friends. I also met Anna Mow at that meeting. She and her husband, Dr. Baxter Mow, and their family had been missionaries in India. Anna Mow was now on the staff of a Brethren Seminary. We became good friends, and I was able to meet many people from India through my association with the Mow family. Whenever someone of importance would be in the Chicago area, she would invite the Indian students from the University of Chicago and from the other colleges nearby to come to her home and meet them. I remember one time in particular that E. Stanley Jones was in town, and the Mows invited a huge group, including me.

When the letter arrived from John Harms with the details for the six-day young people's summer camp at Oakwood Park, I was still thinking that if white young people had a chance to ask questions about Negroes and I could speak frankly and freely as Dr. Nakarai did about Japanese people, it would have the same effect. I wrote to Mr. Harms and told him that I would like to try Dr. Nakarai's method of question-and-answer periods.

Rev. Harms liked the idea and let me use it in one of the first all-camp programs at the beginning of the week. I asked the young people to write questions if they didn't want to ask them before the group. They were as enthusiastic as the kids had been about the Japanese with Dr. Nakarai. It went so well, in fact, that the young people asked for an interest group on the subject with me.

John Harms later shared his perspective of the Oakwood Park Conference in 1935:

"Bringing Rosa Page Welch as a member of the faculty for the Northern Indiana young people's conference meant six days of intimate and informal living together with a black person—unheard of in Indiana at that time. I am sure that if it had been put to a formal vote of any of our governing bodies, that idea would have been vetoed.

"As it turned out we were put to the test on the very first day of the conference. Fortunately, everybody came through, more human and more Christian than before; and I believe that Rosa Page also grew as a result of that experience.

"The dean of women for the conference came to me as the young people were coming for registration and room assignments. There had been some misunderstanding with the camp management about dormitory space which meant a shortage of living quarters. 'We cannot give Rosa Page a room to herself,' she said and suggested that we find space outside the dormitory in the nearby community for her.

"'I thought we had a clear understanding that Rosa Page was to be treated like any other member of the conference,' I reminded her. 'I thought she was to live in the dormitory with other faculty and students.' This posed potential problems because only a few of the group had ever had a peer group conversation with a black person; and none had lived in the intimacy of a dormitory with one! It is enough to say that in spite of crowded facilities, Rosa Page lived in the dormitory. She not only shared a room with the dean of women; she slept with her in a double bed! Finally, it was necessary to assign two girls to the dean's room as well. This may have been a traumatic experience for Rosa Page, and it certainly was for that laywoman from southern Indiana where racial prejudice was more pronounced than in the northern part of the state.

"I have always been grateful for that conference leader. In a dramatic moment of decision she decided to put into practice her Christian belief in the equality of the races in God's sight. She might not have been able to have done that. Indeed, her actions might have delayed or even aborted the wonderful career of Rosa Page Welch as an 'ambassador of goodwill between blacks and whites' which that weeks's conference experience helped to launch."

After everything went so well in northern Indiana, Mr. Harms came to me and said, "Well, Rosa, would you be willing to go down to Martinsville? I don't know what to ask you to expect."

I knew Martinsville, Indiana, like southern Illinois and southern Ohio at that time, could be worse than the heart of Mississippi, but I went.

One large group, along with their beautiful youth leader, were from the church in Huntington, Indiana. They enjoyed the singing and decided that they wanted me to come to their church and meet with all of their youth. John Paul Pack was the pastor, a very open and broad-minded preacher, who knew that the whole church wouldn't feel like the young people did, but let them work it out themselves, showing real wisdom! His wife was the former Adelle White whose father had preached the baccalaureate sermon at Southern Christian Institute the year I graduated. I knew about Huntington, but if these good people were willing to stand by me, I was willing to risk going. However, it wasn't until later that someone told me that the donor of the land on which the Huntington County Courthouse stood had stipulated that if a Negro stayed all night in Huntington the land should revert to the heirs of the original owners. I had no idea I might have been responsible for the county losing its courthouse!

I went alone to Fort Wayne and then took the interurban trolley car to Huntington. I was on this little train, and as we got to the edge of the town everyone was getting off. I was the last one on. As we neared the final stop the conductor turned to me and asked, "Is this where you are going?" He seemed concerned.

I said, "Yes, I am to sing at the Christian Church tonight."

No one was at the station to pick me up and I didn't quite know what to do. I decided not to go into the waiting room as I didn't want to give

46

them a chance to ask me to leave! I know people can get delayed, especially ministers. The ticket agent was walking back and forth looking at me. Finally I went to the door and said, "I'm sorry to disturb you, but I'm expecting the Rev. John Paul Pack of the Christian Church. Would you mind calling him?"

He did so immediately without comment because he wanted me out of there. Rev. Pack came and was so apologetic, but I told him it was all right. He took me to their home and I stayed at the parsonage with them. Everything was so beautiful, and they were so thrilled, for that night I sang to a full and appreciative house. The concert reminded Adelle of the comment her father made upon returning home from Southern Christian Institute: "I heard a young woman sing who has a quality of soul in her voice that I have never heard before."

The next morning Adelle came joyfully up the stairs carrying a tray of delectable food for my breakfast.

"Adelle!" I said, "Girl, I'm not used to this. Nobody, I mean no-o-body, ever served my breakfast in bed before, unless I was sick or something."

She ignored my comment as she placed the tray across my knees and puffed up the pillows at my back. Reassuring me as she looked at me squarely in the eye she said, "Rosa, when I look at you I see no color, for we are sisters under the skin who have the same loving Creator."

6

I Will Answer

THE ever-expanding ripples that are occasioned when a single stone is dropped into a body of water depicts quite well what was happening in my life. The first opportunity for service came to me in the youth conference in Nebraska.

The ripple of contacts extended to national leaders, so I was able then to broaden and deepen my commitment to serve Christ and his church. It was interesting that, as I made the different contacts, not only with national leaders but with state executives of Christian education, more invitations flooded in.

It made me realize more and more that I must persuade Mama to come and live in our home if I was to continue to accept these challenges. Right in the midst of my debating whether to write her a second time, a letter came, and blessed Redeemer, she had made up her mind that her moving to Chicago would be something she could do to help me further my singing career. Mama had a dream that I would use my voice for the furtherance of God's kingdom on earth.

Ripples of opportunities came from the Mows and Brightbills in Chicago. We had become good friends and visited in each other's homes. I even met Madame Pundit's two lovely daughters from India.

Linnie, by this time, was doing very well on the piano and Welch found a wonderful violinist who agreed to teach violin to Gale Page. I was delighted that this particular talent came out in our son. Through him I could see Papa leading the orchestra back home in Port Gibson.

We made arrangements for Mama to come, and she fit into our home beautifully and well. It must have all been part of God's plan.

On one occasion when I was visiting with Sister Anna Mow we talked about Ashrams. In India Ashrams were groups of people who came together to live as a family, to meditate, and to experience a spiritual cleansing. These Ashrams had been organized and promoted by Mahatma Gandhi in India. E. Stanley Jones, a good friend of Gandhi, brought the idea of Ashrams to the United States. He developed a program of study, meditation, prayer, discussion, and listening. No Ashram would be organized where it could not be open to all races and nationalities.

In talking with Sister Anna, I must have revealed my anxious spirit that some day—somehow—some way, I would get to attend an Ashram, for she asked, "Rosa, would you like to attend an Ashram with me?"

"Oh," I said, "I would love to, but I simply cannot swing it financially just now."

"Well," she replied, "I think I can arrange for you to lead the singing in your marvelous way, and that will allow you to attend at no cost."

That is how I attended my first Ashram, held in Green Lake, Wisconsin. I shall always remember E. Stanley Jones that great Christian leader; he influenced my life by his simple yet meaningful understanding of the Holy Spirit. He was really the drawing card, and I went every year after that. The racial situation was being discussed, and they asked me to lead an interest group. We had prayer groups and learned how to lead them. The fellowship was very close; we lived as a family.

My dream of singing at Kimball hall became reality when one night Welch dashed in the door and gasped, "Rosa, Rosa, I have an opportunity of a lifetime for you. My college club wants to sponsor you in a benefit concert in Kimball Hall down in the heart of Chicago." I was so excited that I leaped from my chair and danced around the room, praising God for this opportunity. "Lawd, have mercy!" I had longed for and prayed for such a chance ever since I had started taking voice lessons with Nakutin.

It also meant I must have a new formal; so Mama and I boarded the streetcar and went down to Marshall Field's and found a rich-looking, lovely, deep yellow jersey material which Mama could make into a beautiful evening gown. I do believe Mama was more excited than I. As we rode along on the streetcar going home I heard her say almost to herself, "Lawd have mercy! I never dreamed that I would be making a concert dress for Rosa."

Weeks passed rapidly. At last the hour had come and the great auditorium was filled to capacity. As the curtains opened, I felt that Jesus was standing beside me. I had prayed for God to give me strength and courage to sing my best. Just knowing that Welch and Mama and the children were there made it possible for me to walk out onto the stage with a peace of mind and soul. I felt confident in my new formal Mama had lovingly made me.

For a brief moment I dreamed I was on a great concert stage. Then I was brought back to reality as my accompanist, Gertrude Smith Jackson, played the introduction to the first of a group of arias. It was "Pieta Signore," one of my favorites. A deep silence had fallen over the audience, broken at the close of the aria by what seemed to be thunderous applause. My spirit was lifted higher as I realized they were recognizing my expression of God-given talent. With this kind of acceptance I took new courage as I moved to the next grouping, "Crucifixion," "Are You Ready?", "Down to de Rivah" and "Trouble." Much to my surprise the sound of clapping coming from the upper side seats commenced almost before I had finished the grouping. As I lifted my eyes in that direction, I spotted Linnie and Gale Page just bubbling with enjoyment, their small hands clapping with delight. Following several encores the curtains closed for the final time. I couldn't resist peeking out at the audience, and I saw Mama wiping away tears that had been slipping down her cheeks as they had years ago when I sang "Raggedy Pat" dressed in a tattered dress.

After that we settled back to more normal everyday living. I was glad for the opportunity to look through the mail that had stacked up during those hectic weeks of rehearsal and to sort out my life and thinking. I was so glad to have Mama with us. It was such a joy to know she was enjoying herself and becoming a part of our family.

We were concerned and deeply moved by the tremendous needs and hardships that were being forced upon everyone by the Great Depression. We had endured and survived it so far. It hadn't been easy at times, but somehow God had always helped to see us through. Even though wages were low, Welch still worked for Armour, but there was little money left for anything after the food bill and house payments were made.

The days passed, the excitement of the concert waned a bit. We heard over the radio and through the newspapers the tragic stories of the dust-bowl states. The long years of drought were taking their toll because very little food was being raised on the farms in the nation's breadbasket. While the farmers continued to pray for rain, the poverty-stricken families of the big cities prayed for food, shelter, and jobs.

During this external struggle I was going through a deeper, more soul-searching, indecisive internal conflict. The awareness of a Higher Power persistently tugging at my conscience made me restless and discontent. The lingering ambitions, which were aroused anew by the success of my concert, of singing on stages of great concert halls before applauding crowds was in direct conflict with the experiences I had shared so deeply and meaningfully with those precious young people from our churches. What was it God wanted me to do? What was his purpose to be for my life?

Then one day Mama, keenly aware of my restlessness, said, "Rosa, what's the matter? I can tell that you are struggling with some great decision. Tell me about it, Sister."

We sat down and found ourselves talking more intimately than we had ever done before. It was such a relief to find that I could share my inner feelings with Mama and to hear her say, "Rosa, I prayed all my life that somehow, some day God would see fit to use both you and Lesly in the building of his kingdom here on earth. I hoped you might give time and talent to Christ and his church."

I fell to my knees before Mama and, laying my head in her lap, I cried out, "Oh, Mama, I think you have helped God help me make the decision and that decision is that when God calls I must answer!"

Mama laid her tear-stained cheek against mine and murmured, "Bless you my child, bless you."

In sifting through the accumulated mail, I found two letters of special importance. One was from W. Elbert Starn, Director of Christian Education for the Ohio Christian Missionary Society (the state organization of the Disciples of Christ) located in Cleveland. It would be a chance to renew an acquaintance with Gaines M. Cook who was serving as the state Executive Secretary.

Mr. Starn told me he had visited with John Harms at a meeting in St. Louis. Mr. Harms had recommended me as a person to promote race relations in several Ohio Christian Church meetings.

The reason for his letter was to inquire if I would be interested in going to Ohio, and stated that he and his wife and baby would be attending the annual meeting of the International Council of Religious Education at the Stevens Hotel in Chicago and would be willing to pick me up and drive me to Ohio with them.

I replied that I seldom turned down an invitation to witness for the Lord and yes, I was very interested and willing, and I would plan to ride back to Ohio with them.

The other important letter was from a very talented young pastor whom I had met in one of the summer youth conferences in Indiana. It was none other than A. T. DeGroot, who was then serving as pastor of Park Street Church of Christ in Kalamazoo, Michigan. He accepted my invitation to bring a number of his high school and college age young people to spend a week in Chicago in our home and in the homes of church friends to meet our youth and to participate in the activities of some of their organizations. Blessed Jesus! What a time we had with those young people and the DeGroots.

Years later Mr. DeGroot wrote about this event:

"This was an eye-opening event for our young people! They had lived quite unaware of the achievements and the daily lives of their

51

counterparts. Immediately they wanted to know more about this other part of our USA population, so Rosa later came to Kalamazoo and shared some of her life with the people of our congregation. There were some older eyebrows that were lifted and some reticence on the part of a few to give her a genuine welcome, but with her winsome way and beautiful voice, she won the hearts of a throng of friends.

"Our own family of three—Beulah, my wife, our daughter, Patty—Rose, and I, pursued the opportunity to become better acquainted with the Welch family. When we went to Chicago, we stayed in their home. We must confess that, for us at that time, it was a novel experience to see our two daughters, Patty and Linnie, completely unconcerned about color, play hilariously and finally at some late hour, fall off into sleep! I talked to Mr. Welch about his excellent meat-cutting job, and Beulah conferred long hours with Rosa about affairs of our churches. It was a completely uninhibited experience."

After these delightful exchange visits, Bill Starn called, announcing his arrival in Chicago. His wife, Margaret, and their year-old daughter, Shirley, would be picking me up at the close of his meeting.

We started out for Ohio in their old car. It was a cold winter day and their heater didn't throw out much heat; so the baby and I bundled up in the back seat with a down quilt. The precious baby traveled well, but still the trip was tiring. We decided to stop to eat, and Bill pulled up in front of an eating place. Blacks can usually tell if they are going to be welcome, and I had a feeling this cafe would not welcome me! We were too tired to fool around going from place to place to find one that would serve me so I said, "Just let me carry the baby. They will think I am the nurse."

Most of my white friends simply didn't know what happens to blacks until they travel with one, but we went in and were all served. The embarrassment was usually greater for my white friends than for me, but I surely enjoyed fooling the establishment sometimes.

My first youth meet was in northwestern Ohio at Wauseen in February. Mrs. James D. Wyker was the chairperson for the state youth work committee and was in charge. I stayed with Bertha Park who was the executive secretary of women's work.

Since Bertha Park and Mossie Wyker were both in state positions and wanted to make use of my time in the state, they had all kinds of things lined up to do during that week.

I headquartered with Bertha in Shaker Heights, a very exclusive suburb of Cleveland. Mossie lived farther out and was to pick us up and take us into Cleveland one day for a women's meeting. When we came out, the weather had worsened and Bertha decided she and I should stay at the

Cleveland Hotel so Mossie wouldn't have to take us way out to Bertha's house. Well, I wasn't sure I could stay there, but Bertha went in very confidently. When she didn't return I said to Mossie, "I'm not going to be able to stay here. She is staying in there too long." When she finally came out her face was red and she was just bristling! She told us of the conversation.

"Do you have a twin bedroom?" Bertha asked.

"Yes," was the reply.

"I have a friend and she will stay with me. She is a Negro," Bertha said.

"Oh, she can't stay here. Negroes do not stay in this hotel."

"I am not asking for a separate room. I want her in the same room with me."

"That's all right, but she cannot stay in this hotel. Blacks are not allowed."

Bertha tried everything, but not even the snowstorm would change their mind and she had to leave.

The next decision was to take the interurban train home. Mossie would drop us at the railroad station, and we would eat there. It was crowded but we got in line. By the time we got to the hostess she couldn't afford the time to refuse us; so she took us to a table near the edge of the room, but we could still be seen. A handsome white couple came to a table near us. The man helped the lady with her coat and seated her. They began looking at the menu. All of a sudden one of them looked up and spotted me. I smiled, but they began talking very animatedly to each other. I knew exactly what they were thinking and saying. Sure enough, they got up, put on their coats, and left. I smiled at them and went on eating.

One day I went with Bertha to the office and when it was time for lunch we went to Stouffer's Restaurant which was in the same building. We got up to the cashier, but she informed us, "We don't serve Negroes here." Bertha made the point that most of their staff ate there often and they would remember that Negroes are not served.

The next weekend, Mossie Wyker and I led the youth meet held in the Christian Church in Elyria with 250 registered.

On the day I was to leave Ohio I went with Bertha Park and Mossie Wyker to the state office. When it was time for lunch the entire staff walked over to Stouffer's Restaurant, and we all strode in as if we had always eaten there. Bertha saw my surprised look and winked at me and showed me to a place of honor. This was her way to have the staff thank me for my coming to Ohio, and I couldn't have praised the Lord more for allowing this change of heart to happen.

Enroute back to Chicago, I had arranged to stop off in Crawfords-ville, Indiana, to fulfill a request of former conference young people to participate in their weekend retreat. The young folk at Crawfordsville had asked me to come for their event, but afterwards the church officials wrote me stating they had called a new pastor who hadn't arrived yet. Since I was coming, would I also preach? White people think if a black person can do one thing well, then they are special and can do everything. I was so crazy, I would do anything I was asked to do. Lawd, have mercy, here I was on my way to preach my very first sermon and in a white church! I put the emphasis on the fact that I was a graduate of Southern Christian Institute, explaining that it was one of the earliest projects in home mission work established by the Disciples of Christ churches. I thanked them for the contribution this church, as well as others, had made. The last thing the church leader did was to give me an envelope. I wondered what might be in it but I waited till we were several miles away before I opened it, and there was thirty dollars. O Lord, I never got that much money! I thought, "Oh, I know I wasn't worth that much. I wonder if they made a mistake."

I'll bet I kept that money at least two weeks expecting them to write me and say they were sorry but they had made a mistake.

The Depression had brought about financial difficulties to our Oakwood Boulevard Christian Church, and we were forced to sell it. Fortunately, a Baptist congregation was able to buy it.

While we were looking for another property, a member of our congregation, who belonged to a men's club, allowed us to meet in the club building until we found and were able to buy the church building on Indiana Avenue.

Welch was still directing the choir and our pastor then was the Rev. Richard Davis. We were all delighted that we had found a new church home.

A friend and I had a long talk with our pastor. He went to the church official board and got approval for our ordination.

It was a very meaningful experience that took place during a Sunday morning worship service in 1937. Rev. Davis officiated, giving the charge and the ordination prayer, while the elders of the church participated in the laying on of hands. The experience was beautifully climaxed in our observance of the Lord's Supper.

The spiritual impact of the service deepened my awareness of what it was going to mean for me to give more completely of my talents and my whole life to Christ and his church.

7

Dust — Depression — Disillusionment

THE great dust storms of the Midwest had brought only discouragement, destruction, and disappointment to the farmers. The breadbasket of the world had suddenly eroded into layers of fine silt as it drifted about the farm buildings and forced its way into the homes. Strong winds carried the loose red soil from Oklahoma and Texas clear to the Canadian border. The Depression that we were enduring was diminishing, but it continued to affect the lives of us all. What little the farmers were able to produce brought very few nickels and dimes at the marketplace. Factories had closed, putting thousands of men out of work. The hopelessness of the situation caused desperate people to march on Washington in protest. Franklin Delano Roosevelt's campaign promises kindled great hope and led to his presidential victory. Immediately, things began to shape into some kind of organization. The New Deal, by the late thirties, had put men to work on all kinds of jobs. Bread lines were thinning as people were beginning to find employment. Both the farmer and the factory worker took courage and found new hope.

As the dust clouds continued to roll across the mid-states of our nation, a more serious and threatening cloud was forming on the distant horizon. The Japanese were at war with China, and Hitler was rising to power in Germany, shouting his propaganda about Aryan supremacy.

With the promise of new beginnings in our nation, there seemed to be a resurgence of education and religion. World conditions were ignored.

We were too busy recovering. During this period of new hope in our nation and unrest in the world, my desire to serve the Lord increased.

In the midst of this feeling, a call came from Raymond Baldwin, who was the state executive of Christian education for the Disciples of Christ in Kansas. Having done numerous summer youth conferences under his direction, I was delighted to hear his voice.

Mr. Baldwin was contacting me to see if I would be available to come and serve with him and with the world-renowned missionary, Dr. Royal J. Dye, who had served many years in Africa. He was now in the States on furlough under the auspices of the Home Missions Department of the United Christian Missionary Society. We would be traveling as a team in a program which Mr. Baldwin was calling "Convention on Wheels." Lawd, have mercy! What an opportunity and challenge to work with these two outstanding men. We would be meeting with local people and sharing with them in a worship experience where I would be leading the singing and Dr. Dye would be giving the message. It would mean traveling from town to town, enjoying potluck dinners, and staying in numerous parsonages and homes of church people across Kansas.

I was happy to see that Mama was taking a vital interest in it all. This was not only helping to fulfill her dream for my life, but it was also giving her an added responsibility in our home in caring for Linnie, Gale Page, and Welch as I accepted this kind of lengthy assignment.

As I now reread the diary that I kept of those two weeks when we traveled from town to town in the state of Kansas, I have to smile, at times laugh out loud, and at other times shed a few tears. Welch went with me to the station, and it was with great anticipation that I boarded the train.

I was always pleased when I found a Negro or two in some of the towns and had a chance to talk with them, but my biggest thrill was in renewing friendships with the young people whom I had met in various camps and conferences.

It was surprising to me to meet so many people in the towns with names that immediately had meaning for me.

In Pittsburg, I was a guest in the home of the Dyre Campbells' whose young son George Warren had injured his elbow much like Gale Page had done. I was able to reassure him that it would heal and be much better soon. It was in Chanute that I was pleased to find Mrs. Cobble, the mother of one of our missionaries to Africa. In South Haven, one woman told me I was the first Negro to be in that church and that no Negroes were allowed to stay in town overnight. I told her that I hoped my being there would help the situation. In Pratt I stayed in the nice home of a Negro family. I also met the mother of Stella Tremaine, one of our missionaries to China. It was also in that church that a pretty Negro girl,

Miss Calloway, accompanied me very beautifully. In St. John I met Rev. and Mrs. Rolls, who were former ministers of John Long from SCI. In Sublette we had the privilege of meeting Dr. and Mrs. Lemon, former missionaries to the Philippines, and in Ulysses, Dr. Albert Shelton, missionary to Tibet. In Kingman, I was pleased that a lovely elderly Negro woman came and we sat together. A fine elderly white woman seemed embarrassed by her emotional expression but she was happy and my heart went out to her. She hugged and kissed me and was so glad that she had come.

It had been a tremendous two-week, day-and-night journey across Kansas. Dr. Dye and Raymond Baldwin had been wonderful traveling companions. Dog tired, I boarded the train that took me back to Chicago and my family, with only my train fare as remuneration. Yet, as I jostled along, in my weariness, I found myself pondering many things that had happened. I was deeply grateful for the opportunities God had given us all. As I reflected upon the experiences, I could see the faces of dozens of young people whom I had met in summer camp and conferences. Then, half asleep, I remembered the sweet young girl who was interested in going to SCI and our visit about it. The real satisfaction of a Christian leader comes when youth or adults remember you and want to continue the relationship. I savored the memory of the wonderful people and pastors, some more accepting than others at first, who made up those forty-eight Disciple of Christ congregations.

I began to think how I had come to admire Raymond Baldwin as such a fine Christian leader. I had been impressed by Dr. Dye's deep commitment and marvelous message, but one of the disillusioning things that happened was when I discovered that Dr. Dye was human, too.

In an effort to get people to open their pocketbooks to support missions, he would talk about Africa and his great ministry there, as well as other mission areas. Then he would talk about the South and black people. It infuriated me when he said, "Oh, I can tell you, it is dangerous for a white woman to go through a black neighborhood."

When I got him in the car I had a good talk with him. "Dr. Dye," I said, "I really like you! I appreciate what you tell about Africa and everything, but Dr. Dye, it's more dangerous for black women to walk through a white neighborhood or walk on streets with white men. The white men are the ones who take advantage of black women. That's why we have so many light-skinned Negroes."

It was just like the feeling I got in the car after one of the few traumatic experiences in Kansas, when the pastor's wife in Fredonia put me in a disgracefully furnished attic room. Raymond had sensed something was wrong with me. I had looked at their bedroom and had seen the beautiful coverlets on their bed. I knew by the treatment I received how she really felt about Negroes.

Just thinking about the episode again brought a resurgence of anger and resentment which had filled my whole body that night.

The next morning the woman did serve me breakfast with the others, but as I opened my napkin across my lap, obvious holes again revealed her prejudice. Hiding my embarrassment, I quickly glanced about the table and noticed that my fellow travelers had napkins that were in perfect condition.

The attitude of my hostess began to change somewhat when she learned that the principal of the local junior high school, who had been in the evening service, was so impressed with my song-leading that he invited me to come and speak that morning before a school assembly.

Little did I dream that years later, moments of reconciliation would wipe away the hurt forever. At an International Convention, the pastor's wife, seeing me across the convention hall, literally ran toward me with outstretched arms, crying, "Rosa, forgive me!"

We stood in the embrace of each other's acceptance and forgiveness.

I've always felt it a compliment to be invited by great church leaders to return to serve in a youth camp or to sing a concert in some local church. This feeling was accentuated when a letter arrived from my friend, John Harms.

His letter revealed that he was now the Executive Secretary of the Council of Churches and Christian Education of Maryland-Delaware. He invited me to share in programs in Baltimore, Frederick, and Wilmington, which were still bound by Dixie tradition. Confident that whatever the risk might be, John Harms would stand by me, as he had done in Indiana, I accepted his invitation.

The one event that stands out most vividly in my mind was what happened in Frederick, in an old tradition-bound congregation. All the leaders of the youth conference were seated in the congregation and, as was John Harms' custom, he introduced me last.

Then he whispered, "Rosa, you will have to lead the singing from the balcony."

I ascended the balcony steps and joined the choral group already seated there at the rear of the sanctuary. As I approached the front rail of the balcony, it really looked strange to me for I was looking at everyone's back. I didn't know what was going on, but trusting that the Holy Spirit would guide me, I began to sing, "There Is a Balm in Gilead." Lo and behold, they all turned around in the pews and faced me! I felt they were with me so I went right on giving background on each spiritual before I led them in singing it. Several of my favorites came to mind, and I used "Amen," "Everytime I Feel the Spirit," "We Are Climbing Jacob's Ladder," and "Lord, I Want to Be a Christian." Blessed Jesus! Their singing was as beautiful as any I had ever heard, and I thanked the heavenly Father for their response.

I learned later that the elders had voted that no Negro would be allowed to stand in the chancel of the church. John Harms was told of the decision just before the service where I was to sing. The elders said that a Negro never had and never would stand in the chancel. Strange! This action by the elders came only after they found out I was a Negro. With great insight and wisdom Mr. Harms had saved the situation by quickly deciding I should sing from the balcony. The elders, sensing the spiritual significance of the whole experience, wrestled throughout a prolonged meeting and in the morning were able to tell John that I could lead the singing from the chancel. Lord have mercy!

Dr. Roy Burkhart, a former youth counselor for the International Council of Religious Education, was asked to be a leader in that Frederick conference. At that time he was the pastor of the famous Community Church in Arlington, a wealthy suburb of Columbus, Ohio. Little did I dream that one day I would receive a letter from him, asking if I could come and be a part of his church youth conferences to be held in a beautiful campsite up in Canada. I had never been out of the country before! I was so excited! I replied that I could come.

Canada really made a lasting impression on me in the very first experience I had there.

From the very beginning of my ministry I realized more and more that it was the youth of our churches who, with their daring and adventurous spirits, opened doors that would otherwise have remained closed. These church young people came to know me and enjoy my singing in youth conferences in state after state. They were the ones who enthusiastically and fearlessly invited me to come to their churches. Their pastors, aware of the existence of racial prejudice in our churches, wisely let the youth do the planning while they supported in the background, just as John Paul Pack had done in Huntington.

Among the many young people whom I came to know in those summer youth conferences is one that I shall never forget—Darrell Wolfe, a promising young lad from Hammond, Indiana. I was especially attracted to his beautiful singing voice, and he was one of the first to respond to my efforts to organize small singing groups.

As Darrell recalls:

"I first met this great lady at Lake Wawasee Summer Conference. Although we had good music programs in high school, there was no real spirit for accomplishment. Rosa Page Welch had more charm, more enthusiasm and more excitement than anyone I had ever met before. The singing that she did at conference, as well as the group singing, and the general ability she had to convey a Christian hope was very effective in my own life. No other individual had quite as much influence on my life as did Rosa Page Welch.

"I remember quite well one occasion: some of us pooled our limited resources, borrowed Dad's car, and drove into Chicago to attend one of her concerts. Rosa Page was never just another Negro entertainer! She was not only a teacher of Christian spirit, but also a genuine musician. She was able to hold an audience because of her voice and her interpretation of classical music. The highlight of the visit was the chance to be in the Welch home and to meet her family.

"Rev. and Mrs. Clarence Smail of Valparaiso, Indiana and John Paul Pack, who directed a summer conference, were all graduates of Bethany College and influenced me to enroll there in the fall of 1937. I took with me to West Virginia campus a great deal of ambition and determination to become a minister.

"Knowing how good Rosa Page Welch would be on a college campus, I soon suggested that she be brought to Bethany College to lead a chapel program. I always got such personal satisfaction from people's response to her that I never hesitated to recommend her.

"I distinctly remember Dr. Wilbur Cramblett, President of Bethany College, calling me into his office and asking me about Rosa Page. He very gently explained to me that although they had had Negroes on campus for various programs before, they had never had one stay overnight so had never violated the West Virginia law that no Negro could stay in college dormitories. Since Rosa Page would be there several days and nights, he and Mrs. Cramblett solved that matter by asking her to be a guest in the president's home.

"As usual, Rosa Page completely wrapped the college community around her little finger. Her good nature and ability to implant the Christian hope through her message in song endeared her to the hearts of everyone and affected their outlook and deepened their Christian commitment."

Darrell Wolfe was responsible for persuading Dr. Wilbur Cramblet, then president of Bethany College in West Virginia, to have me visit that campus.

One of the finest places for Christian young people to become acquainted and choose a life mate or lifelong friend is at a summer youth conference. Early one fall I was invited to the wedding of two such fine conferees. Another friend I cherished was Russell Harrison from the Christian Church in Granite City, Illinois. Russell later became the head of the camping program for our total church in North America and was in charge of several hundred camps and conferences for youth of junior high and senior high age, touching thousands of young lives each year.

I had been so busy meeting the many requests of the various white state staffs and local church leaders that I really wasn't conscious of the fact that I hadn't been asked to serve in the church life of my own people. I was made more fully aware of this when I was asked to be a leader in Kentucky for a week. Thomas J. Liggett writes his impressions of that week:

"It was the summer of 1938. Between my sophomore and junior years at Transylvania University, I worked in the camp and conference program of the Christian Church in Kentucky. The regional office asked me how I would feel about working in a Negro summer conference. I admitted that such a possibility had never crossed my mind. With considerable uneasiness and trepidation, I went to that Negro conference to be the leader of recreation and social life. As I entered the campus in Nicholasville where it would be held, I seriously doubted whether I had made the right decision.

"On arrival, the Rev. Robert Peoples (conference director) informed me that I would be working with Mrs. Rosa Page Welch who would be responsible for music and worship. She greeted me warmly, and within minutes had put me at ease. Every word and gesture conveyed a message of total and unreserved acceptance. As the week wore on, I realized that she had sensed my uncertainty on that first day, and in our relationships and common tasks, her spirit of love and dedication had dissolved my fears and overcome the emotional barriers that I had brought with me."

This proved to be one of the richest weeks of my ministry, for in it I realized that black youth had equal potential if only they were given the same opportunities as white youth. The experience gave me renewed determination to help the white youth and adults understand that Negroes are human, too, and deserve the same rights and privileges. From that time on I sang my heart out, convinced in my belief that God's love can heal all separateness and bind all people as his children.

It was in the spring of 1939 that my good friend, A. T. DeGroot, received his Ph.D. from Chicago University. It was good to have the DeGroot family return for an overnight visit, and we all celebrated his achievement.

That fall our paths crossed again deep in Dixie when we all attended the International Convention of Christian Churches in Richmond, Virginia. Again I encountered tense moments when I entered the John Marshall Hotel with Beulah DeGroot. As we approached the doors to the convention banquet, I was denied admission because of the color of my skin. I felt Beulah's whole body become tense as she guided me across the lobby to where her husband stood, visiting with Dr. Roger T. Nooe, president of the convention. In the circle of conversation were other well-known leaders, L. N. D. Wells and C. E. Lemmon. Righteous indignation flared momentarily as Beulah shared with them what had happened. As I've mentioned before, I never failed to marvel at my white friends' reaction in these circumstances.

"A bit of furor ensued, and next morning at the Pension Fund breakfast Negroes were admitted," recalled Dr. DeGroot.

Almost a decade of the Depression and drought had taken its toll, but somehow our country survived. The bold new President Roosevelt dared to initiate programs of work for the unemployed and the discouraged. Many alphabet agencies came into being like the CCC, the NYA, and the WPA (Works Progress Administration) which put 3.5 million men to work building tunnels through mountains for the railroads and highways and sweeping streets in the big cities for $2 a day.

The great truth that "man does not live by bread alone" became evident when for the first time in American history the government began helping the arts and the artists. The WPA hired painters such as Jackson Pollock, writers such as John Steinbeck, and actors such as John Houseman. The arts project was just a small part of the huge WPA, but it became the symbol of the humanity of the New Deal. Many people gained a sense of dignity and a sense of identity in society. People were very grateful for being kept alive. New hope began to surge in the hearts and minds of people.

Mama, bless her, kept our home together by her persistent prayer and good management. She had known poverty most of her life so she stretched the food dollar and, of necessity, continued to sew for the family.

By the grace of God and long hours of hard work, Welch was not among the many laid off at Armour's Meat Packing Company. He continued to enjoy directing the church choir, and together we were able to accept invitations to local churches in and around the Chicago area. Many people seemed surprised to see how we as a Negro couple could so easily be accepted by predominantly white audiences.

I welcomed this interlude to improve and nurture myself and to spend more time with my family and friends.

One of my friends, Winifred Watson Smith, was now attending Chicago Theological Seminary; she and I always enjoyed being together. We shared many laughs as we recalled our experiences in 1938 when we each had leadership responsibilities in a young people's conference in Montana. We were housed in separate cabins, but neither of us had enough covers for the brisk mountain nights, especially for two southern women.

I shall never forget that camp and the contrast of the height and beauty of the mountains. I had never been that high up in my life.

It was a primitive camp so when I was putting my things in the cabin with some of the young people, I thought, *Oh, my goodness, I'll bet snakes will be coming in here.* I was scared.

I mentioned it to some of them and they said, "Oh, no, snakes will not be up this high, but you do need to put your suitcase up on this table or the pack rats will get in it."

Lord have mercy! I was just as scared of rats as of snakes!

It was so cold at night that I wondered what in the world I would do. I became friendly with the camp nurse, who felt sorry for me, and gave me a hot-water bottle every night.

Some of the male faculty members would put on hip boots and go out and catch fish. I was so surprised! We would have trout for breakfast! That was a new thing to me.

I went from the conference to Deer Lodge, Montana, and sang in a program. I met the young single minister, Mr. Harvey C. Hartling, who asked me to sing at his ordination service in a few days. I found out he was the chaplain at the Montana Penitentiary and I was very interested. He asked, "Would you like to go into the prison with me?"

"I would love to," I said. Then I dared to ask, "Do you think they would like to have me to sing for them?"

He said, "Would you?"

I said, "I would love to do that!"

I can hardly describe the feeling that came over me when those huge, heavy, iron doors clanged shut behind us. When those locks clicked, it sent cold chills down my spine. I realized for the first time what it means for every person to be behind prison walls.

The walls in the lobby of the auditorium had beautiful murals painted by the prisoners. We then entered the spacious auditorium and went immediately to the platform. Suddenly the doors opened and the prisoners, with arms folded in front of them, marched in and sat down. Their heads were shaven and no one said a word. In this vast throng of white and Indian men were one or two blacks. Behind them came several women, and finally a group of old men entered who sat in the back. In that group was an old black man.

I had to sing a cappella and my concert lasted about one hour. I did some sacred things and some English things. There was no applause. I figured they were not supposed to.

I announced a group of Negro spirituals and told how they came about. I started out with "Swing Low, Sweet Chariot," and I glanced around and saw that old black man take a big white handkerchief out of his pocket and wipe his eyes, and I thought, *I can't look back there any more.*

When I got through singing that concert, I had applause that has never been surpassed anywhere I have ever sung.

Even after all my travels, that Montana prison concert still remains a mountaintop experience.

Though many years had passed, constant reminiscing with a friend like Winnie added to the joy of having her in our home. The more I shared in the joy of her educational advances, the more I desired to complete my college education and to take more Bible courses. I also yearned to take more voice lessons but could not afford the expense.

Like all the professions, instructors of voice and piano were desperate for more students. A friend, Pauline Osterling, told me the American Conservatory was offering scholarships to vocal students. With a strong sense of anticipation, I submitted my application. To my utter amazement, I was asked to come down for an audition and found an eminent musician, B. Fred Wise, among a group of teachers who were listening to the auditions. Within a few days I was notified that I had received a scholarship to study with Mr. Wise, who was also the vocal instructor at the American Conservatory of Music in downtown Chicago. Blessed Redeemer! My prayers were answered.

8

Voices in a War-Torn World

JUST as we were getting comfortable in our new-found security, like a bolt of lightning, Japanese war planes attacked Pearl Harbor on that day that President Roosevelt said would live in infamy—December 7, 1941.

I was such a pacifist and such a lover of my country that I was torn by the declaration of war. It was a solemn moment when I heard President Roosevelt say, "We now exist in a state of war."

Strange as it may seem, when nations and men are bent upon destroying each other, we find growing out of it a unifying force of cooperation.

It was during this world struggle that churches began to discover common purposes and to combine efforts in worship, education, and mission. Disaster seems to bring a certain unity. State councils of churches, as well as citywide programs, united the cooperating denominations. Life in the churches took on new dimensions. Local churches were influenced by greater numbers of their members attending cooperative leadership events.

Youth conferences and World Fellowship Meets were opening doors for me and calling me into God's ministry. The more they grew, the larger my ministry grew.

When my good friend A. T. DeGroot, now serving on the faculty of Drake University, recommended that I lead the singing for a conference planned by the Fellowship of Reconciliation in Boone, Iowa, I was excited and accepted without a moment's hesitation.

It was here that new voices—voices of great Christian leaders such as F. Laubach, E. Stanley Jones, A. Phillip Randolph, and others—

65

declared their convictions about mending the broken relationships of the world by living out the teachings of Jesus.

One of the thrilling near-home projects was a benefit concert I gave for my home church, now known as the South Side Christian Church. Folks were most appreciative and supportive as once again I sang in Chicago's Auditorium Recital Hall. Critics from *The Chicago Tribune* and *The Chicago Daily News* praised the "delicate timbre" of my voice.

It was summertime and once again youth conferences were called. An invitation to return to eastern Kansas got my consent.

Lois Swick Hawkins, retired professor of Christian Education at Phillips University, who at the time was serving as Director of Christian Education at Central Christian Church in Kansas City, gives the vivid account of one of my first ecumenical experiences:

"In 1942 the Christian Churches of the Greater Kansas City Area had a week's Festival for the world mission of the church. Numerous persons with knowledge and experience were invited to the city where each evening, Sunday through Sunday, they spoke in churches scattered strategically over the city within acceptable distance of all the congregations. Each morning of the week, ministers, their spouses, and other church leaders met for breakfast with the guest leaders, one of whom shared significantly with us each day. These breakfasts were held in the basement of a cafeteria because it was not yet allowed that blacks and whites eat together in "public" places and our constituency included the black churches in the area as well as Rosa Page Welch, a guest singer from Chicago. Each morning Rosa gave the benediction in song.

"Another of the guests was Alexander Paul, who had just returned from China on the first trip of the *Gripsholm*, the Swedish ship attempting to bring home missionaries and western personnel from the terribly troubled area after Pearl Harbor. He had spoken of his experiences of getting out of China, of the suffering he had witnessed, of his tremendous concern for people in the extremely distraught world, of God's presence and of Christians' responsibilities. It was a time of great peril for the whole world and no one was without fears.

"When he concluded, there was not a dry eye in the entire group of some 130 people. After a moment Rosa stood, tears pouring down her face, too. She took a step backward, braced her back against one of the posts which help up the floor above, lifted her face, took several deep breaths, and there came pouring out in beautiful tones Guion's setting for Herman Hagedorn's prayer:

'Lord, in this hour of tumult,
Lord, in this night of fears,
Keep open, oh keep open
My eyes, my heart, my ears . . .'"

I had no more than gotten back to Chicago when at the close of one
of my voice lessons, Professor Wise told me, "Rosa, I have been asked to
lead the singing of the International Convention of Disciples of Christ in
Grand Rapids, Michigan, and I'd like for you to go as my guest soloist!" I
said, "Oh, Mr. Wise, I'd love to go!" My excitement was heightened when
just a few days later a letter arrived from Mrs. Potts, my SCI benefactor,
in Chattanooga, Tennessee, saying she had read in the church paper that I
was to sing at the convention and that she was planning to attend and
how glad she was that at last we would get to meet. She told me what she
would be wearing and wanted to know how I would be dressed in order
to spot me (probably the only black). I was so thrilled at finally getting to
meet this gracious woman who had made possible my musical training.
Yet I dreaded that time for fear I wouldn't meet her expectations of me.

I was wondering where I would stay when a letter came from Genevieve Brown, Executive Secretary of the Adult Missionary Education for
the Disciples of Christ, asking me to share a room with her. O, thank you,
Jesus, for always meeting my needs.

When I arrived in Grand Rapids, Genevieve was right there to meet
me. We were on our way to our room when I turned to see a little white
lady coming toward us asking, "Rosa Page?" I said, "Oh, Mrs. Potts!" I
got to thinking that this would be the first time Mrs. Potts had heard me
sing and I really wanted to do a good job. Well, I went to bed knowing I
was to sing the next evening. I woke up the next morning and I couldn't
talk. I had laryngitis! Lord, have mercy!

Genevieve was so concerned that she called Beulah DeGroot. They
knew how important it was for me to sing, especially since Mrs. Potts
would be there. They tried all kinds of remedies on me. Then someone
told them of an osteopath who had worked on some great singer who had
come to town and had a throat problem; so they took me to him. I don't
know what he did! I was just praying that something would work in time.
They took me back to my room and I stayed until I was to leave for the
evening program. Praise the Lord! I found myself on the platform with
the other leaders of the evening. Hearing the beautiful tenor voice of my
teacher and friend, B. Fred Wise, as he led that great assembly in the
opening hymn buoyed my spirits. Then the president of the convention,
W. A. Shullenberger, preached on the theme, "Voices of the Hour in a
War-Torn World," and it gave me the courage to stand and sing before
my first all-church convention audience. As soloist, I sang "My Mother

Bids Me Bind My Hair," "Were You There?" and "I Walked Today Where Jesus Walked." I didn't know where Mrs. Potts was sitting, but after the closing hymn I discovered her down on the front row. I went to her and said, "Well, Mrs. Potts, I hope you thought it was worth helping me." Mrs. Potts said to me, "It wasn't what I did, Rosa, it was what you were able to accomplish with what I did."

The invitation to visit in the western states in the early forties was another of my dreams realized.

As I sped westward on one of the new Zephyrs out of Chicago, I looked out the window and tried to envision the pioneer families as they traveled in covered wagon trains across the bleak, barren territory where desert and sagebrush were still prevalent.

I found myself wondering how they felt as they confronted what must have seemed insurmountable mountain ranges. Now I was easily crossing the barriers on a modern train, thoroughly enjoying the magnificent view of those gorgeous mountain peaks, Mt. Hood, Mt. Jefferson, and Mt. St. Helens. With the psalmist I could sing, "I will lift up mine eyes unto the hills from whence cometh my help!" This gave me added strength for the task ahead.

I usually spent three to six weeks in an area. Those asking me to come worked carefully and economically to set up my busy schedule during the war years.

I was aware of the vast, booming, war industry. Great ships hovered in the mouth of the beautiful Columbia River, loaded with tons of unknown resources. They could be seen in the Willamette River which cut through the heart of the city of Portland. Many times as I visited with people who lived and worked there, I sensed a feeling of constant fear and dread of an enemy attack. The whole West Coast was vulnerable as it edged up against the great Pacific Ocean.

Mr. E. G. Mosely, a fine Executive Secretary of Christian Education, had invited me to work in summer youth conferences. "Mose," as we all came to call him, had pioneered in youth conferences in the Northwest Region. He was a Cotner College graduate who went West to do his part in the nurturing of youth and adults.

After having met so many beautiful adults and young people, I was thrilled to be asked to go to Washington State to sing a concert in the First Christian Church in Yakima, where Orval D. Peterson was the pastor. The people gave me a great reception. It was such a joy to know the Petersons and to be in their home. I served as songleader for a week-long meeting. Mr. Peterson did the preaching.

I was thrilled to see a black man at the services and when I asked about him they said, "Why, he is a member of our church." I was excited and thankful to God that there was one of our Caucasian churches that had accepted black people.

One of our side trips we took that was most interesting to me was our visit to the Yakima Indian Christian Mission at White Swan, one of our Homeland Ministries. It was a delight to meet Oakley and Lynnette Rhay who were serving on the mission staff there. They had made great preparation for our coming. Lynnette shared a vivid account with me:

"In 1944 many farm laborers were being imported into the Yakima Valley and racial prejudice ran high. David was eleven years old. He was a student at the Yakima Indian Christian Mission. An announcement was made that Rosa Page Welch was coming as a very important guest. When her picture was shown, David said, 'I'm not going to eat with a nigger!'

"In the month that followed we learned all we could about this lovely lady. Negro spirituals were learned and sung with gusto and joy by girls and boys alike—but not by scowling David.

"Finally, on a Saturday, the great day arrived. As the car came down the long driveway we literally prayed that the excitement of the other children and youth would cover David's sullenness.

"The stories she shared were wonderful, but it was in the singing that God spoke to all of us. She was surprised and pleased that we knew so many of the treasures of her race and let our children call out their favorites. In the midst of one session she said, 'I've heard you call one of the boys David. I'd like to sing a special song for him!' Watching David's face as this sensitive, beautiful lady sang 'Little David, Play on Your Harp' was genuine worship, a prayer answered.

"At the close of two days, loaded with all kinds of growing experiences, it was David who was the last to tell her 'goodbye.' As the car went down the long driveway, David paid her the greatest compliment of all. 'You know, she's most as pretty as an Indian!'"

At the youth conference at Seabeck, Washington, I met Allan Lee, a very talented young musician at that time and now the executive for the World Convention of our churches. When I needed someone to accompany me, Allan was the volunteer.

Allan Lee remembers:

"I met Rosa Page Welch while in high school in Washington. In those days we attended CYE Conference at Seabeck. Seabeck was a very special place on the shore of Hood Canal at the foot of the Olympic Mountains. The cabins and main buildings were scattered about the hillside, overlooking a large lagoon. Going up a trail in the trees, one came to the Chapel of the Pines where we attended vesper services each evening at dusk.

"That is where I first heard Rosa Page. I believe she taught a class in worship and the arts and I sat, literally, at her feet in the group as we usually met outside under an evergreen. She was our guest soloist and led 150 or so conferees in singing. How well I remember her singing, 'Steal Away to Jesus,' or, 'Ain't Gonna Study War No More.' But my favorite of them all is one she sang as an a cappella solo called 'The Crucifixion.' I have goose bumps just thinking about it.

"While at Seabeck she sang a concert of some twenty to thirty minutes. She needed someone to accompany her and I was that lucky person. That musical moment at the piano with Rosa Page was the beginning of several opportunities of accompanying her at formal concerts."

After a few days of much needed rest and a visit with my family, I felt the need for my own spiritual renewal and eagerly looked forward to attending the Ashram at Green Lake, Wisconsin, which was always a highlight of my year.

After three years of devastating combat in two major war arenas—the Pacific and Europe—we were moving into booming prosperity once more. The wheels of industry turned faster and faster. Both men and women were working, and everything seemed to beat to the four-word challenge of our President, "We can do it." Hearts were broken and dreams shattered as many people continued to receive the word that their loved ones had been lost in battle. The war waged on, taking its toll.

The whole nation seemed to stir within the womb of prosperity and waited with anticipation for a new world about to be born. We all prayed for peace and the return of our loved ones.

The urgency and the momentum of the times seemed to be reflected in my own schedule as requests continued to be received faster than I could respond. It was early that year that I was invited by the Missouri State Youth Council for speaking and singing engagements in five cities during National Youth Week. The excitement of what happened still lingers in my memory. I never observed a more practical and constructive program of interracial understanding than in Springfield, Missouri. Besides a fine interracial and interdenominational youth organization, they had an excellent interracial council whose members were Negro, Jewish, Japanese-American and Caucasian.

It took real courage and adventure on the part of the sponsors to bring me to the state, but in all those concerts there was not one Jim Crow audience!

W. Elbert Starn recalls the concert in Fulton, Missouri, this way:

"Fulton was in the central part of Missouri which was then referred to as 'little Dixie.' It had been settled principally by persons from Virginia and Kentucky. Some said that this part of Missouri in the 1940s was more 'southern' than the deep south in its attitude toward Negroes. Public schools were segregated. The ministerial association of the city did not include the Negro ministers, nor did the Fulton Council of Churches include Negros in their activities. There were those within the community who were anxious to do what they, as laymen, could do to modify the segregation. In the city there was an interdenominational youth group that cooperated with the Missouri Council of Churches' activities for youth. This council discovered that Mexico, Missouri, was sponsoring Rosa Page Welch in a vocal recital. It was said that this, of course, would not be possible in Fulton because of the attitude of the people. That was a challenge to those youth officers, and they determined that they would have Mrs. Welch in Fulton for a recital.

"They set the date for February 2, 1945, and invited members of the respective congregations to attend. The place chosen for the recital was the George Washington Carver (a black) School.

"Because of our friendship with Mrs. Welch, we invited her to stay in our home. That, we learned later, was very upsetting to some of the citizens of Fulton, including members of my congregation.

"The evening with Mrs. Welch in recital was a very big success. The program was well attended and well received by many of the citizens of the community, both Negro and white. The youth group was happy about its achievement.

Like dominoes stacked for a fall, historical events fell in rapid succession! The first major event came on April 12, 1945, when radios and newspapers screamed the death of President Roosevelt. The President, serving in his fourth term, was dead. We all felt the impact of this great loss. Some, I'm sure, felt that the world would come to an end and the war would be lost—but, immediately, Harry S. Truman stepped into the presidency and took up the mantle. His astute and decisive nature soon cast out the fears and assured us that we had a task to complete—that of winning the war!

The world learned of the death of Hitler. The announcement on May 8 of victory in Europe produced sighs of relief and massive celebrations.

My own appointments multiplied, it seemed, and concert followed concert. I asked the Lord to give me strength to meet the demands.

Agnes Henderson, state Director of Women's Work for the Christian Church in Oklahoma, and Maxine Semones, vice president of the state convention, arranged for a series of concerts in Christian Churches. I remember Blackwell particularly because it had an old ordinance stating that a black person could not stay in town overnight. Jack and Jennie Mae Oliver were serving First Christian Church, and they dared to invite me to do a concert in their church and to be a guest in their home. I had a beautiful experience there with the church filled and people standing.

My next concert was in Ponca City, where Gerald Sias was pastor, and I was privileged to stay in the home of the owner of the meat packing company. After the concert and I had gone to my room he called to me and said, "Mrs. Welch, I know you are tired but won't you come down and visit with us a while?"

As we sat and ate beautiful big oranges they asked me many questions about the racial situation. He asked me how things went in Blackwell. When I told him of the tremendous response, he said that he was pleased because he was born and reared there, and knew that could never have happened when he was growing up.

While I was in Tulsa I stayed with Edward and Maxine Semones and their family. At the dinner table they were discussing flying. I discovered that they owned their own plane and traveled like other families go in a car. I shared my amazement and they said, "Haven't you ever flown?"

"Oh no, I have never been in the air," I replied. Later in the afternoon I looked at my watch and realized that I had to leave to catch a train to Bartlesville, Oklahoma, for my next concert. Maxine spoke up:

"Oh, Rosa, don't worry about the time. Ed is planning to fly you there. It is only a twenty-minute flight. I am to call him at the office in a few minutes to see if the turbulence would prevent flying."

Everyone began to chatter about how great it would be for me to have my first flight. Well, I did not want to fly! Lord, I was so afraid. I did not know the meaning of the word turbulence, but if it would prevent me from flying—I started praying—praying for turbulence! Maxine came back from making her phone call with the announcement: "The weather is good enough to fly. You will have more time now. After he flies you to Bartlesville he will come back and fly me to Dallas where I have a speaking engagement."

As we approached the airport we could see the plane sitting out ready to go. It looked so small and frail. I was so weak that I could hardly get out of the car and walk toward it. They helped me step upon the wing and crawl into the seat. Then he pulled a strap around me and secured me in. Oh, Lord, have mercy! I did not want to go down with that plane! As we took off, Mr. Semones tipped the plane so I could see all the floodwater along the river and I thought, *O Lordy, I can't swim. What am I going to do?*

When the plane landed and he helped me out I felt like getting on my knees and having prayer meeting right there!

Another interesting visit in Oklahoma was when I went to Phillips University in Enid. Dr. G. Edwin Osborne met my train. He was minister of the University Place Church and taught some classes at Phillips. Later a friend, Beth Harader, recalled my visit there:

"Rosa was scheduled to do a concert on a Sunday afternoon. It was hoped that below the Mason-Dixon line Rosa could break down the racial barriers which had been prevalent so many years.

"I was called into the office of Dr. Eugene S. Briggs on the Friday before the concert. He asked, 'Do you realize you are breaking new ground and we have no idea how well Rosa will be received? We have many questions about it, but since she is so readily accepted in the Brotherhood, we'll try it. But don't be surprised if some people walk out of the concert!' The concert, held on Phillips University campus, drew a large crowd. No one walked out. Rosa was called back for encore after encore."

A busy summer followed. I was in Illinois, Indiana, Ohio, Minnesota, Wisconsin, and Tennessee before I went to Arkansas where Paul D. Kennedy, who served as Executive Secretary of Christian Education, had invited me to sing and speak at a summer youth conference. Once again Carroll Lemon was a counselor at this conference, as he was now serving the First Christian Church in Fayetteville, Arkansas.

As often happened, the leaders of the conference were not sure how to handle where I would stay. I told them I would stay in a cabin with the girls.

Lester Bickford, a co-counselor, told me:

"We adults were so concerned about how we could manage to place you in a cabin where you would be 'acceptable' to the girls. And that was not our problem at all—but having to draw straws to decide among the girls, with each begging to have you in her cabin."

So, I was made a co-cabin mother with the other counselor, and we had a very beautiful experience with the girls that week. All I wanted was an opportunity to break down the barriers. Since music is a universal language, my best time for this was when I led singing. I sensed some uneasiness and signs of withdrawing, but I would inject some humor and it helped to break down aloofness.

Grace Shiralshi, who is now Mrs. Kim, shares her perspective:

"We were interned at the Rohwer Relocation Center near McGhee, Arkansas. The state CYF had extended an invitation and camperships for a number of us to attend the week-long conference at Ferncliff, just outside Little Rock.

"It was the first time a black had served on the conference staff and Rosa Page shared herself and her unique talents to the leadership of the camp. I was not in her group but my friend, Joan Ziezler, was. Joan was the daughter of the principal of the elementary school of the relocation center. Her mother was a junior high English instructor and also our Sunday school teacher. Joan was interested in interracial dating as she had a 'crush' on a nisei boy, and found Rosa Page's discussions helpful and reaffirming.

"The whole conference experience was one that I remember as one positive experience that we hold dear from those years of internment."

Carroll Lemon sums up, in his own words, what happened in that camp:

"This was her first young people's conference in the South . . . I can testify to the remarkable, and obvious, and measurable change in attitudes on the part of those young people as the days of the conference went by. Questioning and aloofness and a sense of strangeness melted away until all in the conference loved and respected Rosa Page and heard her message on the meaning of Christian brotherhood and love."

By the time the conference was over and I was riding with Carroll into Fayetteville, he must have felt our friendship secure enough to tell me that he had gotten a phone call from his wife during the week, stating that a lady of his congregation had called expressing fear that I might be staying in their home. She suggested that there was a home in Tincutt, a name for the Negro ghetto in the city, which entertained visiting Negroes. It didn't surprise me at all to hear him say that Mrs. Lemon had plainly and promptly said I would be entertained in their home because of a long-standing friendship.

When they showed me to my room, I fell to my knees by the side of a comfortable bed and thanked the heavenly Father for the experience I had just had with those beautiful Arkansas young people at Ferncliff and for the strong, courageous voices like the Lemons who never failed to speak out where right and justice were concerned. Moments later I arose with the assurance that I could surmount any obstacle, knowing that I was supported by loyal friends, and confident that the love of God surrounds us all.

I could sense that Carroll and his wife were upset and apprehensive about Sunday morning. I offered to stay in the parsonage with the baby but Carroll said, "No, you are to worship with us. It is OK for you to be in Sunday church school the first hour." Carroll regretted that I couldn't participate in the most holy hour of worship, but I understood. I would have my chance in the concert I was to do that afternoon for the student group. The students had prepared well. The concert was overwhelming. Carroll told me later of the feeling that came over him as I sang the "Holy City."

74

"It seemed to me of deep significance when you came to the phrase 'all who would might enter and no one was denied.' This called up in my mind the times when you were denied hotel facilities, comfortable accommodations, appearances in church services, the times when you and other black people found doors shut against you."

Before I left Fayetteville, Carroll commented that my being in the city naturally caused a great deal of controversy. But already a black student had been admitted into law school, sitting behind a rail in classes and using his own library until students saw the absurdity of that separation. Already the university had accepted a football game with another school which had black players. All rejoiced that there were no problems during the game. The university began to recruit black athletes and paved the way for it, the community, and the churches to become integrated. Thereafter, Fayetteville was the first city in the South to integrate its public schools following the Supreme Court decision. Maybe I did help make a crack in the barrier in Fayetteville.

I can remember on the last night how a hush fell over the conference grounds as, under a star-studded sky, we sang "He's Got the Whole World in His Hands" for our closing friendship circle.

Then the momentum of the falling dominoes crashed to a halt with the terrifying news that President Truman had given the order to drop the devastating A-bombs, which literally destroyed Hiroshima and Nagasaki. Its brutal force ended World War II with the surrender of the Japanese on VJ Day, August 14.

Mama had gone back to Mississippi in September to be with Grandma Jo. When Grandma Jo died, I was back in Washington State. I had a real struggle deciding if I should stay on my assignment or go to Port Gibson to be with Mama. I chose to stay, but always regretted that I did not go to my family in that hour.

Honestly, I sometimes felt guilty when I thought of how much I was away from home. But I couldn't help myself. Whenever I received a request and had the time free, I was just driven by a spirit beyond myself.

Gale Page had entered Scattergood Boarding School at West Branch, Iowa, and was a student of violin at the University of Iowa. He was thoroughly happy and so were we. It was an interracial school under the auspices of The Friends United Meeting. Linnie spent Thanksgiving with him. She was graduated from high school and was my accompanist for several concerts. Welch worked hard at the church, on the job, and at home. My sister, Lesly, made a good mama for Linnie when I was gone.

In my date book were 101 major engagements for the year 1945. How many wonderful people I met at each of those places!

9

Agent Of Reconciliation

IN preparation for my long anticipated visit to Chattanooga, Tennessee, the home of my beloved Mrs. Potts, I opened my Bible for inspiration and meditation. I felt definite direction from the Holy Spirit when my attention fell on the fifth chapter of 2 Corinthians. The words that drew my attention led me to ponder anew the real meaning of what God's Word was saying to me about my ministry. I felt added support, not only from my heavenly Father, but from my fellow Christian friends, realizing anew the fact that in Christ we are all messengers of the Good News, agents of reconciliation, and ambassadors for peace.

I was so happy that it would be possible for Linnie, now 18 years old, to go with me as my accompanist. We had great fun and it was gratifying to work out the concert program together.

Going to Chattanooga also meant renewing my relationship with John and Adelle Pack who were now serving the First Christian Church. One fine young woman named Louise, in their congregation, had gone to an Ashram with the Packs. Her father was an outstanding doctor, and the Ashram was the first experience she had ever had with black people on a social level. The Packs had told her about me and after we met we had kept in touch. The reason we were going to Chattanooga was because Louise had asked me to come and give a benefit concert for the black YWCA.

The Baptists had a mission project in the area and Linnie and I were their guests in Bethlehem House. About two hours before the concert that evening, somebody came and brought two huge white boxes with my name on them. I really wondered what they could be and when I opened them there were two of the most exquisite orchids I had ever seen.

We went to Memorial Auditorium to the Little Theatre and, of course, were backstage. We were told that no Negro had performed there before. When I walked out onto the stage to begin the concert I looked at the audience; black and white were all mixed up! I was shocked because you just didn't have any mixed audiences at that time. I found Mrs. Potts sitting on the front row and I was thrilled, for this was the first time she would hear me in a full concert. I was anxious for the concert to be over so I could learn how it happened that here was this mixed audience. Ushers were seating white people on one side and black people on the other when Louise noted what was happening. She said she would help usher and began showing people seats as they came. Nobody left and it was the most beautiful sight I had ever seen.

The principal of the black high school invited me to come over the next morning. John Paul Pack was to give a meditation; so the two of us worked out a joint presentation. They had a black music teacher who led the whole auditorium in singing one or two spirituals I had never heard. She was terrific! I had never heard such singing.

As we were leaving John Paul said to me. "Rosa, I want to ask a favor of you. Tonight our church is having a family church dinner and I would like for you to come and sing for us. I wish I could invite you to come and eat, but you know where we are!"

I said, "Listen, I know exactly what you are talking about! It's all right. Eating is a very small factor. We will plan to arrive at the church about the time you are finished."

Linnie, Louise, and I were to have dinner at the home of the YWCA director. We arrived at the church about the right time. John Paul was giving background for my appearance. It was perfectly proper, for all through the South during those years, southern white people were always willing for blacks to entertain them.

They were all sitting back waiting for me, so I went right up on the platform with John Paul. He introduced me and then I sang. I never prayed so hard for the right songs. I injected some humor and then got them to sing "Amen." That was always a good starter and those people sang it and we had a tremendous time. I sang, "Were You There?" "Sweet Little Jesus Boy," and closed with "Let Us Break Bread Together."

I happened to look over to the edge of the group and there was a little old white lady standing back. She couldn't get up close, but when I looked at her she commented, "I surely did enjoy that singing." I replied, "Oh, I'm so glad you did."

After a while I moved toward her and then she said, "Oh, I liked that singing, but if you were only white!" I threw my arms around her and exclaimed, "What difference does it make? We are all children of God!" She squirmed a little bit but I just held her in my arms.

After they all left, John Paul added, "Rosa, that lady's daughter begged her to go to your concert last night and she refused saying, 'Oh, I wouldn't go anywhere to hear a nigger sing.' She didn't know you were going to be at the church. Her daughter had brought her and she couldn't escape!"

I said to John Paul, "If nothing else had happened the whole time we were in Chattanooga but what happened to that precious old lady, the trip was well worth it."

The amazing thing about it was that I felt God had called me to that situation. I have been in many places where I have seen Negroes become so incensed by the behavior of whites they would rebel. But I have always felt that I was not representing just Rosa Page Welch, but I was representing every black person in America. What happened to me wasn't nearly as important as what could happen to the white people by my having a Christlike attitude. I think about how Jesus was persecuted. They didn't like him either, but he just kept on. More than what was happening to the white people was what was happening to my own soul! I was being cleansed! I'm convinced that God works through people that way. This situation I just told about, proves that one of the greatest needs for us is to try to understand people regardless of race or color. And the best way to understand people is to have some kind of association with them.

I had a memorable experience with James Farmer when we went to Ohio for the Fellowship of Reconciliation to do a week's lecture and concert tour. I used songs about peace and Christian love, both as solos and for group singing. One night the person who was to pick us up after the evening must have forgotten. We ended up sitting in the depot all night long.

Years later when I saw James Farmer again and we were reminiscing, he said that the next time he was with a group and was refused by several places, just for fun, he wrapped a turban around his head and went back to one of the very same hotels and was accepted. My husband told me that at Armour, even Africans and other dark-skinned foreigners could go into the hotels and restaurants, but he, as an American Negro, could not.

As the exciting summer came to an end, I realized that Linnie had matured in many ways. It was now time to send her to college. I was so proud of her musical accomplishments. She had applied at the Oberlin Conservatory of Music in Ohio, and we were awaiting an opening. They had a waiting list and recommended that we seek other places; so Linnie had applied and been accepted at Chapman College in southern California. The thought of her leaving home and going so far away filled me with mixed feelings. How had she grown up so fast? I could now identify with Mama about my leaving home at seventeen to attend SCI.

Just knowing that our good friends, the DeGroots, were living there eased my mother-anxiety somewhat. Dr. DeGroot was teaching at Chapman and I was sure he would look out for Linnie.

We were so grateful when he had again shown his interest in our family by sending Linnie an application for a scholarship. Word soon came that she had been awarded the scholarship and just when we had all arrangements made and she was ready to leave for California, we got word from Oberlin that she could go there. It was a very hard decision, but she went on to Chapman.

Fortunately, I had several engagements in and around Los Angeles, so I was able to visit her soon after the school year began and I stayed a few days with the DeGroots.

After visiting with the DeGroots and getting Linnie settled, I went on to my engagements.

My horizons were widening in my work with the church women. I rejoiced inwardly for their commitment to Christ and his church. My ever-expanding ministry led to other denominations as well. I was delighted when the opportunity came to be with the women in the Presbyterian Church.

It was in talking with Virginia Mackenzie, Presbyterian missionary to Japan, that I learned of the United Council of Church Women. They were to have their Third National Assembly in Grand Rapids in November. She made it sound so good, and I really wanted to go, but I didn't have that kind of money. A woman volunteered to pay all my travel expenses, and I was asked to help lead the singing; so I earned my registration that way.

One of the most amazing things happened at that assembly, which I will never forget. It was just after the war with Japan and no one was allowed to leave the country without General MacArthur's permission. Reverend Mrs. Tamaka Uemura, the pastor of a church in Tokyo that had been destroyed by the bombing, was allowed to come. At this same assembly was Dr. Ilano, a woman doctor from the Philippines. Both of these great women were struggling with how they, each from enemy countries, would appear together. These two women dared to demonstrate their deep Christian witness by agreeing to meet together for prayer before they appeared in front of the assembly. This had a profound effect on the whole conference.

My good friend, Winnie Smith, one of the outstanding and devoted church women of our denomination, was there. Winnie described our reunion:

"When I returned to the States after three and a half years in a concentration camp under the Japanese as a missionary, one of the first persons I saw at our International Convention in Columbus, Ohio, was Rosa Page Welch.

"We threw ourselves into each other's arms and Rosa exclaimed, 'Lawsy me, child! The Lord be praised! I had given you up for dead!'"

The adventurous spirit of youth has always inspired me, and the continued challenges of working with young people led me into deeper ministry. Dennis Savage was such a young man. I had met him in Idaho several years earlier at a youth conference. Now he was serving in our national office. These are some things he recalled:

"Rosa spent much of the summer in youth conferences as a cultural representative for our national office. It was my privilege to be a conference dean, traveling to many states. We were pleased to be together in southern California for three conferences. We had been warned by previous deans that this was one of three areas with the worst behavior problems.

"The youth were sun-tanned, pseudo-sophisticated smarties of Los Angeles and Pasadena. After dealing forthrightly with some mass misbehavior, we had an exciting and rewarding conference.

"One night Rosa gave a concert, and all were deeply moved by her dedicated spirit in testimony and song.

"One sun-tanned youth from a suntan culture of California seriously inquired, 'Do Negroes get suntans?'

"'Of course,' Rosa replied.

"With honest curiosity he queried, 'HOW can they tell?'

"Rosa's eyes danced while she flashed a big smile, 'Why, child! Just like YOU do—when you take OFF your clothes!'

"Uproarious laughter exploded. Rosa had bridged another gap in segregation. Those youth continued to ask all kinds of concerned questions, and attitudes and lives were changed.

"During the third conference, college students and older youth came. It was one of the best conferences possible. The co-president was a cute little brunette from Chapman College, named Mary Lou Khantamour. She sent me into orbit.

"The fall of 1946 I returned to seminary, writing daily letters to Mary Lou at Chapman College. And every day I received a letter. When the students elected Mary Lou to represent them at a post-Christmas conference to organize the Disciples' Student Fellowship to be held in Illinois, I telephoned Rosa and then Mary Lou, asking her to come early and spend Christmas in the Welch home. We announced our engagement day, but it was no surprise to either Rosa or Welch.

"Guests in the Welch home included students, regional, national and world church leaders, and just people. Conversation would ramble in many directions at once, covering a wide variety of topics. Always there came a time when guests would request Rosa to sing. She always responded graciously, but soon had everyone joining in song, It's a good thing that Welches owned the duplex next door, for sometimes the singing, eating, laughing, and talking lasted for hours. No one wanted to leave.

"One day I asked Rosa to meet me for lunch at Stouffer's in downtown Chicago near my office. The hostess politely ushered us to the last table in a dark corner by the kitchen. I politely confronted her, Ma'am, as we came in I noticed an empty table in the front window. We'll sit there, if you don't mind.' With all the haughty, but polite grandeur we could muster, we moved to that table and thoroughly enjoyed our lunch.

"A part of my job was directing United Christian Youth Movement conferences throughout the nation. In 1950 in North Carolina at Lincoln Academy near Kings Mountain young people came from black and white congregations throughout the southeast. Rosa was a popular Christian model for everyone. The president of the conference was a freshman at Davidson College. His parents challenged him that if he came to the conference with 'niggers,' he could not return home, for he would be no son of theirs. He came.

"Rosa had tremendous impact on every youth and adult there. They were living and risking their Christian faith several years before any freedom marches . . .. Many youth said it was their first experience to share deep religious feelings with someone of a different race. There were joy-filled moments and funny situations, too. We were just forming our closing friendship circle when a car wheeled right next to us. A man jumped out and ran to embrace his son. With tears streaming down his cheeks he told all of us, 'Every day your mother and I have been reading our Bible and praying and thinking about you. God seemed to be speaking to us several times through the day that we must change our attitudes. Can you forgive us, son? Can all of you forgive us? It isn't easy to change the way you've been brought up, but we're ready to try.' I thought for a moment we were having a flash flood for tears were spilling down every face. The prodigal father had come to his senses in Christ.

"Two hours later Rosa and I boarded the train for Asheville and Chicago. I was in the air-conditioned pullman car. She was in the old, out-of-date coach with open windows, hot air, and cinders.

"We had agreed to meet in the diner. There had been a recent court ruling that interstate travelers of all races had a right to eat in the dining car. Hostile stares and whispers greeted us as we sat down together, but those black dining stewards served us royally. The black chef and kitchen crew loaded our plates with all kinds of special, delicious food. Our water glasses were refilled after every sip."

Inwardly amused at what was going on, and sensing that Dennis was equally aware of the situation, I momentarily forgot the indignant stares and apparent disapproval of those who were sitting near us in the dining car. I glanced across the table at Dennis and the merriment in his eyes set us off in hilarious laughter. By the time we gained our composure I realized several people had gotten up and left the dining car. As I looked again at my friend I reached across the table and said, "Dennis, I just want you to know, Child, that what you have done so naturally and graciously and sincerely all during these tours together has made possible my own enjoyment and acceptance in many places where I would not have been accepted. I want you to know how wonderful is the feeling one gets knowing that you are safe in someone else's presence. I am sure God will continue to use you to break the barriers that separate his children and I pray that as we continue to serve our Christ we can, by example and witness, demonstrate to the world what the true acceptance and love for all races and all peoples can and should be.

He placed his hand over mine that was clasped in his and said, "God bless you, Rosa; that is my prayer, too."

Dennis continued his recollection:

"Although Rosa had hoped to sing at our wedding, her schedule moved her in another direction. None of us had extra money for travel, so Rosa had a professional recording made which we played at the ceremony. Mary Lou remained in California to complete that quarter of college.

"Mother Page, Rosa, and her sister, Lesly, were always close. They had an intimate understanding and appreciation for one another. Much of Rosa's love for Christ and people was inherited from her Mississippi mother and family.

"The congregation of the South Side Christian Church loved and respected Rosa, but they sometimes felt her suggestions gleaned from her travels were not for them.

"A few critics thought she was hobnobbing too much with the white folks and getting too many of their ideas and ways. The first time I spoke on Youth Sunday at South Side, I was surprised when a staunch member of the congregation unloaded her racial prejudice toward whites on me.

"Rosa and Welch moved into the situation in a tactful, Christian way. Until that moment, I had been ignorant of blacks' feelings toward the white majority. It was a revelation!"

It was a joy to have friends visit us in our home in Chicago. I was always so pleased that Welch and Mama and the children readily accepted the friends who stopped by when they were in the Chicago area.

Such a privilege was hosting the Orval Peterson family from Yakima, Washington, in whose home I had spent so many hours.

Another visitor was my good friend, Jessie Trout, who was serving as the national Executive Secretary for Women's Work in the Christian Church (Disciples of Christ). I had come to know her in many women's events in which we shared leadership responsibility. She spent a night with us and would often call me on the phone when she was in the Chicago area.

One of the most cherished experiences I had was when I served as guest soloist for the Southern Baptist women's annual convention in Memphis, Tennessee. The women from Memphis on the committee for arrangements, housing, etc., wrote me a very sad letter saying, "Mrs. Welch, we have gone to every hotel downtown and we have not been able to find a single one that will take you nor have we found a place for you to eat."

I wrote back, "Please don't worry. If you had found a hotel that would take me or a restaurant where I could eat, I would have been shocked."

Whenever I needed to travel to the southern states on an overnight trip, I would ask John Long, then president of SCI, to get my sleeper reservations for me. The law said those accommodations should be given to me, but the fact was that whenever I tried, they were never available.

The irony of the situation was that after I was seated in the Pullman car and before they made up the beds for the night, the conductor would come through and make up some tale about having to change my accommodations. One particular night I was given a more expensive compartment without charging me another cent just to get me out of the regular Pullman car where there were white people. You see, on a Pullman car you have upper and lower berths, and after they put up the bed, everyone can see who is in the car. I used to laugh about getting better accommodations, but the reason for it made me mad, too. It hurt.

The Memphis committee found me a very nice Negro home in which to stay during my visit in Memphis. In all the publicity they had mentioned my name and that I was singing every evening, but they never said that I was Negro.

They arranged for me to be picked up by cab and told me to come to the side entrance. The Negro driver automatically took me to the back entrance and was hesitant to take me to the side. However, I assured him it was all right and, sure enough, the ladies were awaiting my arrival. We all walked in together, and I could just feel the audience reaction. I looked out over the crowd and saw that each state had a banner with its delegation. I found the Mississippi group, and I prayed hard. When I was introduced, I stood up and sang; then I sat down.

At the close of the morning session a group of excited women were among the first to come up to me and introduce themselves, "We are so glad to see you. We are from Mississippi too." I immediately felt akin to them and thanked the Lord for their expression of warmth and acceptance.

Soon after this Memphis experience, I was excited to be present for Gale Page's graduation from Hannibal, Missouri, High School. I was asked by the principal to present a concert that was sponsored by the PTA.

September 1949 was a busy time for all the family. Gale Page left for Doane College in Crete, Nebraska, where he was a freshman playing in the college band. Linnie was a junior at Roosevelt College in Chicago. At first she was disappointed and unhappy about not returning to Chapman College in Los Angeles, but soon adjusted and enjoyed Roosevelt College.

Having Linnie home and everyone well and busy, I felt compelled to answer a call received from Alaska. Rev. Freeman, whom I had met at one of the Presbyterian conferences, asked me to do a series of concerts in several of their churches and mission stations. Imagine, having been born in Mississippi, I was now going to Alaska among the Eskimos and the glaciers!

As arrangements were being made for my trip, word got around to my Washington friends that I intended to fly from Seattle. They begged me to come early and make another concert tour in Washington.

I did my last concert in Seattle and spent some time with John Paul and Adelle Pack. Adelle had started prayer groups in the church, and this morning we went to an ecumenical gathering. I told them I was on my way to Alaska and that I had to go on a big plane and was scared to death.

I got on that Pan American Clipper, the largest plane I had ever seen. I was overwhelmed by the view. The rugged ranges of mountains and many small islands made an unforgettable sight. As never before I was conscious of the greatness and power of God. I had no fear, only admiration and inspiration.

Sunday was a busy day for me since I sang at the church service and attended a reception later. The next day I went to an Institute and sang for the children and staff. Two Eskimo girls did native dances. I had my picture taken with two of them dressed in their big parka coats and hoods.

Among the many places I visited was Mt. Edgecomb Island. I went to the orthopedic hospital. It was a rewarding experience to visit briefly with many of the children and sing to all of them over the loud speaker.

On the return flight to Seattle I was awed by the apparent endless chain of mountains with snow and then tall, sharp, jagged peaks everywhere. These mountains are so beautiful but look mighty treacherous. There must have been terrific upheavals once upon a time. Never before had the greatness and power of God been more real!!

"O God our help in ages past, our hope for years to come. Our shelter in the stormy blast and our eternal home!" This panorama of mountains!! A truly unforgettable sight.

From Seattle I called home and talked to Mama and Linnie. It would be good to get home. This had been a tremendous trip, but nothing beats going home.

I had not been home long from my travels until Nebraska called again! Carroll Lemon, who had been in Fayetteville, was now Executive Secretary of the Nebraska Council of Churches. He was inviting me to come to a United Christian Youth Movement conference to be held during Thanksgiving recess at Hastings College. I could take the train directly to Hastings and some of the local young people would escort me to the Clarke Hotel. Carroll describes the situation:

"Hastings is a small city whose cultural and religious life is dominated by a Presbyterian college of first rate quality and by large churches and an influential YWCA. I had counseled the local young people to make careful plans for Rosa Page to be entertained in a leading hotel in the city. These young people were shocked when they were told that the hotel policy was not to entertain Negro guests. The experience was educational and soul-searching for the young people and for the chuches of the city, and resulted in winning the consent of the hotel management to receive Rosa Page. The qualification was that someone must accompany her so that she be identified as the person she was. Never mind that most any white guest who came to the hotel for any purpose, legitimate or illegitimate, upright or otherwise, could be received without question.

The young people were there to greet me when the train arrived, and they took me to the hotel and introduced me to the manager. Not knowing the situation, I considered it very thoughtful. My role in the conference was to lead the singing, and I had an opportunity to speak on race relations. That was sufficient.

10

Beyond Boundaries

MORE and more, as I continued to participate in ecumenical meetings, I became keenly aware of a spirit of cooperation and trust that was evident in the United Christian Youth Movement conferences, and felt the spirit of unity among leading church women representing most major denominations. What a marvelous revelation that God wants us all to be one!

The enthusiasm of youth broke not only racial barriers but denominational divisions also. The fervor of the United Christian Youth Movement spread rapidly across the continent and started spilling over into foreign lands as well. Our young missionary candidates were finding it possible and pleasant to join their counterparts from other leading churches in foreign service.

The faithful, dedicated pastors and local congregations were challenging hundreds of our young people to attend camps and conferences. The church was coming alive again. A new surge of interracial, interdenominational cooperation moved the church ahead.

Janice B. Wyatt, who served on the staff of the UCYM, echoed her feelings about the important role of that organization,

"During the 1940s and '50s the United Christian Youth Department of the Federal Council of Churches was a very vital, thriving organization. Youth and youth leaders of most mainline denominations were very active and enthusiastic about what we could do together as united Christian youth. National conferences of youth and their leaders from across the country were held on a regular basis and drew large numbers of young people each year."

In 1949 I was in the thick of the interdenominational, interracial movements, and I loved every tiring minute of it.

Janice B. Wyatt wrote again about the important role of that organization:

"Today, in almost every state, in many denominational and interdenominational staffs, there are effective leaders whose roots stem back to marvelous experiences in the UCYM.

"Rosa Page Welch joined with other dynamic adults to lead church youth. The depth of her Christianity shone as a beacon to hundreds of youth from across the country. She was very generous about sharing her great talent to enhance our programs and worship services."

I was invited to Lynchburg College by Riley Montgomery, who had been a pastor in Chicago and whom I knew well. He was now president, and Lura Aspinwall, with whom I did my very first conferences, was now on the college faculty. Those two dared to invite me, and I ate in the dining room. The young people who waited tables were reluctant—for a white person serving a black person was unheard of. Those white students had never had the opportunity to meet and know a black person, and after we had sung together and laughed at ourselves we really had a beautiful experience together. Journeys from there took me to Moberly, Missouri, for a council of churches' conference and then to the Colorado-Wyoming state church convention of Christian Churches.

A long-distance call from Little Rock, Arkansas, informed me that I had been chosen as one of two persons to be an honorary member of Sigma Gamma Rho sorority. This really took me off my feet! It is the most significant honor that has come to me from my own people, and I was especially grateful.

I was asked to be the leader of singing and one of the soloists for our Disciples Centennial International Convention meeting in October of 1949 in Cincinnati, Ohio. More than eight thousand delegates were registered. I have never felt love and cooperation more than from that group. I had met so many of them in conventions, youth, and adult conferences, and in their local churches during these fifteen years of service throughout the country and in Canada. Every moment of that convention was great, but Friday night when eleven young people, one a Negro girl, were commissioned to foreign mission service, and Saturday night when a thousand young people, many of whom I've watched develop through youth conferences, knelt in dedication of their lives to Christian service, and Sunday afternoon when more than 15,000 people jammed Cincinnati Gardens for that marvelous interfaith communion service—these were the highest moments for me.

One of the eight thousand delegates, Rev. Hubert Sias, shares his impressions of that convention.

"It was at the Centennial Convention that I first heard Rosa Page Welch. Her solo during the first evening session was, 'Spirit of God, Descend Upon My Heart.' The next evening, when some one thousand young life recruits were the principals in an inspiring dedication service, immediately following the Call given by the always challenging Dr. Royal J. Dye, Rosa sang 'When He Calls Me, I Will Answer.' The highest moments for me were the final and climactic communion service on Sunday afternoon. A huge white cross dominated and glorified the chancel area. Convention President Dr. Frank E. Davison presided over this beautiful service. The large congregation sat in rapt reverence as the sacred elements were received, and Rosa Page Welch from a hidden spot behind the cross filled the huge assembly hall with her glorious voice and the moving spiritual, 'Were You There?' Nearly thirty-four years later I thrill to recall the wave of the Spirit which filled me and beautified that experience of the supper of our Lord."

I spent two glorious weeks at Mt. Sterling, Illinois, at the Christian Church, leading singing for services every night and every Sunday morning with Norma C. Brown preaching. She had been an inspiration to me for years. She later was called to Eureka College in the Department of Religion.

My concerts at the University of Dubuque, singing and speaking for the YWCA International dinner in Peoria, World Day of Prayer services with the Indianapolis Council of Church Women, and weekends with Disciple and Congregational Student Guilds at Ann Arbor, Michigan, made the Brotherhood Month of February truly memorable.

Our Twelfth Street Christian Church in Washington, D.C., with Rev. and Mrs. Witfield, was trying to earn funds to erect a new building. She either asked me or I offered to give a benefit concert. In order to have a bigger place she approached Rev. Warren Hastings at our National City Christian Church. He was persuasive enough to get the consent of the majority of his people, and they arranged for the concert. He even had me sing during their morning worship service. That afternoon concert was one of the biggest integrated audiences that I had ever had in the whole United States. Some of the best-known black people were in attendance.

The black newspaper commended Dr. Hastings and the congregation for allowing that concert to be held in Washington, D.C. It was a pioneering adventure.

There were concerts in Dallas and Ft. Worth, Texas, and another pioneering step was taken after my concert at Texas Christian University. A. T. DeGroot, now Dean of the Graduate School of Arts and Sciences of TCU, said that after that concert he succeeded in pushing through a motion to end the existing segregation which kept Negro students from campus classes. The next year after I was there, classes were open to Negro teachers who were working on graduate degrees.

Gale Page came home for his birthday. He had a job, but expected to be drafted into the Korea War. My concern for all young men and boys everywhere was too great for me to pray just for my son. I hoped that he might realize the futility of war and violence in any form. I wanted him to feel as I felt that all people are related and God is the Father of us all.

Home and family were comforting, but the date book filled up and I was off and singing at the state convention in Nebraska.

It was during that time in Nebraska that I was asked to sing a concert in Grand Island at the First Christian Church, where C. C. and Mabel (Niedermeyer) McCaw were pastoring. Newspaper publicity attracted quite a group of Negroes in the area who came to my concert and were ushered to the balcony.

From there I went to Lake Koronis for an Evangelical United Brethren Assembly. In no time at all I was a "Presbyterian" at the Iowa Presbyterian Synodical meeting on the campus of Iowa State in Ames, Iowa. Another of the most thrilling and inspiring experiences of my life was the privilege of attending and singing for the World Conference of Christian Education at Toronto, Ontario.

Dr. Jessie Bader was the first Secretary of the World Convention of Disciples of Christ. At one of the conventions held in Buffalo, New York, he asked me to sing, and Linnie accompanied me.

Every morning a different leader led the devotional, and one day Dr. Bader said to me, "Rosa, you will lead us tomorrow morning." I didn't feel qualified to lead all these great people such as my friends Anna Mow, Paul Macy, Jessie Bader and the others. I prayed hard and as I reached for my Bible it opened to Luke 4 and verse 16 caught my eye. "The spirit of the Lord is upon me, because he has anointed me to preach good news to the poor. He has sent me to proclaim release to the captives and recovering of sight to the blind, to set at liberty those who are oppressed to proclaim the acceptable year of the Lord." Blessed Redeemer! How that scripture spoke to me and deepened my commitment and lessened my fear of leading the devotional time.

Dr. Bader was a deeply spiritual man and a powerful speaker. This great Christian leader was willing to try many approaches and was very innovative. He had a part in instituting the worldwide observance of Holy Communion on the first Sunday in October.

I was in Cincinnati for the United Council of Church Women's biennial before I left for Cleveland and the history-making Constituting Convention of the National Council of the Churches of Christ in America. A great honor and a great privilege was my opportunity to serve as leader of the singing for this occasion.

I remember the closing night service of installation and consecration in the huge Cleveland Public Auditorium. We had beautiful bulletins, long, printed with pictures of many well-known people representing various groups in the new organization. Rev. Eugene Carson Blake gave a very challenging sermon on "The Cost of Discipleship." The people had been singing so beautifully, and while I was sitting up there I thought I would like to lead these people in singing Mallotte's "Lord's Prayer." That thought just stuck in my mind and I kept praying about it. Dr. Nolte was presiding and sitting beside me so I wrote him a note. "Dr. Nolte: I notice you have a wonderful hymn as the closing before the benediction. I wonder if you would permit me to lead the group in singing 'The Lord's Prayer' instead?" His eyebrows went up and he leaned over and whispered to me, "You will sing it by yourself?" "No," I said, "Don't worry; it will go all right." I am sure it was with reluctance that he consented.

When the time came, I stood up and I did what I usually do when I'm going to lead a group in singing. I said, "I know you are used to hearing this wonderful song as a solo, but we can all sing it together. All I ask is that you follow my direction."

I think everyone in there was shocked when I made this announcement. I had them all stand and I have never heard it sung more beautifully! Six thousand delegates, mostly men and trained clergy at that, but there were just enough women's voices to balance it beautifully. We all felt an overpowering sense of unity under God.

Some time later in Chicago I saw Dr. Eichelberger, a big black American Methodist Episcopal Christian educator. When he saw me he said, "Rosa, how do you do it? Come here, Girl! When you got up in Cleveland on that last night and said you were going to lead us in singing Mallotte's Lord's Prayer,' I said to myself, "Lord, have mercy. We've been so proud of Rosa all through this convention and now she is gonna spoil it. But, Girl, let me shake your hand. It was tremendous!'"

We had a big laugh right there in the lobby.

When Robert Thomas became pastor of First Christian Church in St. Joseph, Missouri, he relates that:

"One of the things I did early on was to invite Rosa Page Welch to be the guest leader for a World Day of Prayer service. She stayed with

90

us in our home, did a number of special programs for the people of our church, and the Christian Women's Fellowship in addition to the World Day of Prayer. Believe, me, it was a breakthrough in St. Joseph!

"My wife took Rosa Page on a shopping trip. They broke color barriers all over the place. Rosa knew what was happening and it was a beautiful experience all around.

"We had known Rosa Page in Chicago when I served as a member of the faculty of the Chicago area youth conference. The young people loved her, of course, and it was one of the rich experiences of my life to get to know Rosa Page and to share with her during these exciting times."

In the past few years, I had been carrying on my personal crusade for interfaith, interracial Christianity. It was exhilarating, but it made me a little dizzy when I wondered where and how far this crusade would take me. I hadn't counted on a prize along the way. But, blessed Jesus, it came!

A telephone call late one afternoon brought me great joy. The Executive Secretary of the National Conference of Christians and Jews, Dr. L. K. Bishop, was on the line. I knew him well because he arranged for me to go to St. Louis to speak for the Jewish women's organization, and then had sent me on a tour to South Dakota and to Omaha, Nebraska, where I appeared at Creighton University. This time he asked if I could go to Drake University in Des Moines, Iowa, which was one of our Disciple institutions, to receive the Distinguished Service Medal from the National Conference of Christians and Jews. I was so surprised and humbled. It was really a very touching ceremony. I was surrounded by an audience of many of my friends, both Christians and Jews, such as Dr. Henry Harmon, President of Drake University, and who placed the round silver medal on a beautiful ribbon around my neck On it was inscribed my name and date and the words, "Service in the Cause of Brotherhood."

The oneness of the Christian church, extending beyond all boundaries of race, color, or denomination, was one of the most immediately apparent experiences in my attendance at the Student Volunteer Movement's 16th Quadrennial Convention in Lawrence, Kansas. The last night in a watchnight service on New Year's Eve, in the darkened auditorium (at the University of Kansas) students of ten nations knelt, one by one, in front of a lighted cross and prayed in their own language for the needs of their people. They had given up most of their holiday season to search for Christian answers to world turmoil and personal uncertainties.

I was pleased to hear again Dr. Frank Laubach, the pioneer missionary educator whose literacy method has helped millions learn to read. His message was, "We must help the desperate nine-tenths of the non-Christian world out of their hunger and misery before we can preach to them."

Dr. John R. Mott, Nobel peace prizewinner, received a scroll expressing deep gratitude for the outstanding leadership he has given Christian students around the world. He had attended every Student Volunteer Movement Quadrennial since the first one in 1891 when a meeting of 251 college students at Mount Harmon, Massachusetts, organized the group.

Dr. Kenneth Scott Latourette of Yale University's Department of Religion, and President of the American Baptist Convention and a leading church historian, presented the scroll and expressed gratitude for this ecumenical movement which was drawing together Christians around the world.

We leaders formed a mutual admiration society in Lawrence, Kansas. I absorbed their messages and they listened while I led the singing. Little did I know that this was the very shadowy beginnings of a widening world for me.

With the increasing importance of foreign affairs in our national life, it was encouraging to see a new spirit of optimism and a growing sense of cooperation among the foreign mission interests represented at the second annual Assembly of the National Council's Division of Foreign Missions, held in Toronto, January 3-6, 1952. More than 75 mission boards and agencies of 38 United States and Canadian denominations were represented by the 400 delegates. The demonstration of togetherness on the part of the churches' foreign mission agencies helped to strengthen the moral position of the church.

It was interesting to learn that the number of foreign missionaries had doubled from the pre-war years, and there were more than 15,000 Protestant men and women abroad. More than half were college graduates, and the majority of the leadership for the assembly was provided by the younger missionaries. It was very gratifying to me to hear most of them appeal to the churches for positive action on the race issue, both at home and abroad, saying that unless this problem is resolved here, there is no point in our going to Africa because we won't be able to solve the racial problem there. Rev. Tracey K. Jones, a thirty-four-year-old, second-generation Methodist missionary said, "If we cannot say we are one people, then we are irrelevant to the needs of our times and the needs of people around the world."

One day as Margaret Shannon, Executive Secretary on the missionary staff of the Presbyterian Church USA, and I were visiting, she said "You know, Rosa, we are thinking about sending a deputation of women to the Philippines, and I think maybe you ought to be on that team. Would you like to go?"

I told her I would like to do anything she thought I could do.

That evening we sat in our denominational group for the meal and, of course, I was with the Disciple group. I happened to be sitting next to

Virgil Sly, who was then the Executive Secretary of our Foreign Mission Board. I was just bursting, and the thought came to me that they say men can keep secrets; so I turned to Virgil and said, "Virgil, I have always heard that men are able to keep secrets and because of my respect for you I am just bubbling over with something I would like to tell you. Are you sure you won't say anything about it?"

He scratched his head and said he guessed so. I told him what the Presbyterians were planning and I'll never forget his reply.

He put his head down and then commented, "Well, we can't let the Presbyterians do all that and we not come in on it."

My next assignment was to lead singing for the board meeting of Church Women United in Green Lake, Wisconsin. I took the train to Milwaukee and, lo and behold, Edith Sampson, an attorney, got off the same train. We introduced ourselves, and someone from Church Women United met us. We visited all the way to Green Lake. There she told the whole board about her many experiences on her world tour. She had been asked many questions on the tour about the racial situation in America. As a black American, her answers made a marvelous contribution.

Edith had to leave, and Mossie Wyker started the business meeting. During the discussion a woman from Des Moines, Iowa, got up and stated, "We really enjoyed and are inspired by what Attorney Sampson told us about the contributions she was able to make as a black person on this world tour. If a woman in the secular world could make that kind of impression on people of other parts of the world, what would it mean if a woman involved in Christian service, a Christian woman, would make such a tour? And who could do a better job than Rosa Page Welch?"

Shortly after that meeting our Disciple International Convention met in Chicago. The ministers' wives had a beautiful luncheon and invited attorney Edith Sampson to speak. Well, our Disciple women heard about Edith's trip and what Church Women United and the Presbyterian women were wanting to do. Alberta Lunger, who was president, said, "I think we as Disciple Christians should support this effort and Rosa Page Welch who is one of us."

We were doing some things with the American Baptists in that convention, and I remember singing for the joint communion service. Fran Craddock was there and said that my singing, "Let Us Break Bread Together" made it for her "the most beautiful and meaningful communion service I have ever experienced."

As a result, the American Baptist women also became sponsors. The whole idea just seemed to gain momentum, and more and more countries were added until it included seventeen countries. Lawd, have mercy!

I was in and out of many events, one of which Paul A. Crow remembers vividly in an experience he had that summer. He says, "I made my decision to enter the Christian ministry while Rosa Page Welch was singing 'Let Us Break Bread Together On Our Knees' at the North American youth convocation at Champaign-Urbana, Illinois. During the closing communion service, as Rosa sang, it all fell into place calmly. No apostolic flashing lights, just the spiritually lyrical voice of one of God's great saints, telling of God's embracing love for all people."

This life-changing moment has led Dr. Paul Crow on a life-long journey of ecumenical ministries throughout the world, culminating in his present position as president of the Council on Christian Unity.

I had some very interesting experiences, but most of my energies centered around getting ready for the world tour.

My family knew that when my mind was made up, nothing would change it. I really wanted to go, but I had some reservations about it, too. Welch commented again, as he had done so many times before, that I should be careful and not say anything that I would regret later. My family was so excited. My mother made me two nylon dresses that I could wash out at night so they would dry by morning. My cousin,

Emma Lee, was living with us then, and she remembers that one day in my excitement I ran out the door to catch a streetcar and suddenly realized I had forgotten to put on my skirt. There I was with a suit coat and slip! I had to rush back into the house where we all had a good laugh while I put on my skirt.

The thing that began to cause me the most concern was my hair. "Blessed Redeemer, what am I going to do about my hair?"

I was beginning to realize that there wouldn't be any beauty shops in Japan or probably any other country that would know what to do with my hair. A group of lovely black women took me out to lunch one day, and as we talked I said, "I'm concerned about my hair."

One of the women who had been to Europe on a trip said, "Oh get yourself a permanent. I went to Europe and stayed three months and didn't have any problem."

I said that I had been reading about these permanents, but I couldn't believe that they would work on our hair. She assured me that they did and told me about the Angel Beauty Shop where she had gone. I had seen that shop and it wasn't too far from my home. I asked her what it would cost and she said $25. I thought to myself, "Now where am I going to get that kind of money?" In the next few days a black Baptist church had me come to speak and sing to their women and they gave me $13. Then my church had a reception and took up an offering and gave it to me and that came to $12. There was the total amount; so I reluctantly went.

I still didn't have any confidence. I told the hair dresser, "I am going abroad for several months. You were recommended to me."

"Oh," she said, "I'll take care of it."

It was August and hot and humid. In two or three days I was disappointed over my hair; I went back and told her, "Look at my hair. I told you I would be gone for several months." She took one look and said, "Oh, I'll give you a touchup."

Another great concern was over Gale Page's being drafted into the army during the Korean War. He had to report for basic training. I felt compelled to write a letter explaining that as a Christian mother I had tried to instill the belief of non-violence. I addressed my letter "To Whom It May Concern" and requested that if possible my son Gale Page not be put into a position where he would have to carry a gun.

Blessed Jesus! I was so relieved to learn that he was assigned duty in the PX and never was in combat.

The very idea of having the opportunity of sharing the Good News through my God-given talents with God's children all around the world lifted my spirits. I felt God's direction as final preparations fell into place and I found myself humming snatches of the prayer hymn, "Precious Lord—take my hand,—lead me on . . ."

Rosa, 1948

1952

Rosa singing at the International
CYF Convocation in Champaign-
Urbana, 1951, accompanied by
Mrs. G. O. Taylor.

Rosa at the youth section of the 1953 Portland, Oregon International Convention of the Christian Church.

Rosa with Fred Sawyer and Dr. Don West.

"Sometimes it causes me to tremble—tremble—tremble. . ." 1952.

11

Ambassador Of Goodwill

IT all seemed like a dream—one that first germinated for me years earlier as a student at Southern Christian Institute—listening to the great missionaries of our denomination, and later meeting great Christian persons with whom I had been privileged to share leadership responsibilities. Now I was being sent out by the Church Universal. The Great Commission of our Lord took on deeper significance as I heard again his words, "Go therefore and make disciples of all nations." A newly-felt assurance crept over my very being as I read again his promise . . . "And lo, I am with you always, to the close of the age."

Saying goodbye to Mama was the most difficult of all. A beautiful smile of pride and joy illumined her face; yet as she took me in her arms I felt her aging body cling apprehensively to mine. "Rosa child, you are going so far away—but I'll pray every day that our heavenly Father will guide you and keep you in his care."

"Oh thank you, Mama; you take care too!"

As my plane took off I could see Lesly, Linrie, Welch, and Emma Lee and many friends waving their goodbyes.

Mission Number One — Japan

As I came off the plane in Tokyo, Japan, there was Kenneth Hendricks standing at the bottom of the ramp. Waiting anxiously behind the fence were his wife, Grace, (Kenneth and Grace were our Disciple missionaries who had been in the field the longest); Jessie Trout, executive for Disciple women's work; and Lin D. Cartwright, editor of our Disciple paper, *The Christian-Evangelist*.

Lin Cartwright, H. C. Shorrock, K. C. Hendricks, Rosa, Grace Hendricks, Betty Ellis, Daisy Edgerton, Jessie Trout, Aigi Kamikawa.

I was a guest in the Hendricks' home. Such warm cordiality and welcome! After we had talked awhile, Mrs. Hendricks took me down and showed me where the bathroom was, and showed me how to bathe in a Japanese bath. There was an oval-shaped tub and it was deep and full of hot water. Mrs. Hendricks said, "You will take this basin (which was small), and dip some water out of the tub and cool it to the temperature you want. Here is some soap; you soap yourself and scrub and then rinse yourself off with this dipper, taking water from the tub. Then you climb into the big tub from this little stool and just sit and relax in the water for about fifteen minutes. Please don't let the water out of the tub, for the whole family has to use it." Then Mrs. Hendricks left. I got along fine with all my washing and rinsing, but when I stepped into the tub, the water just took my breath away. After a while it felt so good I didn't want to get out. I looked forward to those Japanese baths from that first night on.

The genuineness of the Japanese politeness and friendliness is so impressive. To recall the curtseying or bowing is an unforgettable memory.

Don West sent word ahead to let me rest for a couple of days, and it was so thoughtful of the Hendricks and Jessie Trout to arrange for a quiet spot for a retreat up in the mountains. I quickly wrote some letters so Dr. Cartwright, who was leaving for the States, could mail them there for me. Among them was a card of congratulations to Linnie and Jake for their wedding day. Mrs. Hendricks went with me on the trip and Jessie Trout accompanied us to the railroad station. Crowds of people were loading and unloading. I had never before experienced the helpless feeling of not being able to converse because of the language barrier.

Expressions of friendliness, interest, sympathy and gratitude coming from the heart stamp themselves in the countenance, so I felt their welcome, their friendliness and their kindness and I tried so hard to let mine be known in similar ways also.

The shrill whistle blew and we were off.

The orderliness, artistry of the planting, the neatness of the cottages and homes were all indications of the love of beauty and the artistic mind of the Japanese.

The first full morning on the retreat I awakened very early and just couldn't go back to sleep. I tossed and turned; thoughts and anxiety about home possessed me. I found myself overcome with sorrow, and just cried and prayed to God for relief and courage to face whatever came. I prayed for strength and the will power to surrender all my family and situations to his keeping. A strange thing happened. I became quiet inside and listened to the Holy Spirit, and God calmed my soul in a miraculous way!

We returned to Tokyo, and my busy schedule began. So many experiences! Here are a few.

One day Mrs. Hendricks took me to a primary school where she worked. The little children were all dressed in crisp uniforms. They put on a program as a response to my singing for them. A little boy, who looked no older than six years, stood up there with a baton and directed the children in their songs. It was one of the most delightful things I have ever seen.

At one of the churches I met a young minister and his wife. He had been brought up in the slums and lived under a bridge. We saw some terrible slums; this was soon after the war, and there was so much destruction. After this young man became a Christian, he was so dedicated that nothing was too great for him to sacrifice. He had been brought up here and he chose to work among the people in the slums. One day when I was going somewhere on an elevated train, I looked down and saw the little white building with the blue cross on it. I can see that church now where this young fellow pastored.

It was some weeks before the World Christian Student Conference was to meet in India. In Tokyo I gave a concert to raise funds for the YWCA to send their delegates. I remember Naomi gave me a beautiful evening gown which she made from a kimono. It was very lovely. And, of course, the people were glad when I walked out on the stage dressed in a garment that was Japanese.

One of our missionaries mentioned a leprosarium. Would it be possible for me to go to see it? I asked. I had never seen anyone with leprosy.

Arrangements were made for me to visit the compound. We arrived and stopped at the medical building. One of the doctors got in the car with us. We drove around this huge compound with many buildings, but no people were in sight.

We came to a small building where the doctor explained that most of those who were not bedfast were gathered to see a movie. I asked, "If they are gathered together, do you suppose they would like to hear me sing?" I was always eager to sing.

The doctor assured me they would prefer live entertainment to a movie. We went in, and there were all these people sitting on the floor. I began to sing. A Japanese friend had just taught me one of their lovely national folk songs, "Moon Over the Deserted Castle." So I sang it for the first time for these people. The applause was terrific. I discovered that any outsider who would take time to learn how to greet the people in their language and learn one of their songs was instantly accepted. From then on, in every country I visited I tried to learn to say hello, goodbye, and thank you in the language of the people.

Nearly every mission compound or medical center had a colony of lepers and I always asked to sing to them.

After a visit to a girls' school, Virginia Mackenzie told me about the occasion from the girls' point of view.

"Rosa, when you came to Japan after the war, our school girls had never seen anyone of the black race. And the rumors they had heard of American Military Police in Tokyo and Yokohoma did not prepare them to meet even a black lady without some feeling of withdrawal. However, when you began to sing for them, your voice and personality opened their hearts completely. And to this day they remember the loving response they felt. All of us recall our special gratitude as we welcomed you. It gave us a sense of true Christian unity. Material healing had been made with the rebuilding of our school, but the type of healing you brought was much more needed and all the more precious. Unforgettable!!

The accompanist and interpreter during my travels in Japan, Hana Kawai, was helpful and tried so hard to get me to rest between concerts; she understood the energy one expends in presenting a concert two and three times a day, day after day. Hana later shared her insights:

"Japan in the early 1950s was not Japan as it is today with its modern transportation facilities; so traveling to some of the out-of-the-way places must have been quite a new and inconvenient experience for Rosa. We first went to Kanazawa, an ancient castle city where Buddhism is still very strong, but there is a Presbyterian girls' school there. The concert was held in a public hall and was a great success.

102

Our last concert before returning to Tokyo was at Doshisha University in Kyoto, and as the train was not running according to schedule, we had to go straight to the hall and leave immediately after the concert.

"We took the night train with its simple, triple-deck berths. At that time to travel on a train with a foreigner, especially a black woman, attracted a great deal of attention. My worry was unnecessary because Rosa's personality charmed all the people around her.

"Besides the classic songs which she sang, such spirituals as 'He's Got the Whole World in His Hands,' 'Let Us Break Bread Together on Our Knees,' and 'Go Tell It on the Mountain,' were new songs to me and now whenever I hear them, I can see Rosa's dignified demeanor and hear her beautiful voice.

"It is a custom in Japan to give gifts besides an honorarium to the performer and, I can still see the glow in Rosa's eyes when a pearl was presented to her."

Before I flew to the Philippines, Hana Kawai, who knew I was going, said, "Rosa, since you are going to the Philippines, I wish you would take a message from the Japanese Christians. We didn't know the terrible things our soldiers did in the Philippines. All we heard and all we read was how wonderful our soldiers were and how cruel everybody else's were."

I said, "Honey, that is war. War makes brutes of men, and people at home don't get the facts. Our servicemen did the same things."

On my last day in Yokohama I had an opportunity to go to one of the orphanages where the "war babies" were. I saw so many beautiful children. We went out to the playground and many of them (all colors and mixtures) rushed to me, looking up into my face as they clung to my skirt, saying, "Momee, Momee, Momee." It was difficult to keep back the tears.

As I sat on the departing plane waving to friends I prayed, "Oh, God, may I always be worthy of the love, the friendship, and appreciation expressed by the people in Japan!"

Mission Number Two — The Philippines

As we landed in the Philippines I greeted everybody; then two Filipino ladies took me by each arm and rushed me to the women's restroom where both of them opened their little pocketbooks. We could not communicate, and I had no idea what was happening. One took out a pencil and paper and the other a tape measure; they started taking my measurements. I still didn't know what it was about, but we came on back to the missionaries. I had the nicest guest room in the home of Mr. and Mrs. Young, missionaries who were working with the American Bible Society. That evening I really started worrying about my hair! My hair looked worse than when it was in its natural state! I couldn't do anything with it!

(From *Blue and Silver*, student newspaper of Philippine Christian College:)

"Singing for the first time since her arrival in the Philippines, Mrs. Rosa Page Welch, famous Negro mezzo-soprano, was welcomed by the entire student population during a chapel-convocation held in Ellinwood Church.

"She acquainted the students with the origin of the Negro spirituals which have now become an important part in the culture of America. 'True Negro spirituals are the songs sung by my ancestors during the time of their slavery, and in these songs they expressed their trials and tribulations and also their joys, seeking to find comfort and relief through them.'

"When she started to sing, the students were awe-struck with the beauty of her clear and unrestrained voice, which rose and fell in excellent crescendo and diminuendo. After singing a number of songs, she led the students in singing some of the best loved spirituals. She delights in leading sacred songs and has an amazing talent for leading untrained voices into harmonious chorus.

"Mrs. Welch, who is an accomplished artist, does not sing merely for the sake of the music, but because she knows that music expresses the spirit of man, the spirit that is capable of glorifying its Maker.

"We are grateful for her efforts to bring good music to the common people. Mrs. Welch does not come from a privileged class, and does not consider good music as belonging only to those who can afford to hear it. It is a joy to hear a voice that moves, and drives home the simple message of upliftment, a voice that understands and expresses what is in the human soul. May she continue to sing, for the people and for God."

As a surprise, all those measurements turned into the most beautiful Filipino gown for me to wear the next evening for a gala garden party in Manila. There were many American missionaries from different denominations, and all of these beautiful Filipino women dressed in these gowns. I still have mine. Since I was the color of many of them, they were very pleased to see me in this dress. I still worried about my hair; it took all the hairpins I had to pin it down!

In my speech I brought greetings from Japan. You could almost feel the atmosphere! And then I brought the greetings from Hana Kawai. I went on to say that I knew what it felt like to have ill feelings directed toward me, but we all make mistakes.

After the program a group of Filipino men and women gathered around me and started talking.

104

One person said, "It is very interesting to us that the Japanese have sent a message like that, and we are thankful."

Another man said, "Mrs. Welch, it is very hard. I know we should forgive, but it is very difficult for me because I saw my whole family massacred by the Japanese soldiers."

Another man said, "It is easier for me, but I'm thankful for this message; it was a Christian Japanese officer who helped my family get to a safe place." But there were tears.

One night I visited a community where the Americans had dropped bombs that had practically wiped out one village. I was taken to the home of a young Filipino couple. When we went in the door I almost stumbled because they had not yet been able to put a new floor in their home. Here I was in the community that had been bombed by Americans, not the Japanese. I was shocked when I went to bed that night to notice for the first time that there was a roof over the house but they had not yet rebuilt the walls. I found myself trying to imagine what it must have been like when the bombs were dropped.

While I was visiting the Philippines I met the Managbanag sisters who had studied at Phillips University in the United States. Two of the sisters had married and lived on another island. When they heard I was coming, they took a slow boat and arrived at the same time I did in Cebu City where there is a large mission hospital. The other Managbanag sister worked there as a nurse.

Norwood and Wilma Tye, at Baguio way up in the mountains, entertained me for a couple of days. I really enjoyed doing my concert for them. Everywhere I went, the churches and schools were crowded and the people so eager, so sweetly appreciative and generous.

Presbyterians and Disciples were working beautifully on my schedule and we were all one grand, happy family. I was greatly impressed with the unity and cooperation of the Evangelical churches.

Before I left the main island of the Philippines, the Christian women honored me with a tea. Even though the women sponsored it, the men were there too. Men seemed to be very proud of their wives in the Philippines. I have never met or observed such great enthusiasm, zeal, and joy in just being a Protestant Christian as I observed in the women of the church.

At this tea I became Rosa Pagina Uvas when I was adopted as "Daughter of the Philippines" in "fitting tribute and tangible recognition of her untiring and sincere devotion to the cause of God's Kingdom and world peace." The document was signed by representatives of the United Church of Christ in the Philippines, the Philippine Federation of Christian Churches, the National Women's Association of the UCCP, and the United Council of Evangelical Church Women. They even presented me with official adoption papers. I was told the only other American woman to receive that honor was Mrs. Franklin D. Roosevelt.

George Earle and Margaret Owen who were then missionaries in Manila shared the following clipping which appeared in the *Christian Century*, dateline Manila:

"No one ever so completely won the hearts of the Philippines' Protestants as did Rosa Page Welch of Chicago during her recent visit to the island. Through the universal language of music, the widely-known Negro church leader and singer was at home in and understood by all religious, racial, and cultural groups. Her charming personality, her rich mezzo-soprano voice, her ability to lead any congregation in enthusiastic group singing, her interracial understanding, her quiet dignity and gracious Christian spirit made her an ideal ambassador of goodwill."

When I went back to Manila, after my visit to the southern islands, Dr. Ilano met me. I said, "Oh, Dr. Ilano, what will I do about my hair? I am so ashamed for my American friends." She offered to take me to her beauty shop. They gave me a shampoo then put me under the dryer, and I could just feel my hair bush out. Dr. Ilano had gone to treat a patient and I could not communicate with the beauty operators. I looked all around and finally found some Brilliantine cream in the display case. Through sign language I was able to obtain a jar of it just as Dr. Ilano came in the door. She took me home and I got my hair under control.

Mission Number Three — Hong Kong

My flight to Hong Kong was early in the morning of a very beautiful day. From the air I could see it was a beautiful city and port. Mr. Walline, Executive Secretary for all missionaries who had to leave China and relocate in Hong Kong, met me and we took rickshas to the Grand Hotel. After lunch, the Wallines took me to the True Light Middle Girls School where I met the lovely principal and sang for the girls. This was a very famous Christian girls' school in occcupied China that was moved to Hong Kong.

That afternoon I met Mr. and Mrs. Frank Price, Presbyterian missionaries, who were released from the Communists after being interned two years. Later all the missionaries came who had been working in occupied China and were now in Hong Kong. It was most interesting to sit and observe these missionaries asking the Prices how the Christian Chinese were faring. We heard their account of injustice behind the Iron Curtain. I sensed many mixed emotions, Mrs. Walline asked me to sing. I prayed for some song that would release them from their anxiety about the China they had to leave. It was a very emotional time. I started with

106

Guion's "Prayer," "He Never Said a Mumblin' Word," and "He's Got the Whole World in His Hands." Since I was sitting next to Dr. Price, I asked him, "Dr. Price, what would you like me to sing?" He shyly said, "I was hoping you would sing 'Nobody Knows the Trouble I've Seen.' I thought of it so much during the two years in China." I was so glad that I could lift their hearts with song.

A group took me to the peak that overlooks the city. Looking back we saw the most beautiful view of the harbor and the city. At the top we were more than 1,100 feet above sea level. What a magnificent view. We watched the sunset as it seemed to drop into the inland sea with those tiny launches dotting it. A group of us had a picnic up there. We had relaxed fellowship until dark, then we went into a teahouse and had tea. We could see that the Moon Festival was going full swing, with balloons, colored streamers, whistles, and lots of laughter.

I had wanted to see the British hospitals; so when we came down on the tram we went right to the maternity ward. Then we went up to the roof garden where as many of the nurses and doctors as possible gathered, and I was honored to sing a whole program.

I met Dr. John Hays, one of our Presbyterian missionaries who had just been released from prison in China after a year and a half. We had lunch and interesting fellowship interspersed with Dr. Hays' fine sense of humor. I asked him what his favorite song was, and he requested "We've a Story to Tell to the Nations." Of all the times I've sung this hymn with many young people in their camps and conferences, it had never meant to me what it meant as I sang it for Dr. Hays. He sat looking in the distance as though he could go right back into China to finish telling the story of Jesus Christ, even if it meant going back to jail.

In only two days and two nights I had some unforgettable experiences, but then it was time to go to another country.

I flew British Overseas Airlines, and the plane was very spacious; the services were very elaborate. The stewardess and I had a wonderful visit, such as I'd never had before with a total stranger. I never felt more that God really spoke through me. Because of the tragedies in her life, she'd given up her Catholic church and questioned God a great deal. Shortly before arriving she said, "I want to thank you for the way you helped me. I'll think about what you said." I answered, "You helped me too, and we'll both thank God for our meeting."

Mission Number Four — Thailand

We landed at the Bangkok airport, and Mr. Horace Ryburn, Executive Secretary of the Presbyterian missions, and Miss Vida Rumbaugh were there to meet me. When we arrived at Vida's and Jean Belejean's home where I was to be a guest, there was a nice group waiting with cordial greetings and loads of food and fruits.

Margaret Flory's plane arrived and we all went out to welcome her. She was coming to the Presbyterian missions which were strong in Thailand because they were the first to do mission work there. We visited some areas together and at other times we went our separate ways. I had first met Margaret Flory in a Disciple Youth Conference in Ohio and had worked with her in the States in Presbyterian and Church Women United work.

As Margaret Flory says:

"Many of my memories cluster around a memorable journey we made together over several months in late 1952 and early 1953, beginning in Thailand and moving through India, Pakistan, and several countries of the Middle East. Schools and colleges were the locale of our pilgrimage. The occasion was usually a school assembly. Rosa would open with a few spirituals, explaining that the spirituals came out of the heart-throbs of an oppressed people. She would divide them into the songs of sorrow and the songs of joy, and she'd fill the whole hall with beautiful music and haunting messages. Then I would follow with a message. Her final solo, adapted each time to the occasion, was the summing up and the sending forth note. Her reportoire was vast but of course, I had my favorites: 'I Ain't Gonna Study War No More,' 'Go Tell It on the Mountain,' 'Steal Away To Jesus.'"

My interpreter was a woman who had started a girl's school here. Usually my interpreter would repeat after each sentence. I began my sermon and then turned to her and she said, "That's all right, Mrs. Welch, you go right on and do your whole sermon." I couldn't believe she could recall it! When I was finished, she stood up and put in all the inflections, all of the emotions I had used and she did that sermon as well or better than I did. In fact, she outpreached me with my own sermon!

After church a Thai family and I went home through streets of tiny crowded shacks. The canals were filled with filthy looking water and shanty boats where people lived and reared their children. I just don't know how to describe it, but I do know how miserable and helpless I felt and how my heart went out to them.

The daughter of one of the church families painted a very interesting and attractive poster. Her imaginative drawing of me was really interesting. My skin color matched the Thai, but she sketched me with hair that was beautiful, black, straight, but curled on the ends. My hair had become thick, and refused to become smooth, even with the application of my expensive Brilliantine! It had caused me untold consternation and I had done every single thing I know. I felt that I would really be on my own when I reached Africa. I wondered if I would look so much like the natives that the Belgian government would send me back to America!

Vida had helped set my benefit concert for the Thailand Rotary club to aid in their purchase of an iron lung for polio victims. I was introduced as the honored guest of the day and the applause was very warm and generous. I wore the beautiful print Filipino dress, Japanese crystal jewelry, and Thai orchid corsage sent to me by a U.S. Ambassador.

Here was an American Negro Protestant singing in a Roman Catholic auditorium to at least three different religious groups for a common cause. It is marvelous how God can and will use us. Our Disciple missionaries, Ms. Edna Gish and George and Margaret Cherryhome had come from Nakom Patom, thirty-five miles away. I was so glad to see them.

Margaret Flory and I had an interesting experience in Bangkok. Genevieve Lim, the daughter of a Chinese family, worked in the Presbyterian boarding school and we became good friends. Mr. Lim was observing his sixtieth birthday, and for the Chinese that is a very important birthday. All of the missionaries were invited, even though only two daughters of the whole family were Christian. The rest of the family were Buddhists. Their house was very big and it had a huge veranda that went almost all the way around the house. I sang "Bless This House," and the family was appreciative.

Vida had me teaching some of her music classes at the school, and I really enjoyed discussing different things and leading them in singing.

I gave a concert on the seminary campus at Chengmai and the professor who interpreted for me had just come back from the States with a doctorate from a Presbyterian college in Wooster, Ohio. I had been on the campus and knew that a lovely bronze statue of Abraham Lincoln was there. I always gave a little historical background of the spirituals before I sang them. I was explaining that many of them came about during slavery and that they were the heart-throbs of my ancestors. I stopped to let the professor interpret what I had said for the Thai people and all of a sudden he said in English "Abraham Lincoln." I jumped because I hadn't said a word about Abraham Lincoln. Then he said "1776" and I jumped again because I don't fool with dates. I was wondering what this man was telling these people. The missionaries saw my distress and they smiled, so I went on, but as soon as I got back to the mission house I asked, "Will you please tell me what that man said to those people. I did not say anything about Abraham Lincoln nor did I use any dates." They laughed and laughed and finally explained, "Well Rosa, he has just gotten back from the States and he made a special study of Lincoln, who is a most revered American here. He just took advantage of the opportunity to share what he had learned about this great man."

The Disciples had a good-sized hospital in Nokon Potom. One evening they set up equipment so I could sing and be heard all over the grounds. Many people from the community came and heard the concert, too.

I did a formal concert at Chulalanghorn University, the big government school in Bangkok. I met the older students in the morning. I sang for them and then we sang some songs together.

There was a message later from the head of the school, Achorn Chuan, expressing thanks on behalf of church officers, saying I had helped them in many ways:

—I had encouraged them to have faith beyond their discouragement;

—I had helped them see that people around the world are the same regardless of their nationality or skin color;

—I had taught the children songs that they could sing expressing either joy or sorrow; and

—they were thankful for my being an abassador of goodwill not only to the Christians, but to the whole community.

I was in Thailand about six weeks and traveled to many places. While I was in Bangkok, I met an outstanding young Christian leader from Burma. He could not understand why I was not scheduled to visit his country. I tried to explain that my schedule was made up by other people before I left America. However, since I had two unscheduled days I told him I would be happy to do whatever he could arrange. He was the executive secretary of student and youth work for that part of Asia and wanted me to do a benefit concert to raise funds to send their delegates to the World Christian Student Conference.

Mission Number Five — Burma

My flight to Rangoon, Burma, was delayed, but I finally got out and was so surprised to find friends at the airport to see me off. When I arrived at Rangoon, the youth leader met me and took me by my accompanist's home. We went over my program and then went to the YWCA where a woman in charge showed me to a comfortable room. I later had tea with several of the students and leaders. I was so surprised and pleased to meet Sister Ruth Christopherson. We had known each other in the Ashrams and she was now a missionary working in the YWCA.

After going through much red tape at the immigration offices, Ruth took me to the Baptist seminary where I spoke and sang for and with the students. Some of them were from the Karin tribe way up in the hills of Burma. Their voices were so beautiful that I asked them to sing for me.

Soon after, I left for India.

Mission Number Six — India

I changed planes in Calcutta but had to go through customs, even though I was there only one hour. I waited up for Margaret Flory who arrived later. In the afternoon we left for Debra Dun and had tea in a beautiful garden facing the majestic Himalayas. Margaret and I gave our program at the school the next morning before we left for Landow. We took a breathtaking drive up the majestic, exquisite Himalayas, then we finished the frightening trip in rickshas. It was depressing to utilize the coolies this way. These men have poles that rest on their shoulders and passengers sit in something that looks like an old-fashioned buggy fastened between the poles. I finally couldn't take it anymore. "Let me walk the rest of the way," I begged. The missionaries said, "Well, Rosa, this is what we always have done." And before I could stop myself I had blurted out, "You mean to tell me that you missionaries have been coming up here all of this time and you haven't discovered any easier way to get up to this school?" Then after we got into the buildings I saw all of the furniture, even a grand piano, and I knew the only way it got up there was that those men brought it on their backs. But of course, they said that it was a way for the men to earn a living. I learned that their average life span was thirty-seven years. I found one Disciple nurse, Elizabeth Hill, who worked there. I was in London several days and did a concert for all the students. They were children of missionaries, as well as outstanding Indian and European children.

When we got to Moga on our way to Jullundar, I had a cable from Mama informing me of her brother, my uncle G.W.'s death. It was such a shock. He was my favorite uncle. Again, I felt so very far from home and my loved ones.

When I visited the big government university at Allahabad, I was a guest in the home of Dan and Isabella Caleb. Dan was a professor on campus. Isabella and I became like sisters. She taught language to the missionaries when they first arrived and was a charming woman. They had a beautiful dinner party in their home and invited a large group of staff and government people. One of the professors in the department of social sciences, who was a Caucasian American, asked me if I would be available to speak to an assembly one morning. I assured him that I would like to very much. At the time there was much talk about communism, and the students were very rude and asked if the United States wasn't really a Communist country and then asked about the racial situation. The professor was so shocked and embarrassed that he threatened to stop the whole program. I begged him not to stop the questioning, for this was my reason for making the trip. My mission was to bring understanding about my nation and the truth about what the United States endeavors to do.

"They can't hurt me," I assured him. All the missionaries and all the Christians in the school were happy that I was able to meet the challenge.

Margaret Flory described the Christmas Eve we shared:

"We spent Christmas 1952 in Mainpuri with two marvelous missionary couples, John and Agnes Weir and Sarah and Calvin Hazlett. On Christmas Eve we worshiped in a small church where the Christmas tableau was presented by those whose skin color and robes were most appropriate. Our candles were lighted by a central Christ candle in the manger. Rosa sang, 'Oh Mary, What You Gonna Name That Pretty Little Baby?' and 'Go, Tell It on the Mountain.' We went out into the dark carrying our lights with us. In the meantime the whole neighborhood was lighted up by hundreds of little *divali* lights on roof tops, on stairways, on window sills. Standing in the middle of this festival of light, Rosa sang spontaneously to everyone's joy, 'This Little Light of Mine, I'm Gonna Let It Shine.' That was the special gift she had, of divining instinctively what message was needed and doing it with eyes luminous and head thrown back."

Margaret and I had prayer together. It was a never-to-be-forgotten experience. As we prayed for our friends and loved ones, they all seemed so close. As we thanked God for his precious gift, the baby Jesus, we seemed nearer him. Thoughts of my child, Gale Page, somewhere so far from home, of Linnie who was expecting a child, thoughts of others of my family who perhaps were feeling the sting of separation, all these piled in on me and caused tears. But then, there was a nearness that none of us have ever known before! I had such mixed emotions. There was an awareness of my own maturity, yet an empty lonely feeling as I realized that my stewardship in this privilege of child rearing was about finished. Now all I could do was pray, pray, and pray that somehow they may have caught a spark of the love of Christ, the faith, through needing greater strength, the compassion, zeal and enthusiasm for the peace and understanding of peoples everywhere and the inner peace which passes all understanding, which possessed my own heart and soul. May it find a kindling in their own hearts and souls burning with a brilliance that will reach out and up to God through humble service to him and all humanity.

Christmas morning we were awakened early by the bands playing. We got up and exchanged Christmas greetings and after breakfast exchanged gifts. Then we went to a worship service, presenting white gifts which were sent to Pakistan. As each person marched up to present his offering in the gorgeous white basket, three girls beautifully sang, "I Surrender All" and the congregation joined in the chorus.

In Agra, Margaret and I went through the magnificent Taj Mahal. On Sunday I sang a sacred concert at the Free Church in place of the sermon, and was surprised to see Dr. and Mrs. Frank Laubach in the congregation. Margaret and I had a lovely flight to Madras, where we stayed at Madras Christian College. A wonderful biblical play was given by Madras Christian students just after a real Indian dinner in the garden.

In addition to singing for the Student Conference south of Madras I gave a concert at the cathedral in Madras.

Next we were off to Vellore where we were guests in Dr. Scudder's bungalow at the medical college campus. At dinner we met the charming Dr. Ida Scudder, founder of this great hospital. After dinner we did a program for the doctors and nurses. At that time there were more women studying medicine than men. Dr. Scudder's father was a doctor, and he became disturbed because he saw so many Indian women die for lack of medical attention, for the custom in India did not allow male doctors to treat women. Dr. Ida Scudder studied medicine in the States, then came back and started this hospital and school for women.

India is such a vast country. They have many leprosariums. As we went along and saw one, I would say, "Oh, let us stop and sing for them." I would sing some of our old hymns that the missionaries had taught many of them in their language.

A Presbyterian missionary took me on a sightseeing tour. It was during the cooler months near the end of January, near dusk, when we passed a family. A father and mother and three children were leading a cow into their little one-room house. I knew the cow was considered sacred but I said, "My, goodness, why are they taking a cow into the house?" My guide said, "Rosa, you have on a woolen suit and you say you are still chilly. This family is taking the cow into their house because tonight the whole family will be sleeping next to it for it is the only heat they have."

We got to India the last of October, and we were there until the first part of January. We saw so much poverty there! At the railroad station, especially at night, there were so many people—going somewhere—and they didn't have a place to stay so they just stopped at the railroad station! They stretched out and went to sleep everywhere.

Mission Number Seven — Pakistan

From India we went to Pakistan. We were there about a week. I was practically exhausted. As we approached Pakistan something happened to me. I had been suffering a head cold. The stewardess gave me two little white pills. By the time we got on the ground, I was worse. The missionaries were there to meet us, and I didn't tell them how I felt at first but finally had to admit, "Right now I must have the chance to go to bed. I really would like to see a doctor." We stopped by the hospital, but the doctor was busy so she told my hosts to take me to my room and put me to bed and she would come as soon as possible. After an hour or so she came and examined me and said, "I guess you will stay in bed." She gave me B-12 shots and had an Indian nurse care for me for about two days.

When I recovered, I sang for the students at Kinaird and then at Farman College.

I had a trying experience at the airport as we were leaving. For some reason the officer insisted that the man receiving tickets and weighing luggage, re-weigh mine; I had to pay $27 for overweight. In customs they went through my things like they had never done before, and they never ever opened Margaret's bag. I couldn't understand it. I had to pray hard to keep a Christian attitude no matter what happened.

Mission Number Eight — Lebanon and Palestine

We landed at Basra, Iraq, for about 45 minutes. We had tea and saw Moslems praying with faces turned toward Mecca. Then we took off and soon landed in Beirut, Lebanon. Such a beautiful city! There was a beautiful sunset on the magnificent blue Mediterranean Sea with the majestic snow-covered mountains and rolling green hills in the foreground. An unforgettable sight!

I sang with a large group of students in the girls' dorm where we had a wonderful time and some good conversation. I rehearsed some songs for my concert with my accompanist and then we were guests for dinner in a Syrian home.

One day after breakfast we left for a refugee camp. It is an unforgettable sight. The contrast between the poverty and suffering and the modern, comfortable apartment buildings in the city was disturbing. The tents were getting old and they were tattered and torn and patched. I didn't know what to say. Most of them were Arabs and I didn't speak the language. I smiled and bowed and tried everything I could to express how glad I was to see them. I shook hands with an old man at the door of his tent and along came a stout, pleasant woman. I offered her my hand. We shook hands and she walked along beside me and talked in lively Arabic. I smiled and caught her arm. She put her arms around me and continued talking. When we got down the hill, the people were lining up because Church World Service was providing a meal. Women were bringing their children with their tin cups, and I wanted to do something so I asked the missionary if I could sing. I started singing and of course the people who were serving the food out of courtesy stopped and I happed to look to my right and there was a tall woman with a baby in her arm and a child holding her hand and she looked so disturbed as if to say, "Oh, please get through so they will serve us." I realized this wasn't a good time to sing and stopped.

Soon we flew to Jerusalem. a man on the plane pointed out places of biblical interest. We took pictures of the beautiful snow-covered mountains, the Sea of Galilee, the Dead Sea, the Jordan River and Damascus. It just didn't seem real to be in the Holy Land. We were taken by car from the airport to our hotel, The American Colony, where we were within walking distance of the Garden Tomb. A guide took us first to the spot where we could see Golgotha, the crucifixion hill, place of the skull and the city wall. Then he took us through the beautiful little garden to the tomb. We went through the small opening into the tomb and stood beside the place where Jesus was laid.

All the thoughts, memories, and imagination crowded in on me and I tried to visualize all I'd ever heard. learned, and tried to understand. As I went out I prayed that God would give me courage anew to go out and tell the Good News with new meaning. We went to the office, signed the guest book, bought some mementos, talked to the warden and then as if something pulled us, we went back to the tomb. I went in again and came back and sat in the garden to meditate. The song, "Were You There When They Crucified My Lord?" just had to be sung. Margaret read scripture which brought alive the scene again; we prayed and talked and meditated till it began to get dark and reluctantly we left.

I thanked God for this marvelous realization of walking and standing where Jesus had walked, seeing where he was crucified, where his body lay. I thanked him for Simon the Cyrenian, a black man who had borne his cross and expressed love and sympathy rather than hatred. I love this section of the world. The people seemed especially warm, friendly and unbiased, and I've seen people who resemble people (in color and features) of every race and nationality I've ever known. There's a peacefulness unexperienced anywhere else, and this spiritual experience fills me with deep humility and gratitude to God for this glorious blessing and privilege.

We flew back to Beirut, and I went to the community school where I spoke and sang for children, mostly American.

Margaret was busy packing as she was happy to be going back to the States. I hated to see her go, but it had meant so much to have had so many experiences with this dear friend.

The next morning I did a chapel program at the college, and afterward a teacher from the English Syrian school took me to the school for junior girls where I sang a part of my concert program. As I looked down near the front there was a beautiful little dark-skinned girl with long braids and great big black eyes that were kept on me. I wondered who she might be. The principal told me that the child was the daughter of the King of Kuwait.

Mission Number Nine — Egypt

My next stop was Cairo, Egypt, after a very beautiful flight over rich oil lands and vast amounts of desert. After going through customs and working out my travel papers and money exchange, a guide from the Air India office offered to take me sightseeing. We saw the pyramids and the sphinx and then the museum of ancient Egypt, including King Tut's coffin and other contents of his tomb.

Mission Number Ten — Africa

On the way deeper into Africa, I didn't sleep very well. We landed at Juba for refueling. I saw my black brothers filling important clerical jobs at the airport, and I was so proud of them. I was longing to have a word with them, but I could not speak French, and I assumed that they couldn't speak English so I just smiled. Before long the air officer who was on the plane came in and I rushed to tell him how happy I was to see these people and how I wished I could speak with them. He assured me that they knew English. I was so elated that I ran over and shook their hands and told them about my trip, and they seemed pleased. We began flying again, this time over the thickest and most extensive jungle I had ever seen.

We landed in Stanleyville and had to get off the plane and go through customs. The first official started talking in French, and I said, "I'm sorry, I do not understand. I speak only English." Another man picked up and said he understood English. So, they said, "You will continue your flight tomorrow morning at 7:30." I said, "Tomorrow morning! Where will I stay?" This was the first time in the whole trip I began to feel as if I were back in the United States. And I thought, *Blessed Redeemer, what will I do? I don't know any Africans! I don't know anybody here.*

Just then someone said, "Mrs. Welch?" I looked around to see a white man dressed in khaki shorts and shirt and he said, "Mrs. Welch, I am a chaplain. The Baptist missionaries had to be away and they made arrangements for us to take care of you until tomorrow when you continue your flight." Oh, I felt like falling on my knees and having a prayer meeting of thanks right there. During a meal the chaplain said, "Mrs. Welch, we noticed by the newspapers that you will be doing concerts in the Brazzaville and the Coquilhatville area, and we would like for you to sing for the Europeans." By that time I knew that Europeans were white people whether they were Europeans or Americans. "I would be very glad to sing for the Europeans, but would it be possible for me to sing for some Africans, too?" I asked. He said, "Well, I think perhaps we can arrange it." When we went to the African church there were already about fifty or so people, and they never stopped coming. The drums! They had beaten out the message—they were coming from every direction. I stood up to talk. I always brought greetings from America, from Christian churches in America, and from the black people of America in general, and then I sang for them. I first told them how happy I was to be there. I told them this was a childhood dream of mine to come to my ancestors' land. I said, "I am not only your sister in Christ, but I am your sister in the flesh. My ancestors came from this land, too." But of course, I had to wait for interpretation. The Belgian chaplain translated and when he got through, a concerted groan went through that whole audience. I found myself wondering what in the world had this man told these people! I almost became angry because I thought he told them something I didn't mean. I thought the groan meant they were dissatisfied. Finally I got through the program, and I said to the chaplain, "What in the world did you tell them a while ago when that sound went through the audience?" He smiled. "Mrs. Welch, whenever you hear that sound go through an African audience, it means they liked what you said."

I surmised that God was in the whole plan because my hair wouldn't act right, but being in Africa with my hair in its natural state helped identify me with African women. I was perfectly content to be in Africa with my hair kinky. I really was surprised when I got to Africa to discover that I was more of a curiosity in Africa than in any other country where I had been!

One time I spoke to a group of women, and the missionary of course had to interpret for me. They were asking questions through the missionary to me and I was giving the answers or asking questions through the missionary. After a while, they asked a question and the missionary turned red and she didn't ask me right away. And I said, "What did they ask you?" And she said she didn't know how to ask me. And I said I didn't care what they ask me; they couldn't hurt me. She said she was really embarrassed. I said, "Please tell me." She said, these women seeing us talking to each other and understanding each other, and we are dressed alike, these women want to know, "Is she white like you?" They were not basing it on the color of the skin, but on customs and actions and how you respond and react, that is how they tried to identify with me.

Soon I flew to Coquilhatville, now having an African name since names changed when countries gained their independence. When I got to Coquilhatville there were some of our American Disciple missionaries whom I knew. I felt more at home and I was so thrilled because there was a big stack of mail waiting me. The missionaries' names were Mr. and Mrs. Russell, Mr. and Mrs. Caldwell, and Edna Pool—and many others. The house I occupied looked right over the Congo River. This was exciting. The first time we met in the Congolese church it was overflowing with hundreds of people. There was an old man who was one of the first Christians. He was so proud of me and he made the introductory remarks, greeting me.

Coquilhatville, now called Mbandaka, is right on the Congo River. To go from Bolenge to Coquilhatville, we crossed the equator. The Congo River was beautiful and placid that day. It wasn't really wide; we could look across it. Then we went to Leopoldville, which is now Kinshasa, I was in Leopoldville where the Baptists and the Salvation Army had wonderful missions. The Baptists had a large school and the only hospital. They had just finished the first building of the new government hospital. I went into the hospital, and one of the first patients I saw was a little old black woman sitting up in bed just grinning and trying to say something to me. She was so happy! I asked about her and they told me the missionaries had found her in the corner of her hut with a leg that was practically rotted off. They took her to the hospital and amputated her leg. But now she was well again except for that leg, and she was sitting up praising God. The American Baptist school and seminary had a fine music department.

In Leopoldville, I celebrated the 75th anniversary of Protestant missions in the Congo. I was on the program on that very hot day. Of course, those on the program were government dignitaries, officials of Europe, our American consul, and a Protestant minister from Belgium. On the platform also were a few African men.

As I sat there, I was excited about seeing all of these African people, the most I had seen at one time. There must have been about twenty-five or thirty thousand of them. At the beginning of the program about four or five thousand African students who were representatives of all the Protestant mission schools marched in review all around the stadium, where the people on the platform could see them. It was thrilling to see thousands of children swinging their arms, their heads and shoulders erect, marching to the rhythm of a marvelous African band. I was thrilled because here I found myself in Africa, the land of my forefathers.

I was sitting there noticing that even when the dignitaries got up, nobody said anything about them or who they were. They just spoke and sat down. And I thought, *Well shoot! I want to be able to tell these people who I am and where I'm from.* I said a little prayer, "Lord, if I'm supposed to say something, please let me know."

Then I whispered to my Salvation Army friend, "You know, I would like to have you interpret for me when my time comes because there is a little something I would like to say before I sing." Of course, he got all flustered, whispered, "Well, tonight at the mission meeting you may say something."

I knew that meant he was not going to interpret for me. I wanted to talk to black Africans. So, when my time came, I went up to the microphone. I looked at the Secretary of Missions and beckoned to him. I knew that was definitely against protocol, and I didn't get any response!

118

Then I called his name and asked him to interpret for me. Of course, everybody in the stadium heard and there was nothing he could do but come up reluctantly.

"All I want to say is that I bring you greetings from the United States of America. I bring you special greetings from the Protestant churches of America, on this goodwill mission. I bring you greetings from the Christians of America. But I bring you very special greetings from American black people. I am so happy that I am in this land of my forefathers, too. I am going to sing a group of songs for you. The first one I will sing will be a Negro spiritual. These were the songs that were born in the hearts of my ancestors during the days of slavery. My people were able to sing them because there had been white ministers who recognized it enough to teach them the gospel of Jesus Christ by reading the Bible to them. Later my own people, the slaves, who had learned a little English, learned how to read the Bible for themselves. It was a great source of strength and hope and faith for them. And out of their knowledge of the Old Testament of the Hebrew people as well as the New Testament, especially as it had to do with the sufferings and even the death of Jesus Christ, these songs were born in the hearts of my ancestors. One of these spirituals 'Swing Low, Sweet Chariot' we think came directly from Africa because it seems to be based on an African legend. After that I will sing 'One World, Built on a Firm Foundation' and then 'Were You There When They Crucified My Lord?' And as I sing it, I want to say I do not believe that my ancestors were thinking about any one particular group of people who crucified our Lord. But they thought of it as relating to every one of us, even to this day, who say we love God through Jesus Christ, who, when we fail to live up to the highest we know of the Christian way of life, we too are guilty of nailing the nails." I sang and when I finished, like the others who were on the program, I sat down.

Our American officials seemed very thankful for my being there. Consul Alberts had made arrangements for me to sing in Brazzaville at the Roman Catholic Cathedral.

Brazzaville was across the Congo River in French territory. We had to cross the river on a boat. Consul Alberts, of course, went with me. The trip across the river was interesting because for the first time since I had left the United States I was reminded of discrimination. In that part of the Congo everything was separate. At the ticket office there was a window for blacks and a window for whites, so Consul Alberts got the tickets. When we got on the boat, there was also an area for the black people to sit and an area for the whites. When we got on I saw the Africans sitting back there; so I deliberately went back and sat with them.

Consul Alberts motioned to me and said, "Mrs. Welch, you come and sit with me." I knew I could because I was a visitor and was with white people, but I said, "No, I would like to sit back here."

And I stayed back there and bless his heart, he was embarrassed. He knew I was reminded of what happened in the United States. At Brazzaville, we went to the cathedral for the rehearsal. The beautiful cathedral was in the process of being built in African style architecture.

I heard several missionaries were not happy about Consul Alberts' taking me to do a concert in Brazzaville. So, I made it very plain to them that I was not given any particular directions as Ambassador of Goodwill for whom I was to sing. I also learned how human missionaries are. We have made little gods of our missionaries all through the years. We thought anybody who left America to go to these backward places had made the greatest sacrifice that anybody could ever make. I don't think missionaries always appreciated it, but we did it because we at home had this kind of attitude. Well, I remember when I thought if you went out as a missionary you were a perfect Christian, but I have learned that missionaries are human beings, too. None of them are perfect as none of us are perfect. You loved them more because you knew we were all alike. I met a lot of wonderful missionaries who inspired me and challenged me.

The harmonization of men's and boys' voices at the concert was absolutely magnificent. It was so moving, I wished there was nothing but that on the program. That was a wonderful night; I did the solo part and they did this harmonized background and then part of it they would sing with me.

Plane and boat schedules worked against me so I didn't meet Dr. Albert Schweitzer. The late Emory Ross, who was a very close friend of Dr. Schweitzer, knowing that I was going to Africa, made arrangements for me to go to Lambarene to see him. I was so excited, but the plane was late and when we landed in Gabon the last boat going to Lambarene had already left. I couldn't keep the tears back.

I had several experiences back in the bush.

One was at our Mission in Wema. Messages were sent by drum; so as we were making our way to Wema there were people who came out of the jungle and waved at us. They told the missionaries that they had heard about me and they would like to hear me too.

We went from Wema to Mondombe where Ned Roberts and his wife, as well as Gertrude Shoemaker had a home and I went to the leprosarium with Hattie Mitchell and sang for the lepers. On Sunday morning Pastor Ntonga preached. I have never heard more powerful preaching anywhere in my life! Pastor Ntonga had my vote of confidence for winning Christians in Africa.

At the end of one of the services, the names of the candidates for baptism were called. As they were called, they went out and formed a line, two by two.

Finally everybody was called and there were six or eight people left, men and women, and they came rushing down the aisle, talking to Pastor

Ntonga seriously. I saw Pastor Ntonga shaking his finger. Ned was standing there and I asked, "What's happening"?

He smiled, "They came down to tell Pastor Ntonga that he had not called their names but they were to be baptized too. Pastor Ntonga told them he had checked on them and they had not lived up to the standards. They had to go back and do some more living. And when the pastor came again, if they had met the standards, then they would be baptized."

I said, "Lord, have mercy. I wonder how many preachers in the United States would do that!"

Ned Roberts relates this incident:

"Her visit there was wonderful. About a month later, Jewell went out to the school to teach a women's class and as she approached the room she heard the Amen chorus being sung and was most pleasantly surprised to find one woman's two-year-old son standing before the class directing the singing in perfect rhythm. They are taught the rhythm of the drums before they are a year old.

"On Rosa's visit, my wife, Jewell, and I met her half way between the mission stations of Wema, where we had been visiting, and Mondombe where we lived. She wanted to experience traveling and living in the bush or jungle villages, so we took her on a three-day tour of villages, churches, and schools of the equatorial rain forest area.

"Her fame as a beautiful singer of the Good News had gone before her. The jungle drums announced her presence and alerted each village of her coming before we arrived. The result was that whole villages had turned out and were blocking the jungle road in eager anticipation of her coming and her singing for them.

"The tunes of the gospel songs she sang in English were well known by the Christians and were received as the messages of the apostles of the Day of Pentecost in their own languages of Lonkundo, Lalia and Lingala. There was great joy and celebration in the worship and praise.

"On the third day we headed for Mondombe, but the progress was extremely slow as in each village the crowds awaited the marvelous Wembi (The Singer). We had hoped to be at the station for the evening meal, but gave that up because of the demands for Rosa to sing, and she never refused, although she was becoming extremely weary.

"It was nearly 9:00 p.m. when we approached the mission station. We warned her that the greatest crowd yet would be waiting for her when we arrived, including hundreds of students, mission staff of schools and hospital, surrounding villagers as well as residents of our leper colony. She wearily groaned, 'Surely they won't want me to sing tonight. I simply cannot sing another word.' The crowd was bigger than we expected and their expectations of a concert greater than we anticipated. We tried to explain that the Wembi was too tired and needed rest, but she would sing for them the next day. That was very unsatisfactory for the many who had walked for miles and would not be able to come back the next day. When the situation was explained to Rosa, she reluctantly agreed to sing one song. She mounted a stand and as she began to sing her spirit was rekindled, her tiredness melted away and she sang more beautifully than ever.

After visiting a leprosarium in Mondombe, we went to Bolenge. The Russells were the ones I stayed with in Bolenge, but I cannot talk about our work in what is now Zaire and especially Bolenge and Coquilhatville without talking about Walter Cardwell and his family. Walter was the field secretary and took me to see, feel, and understand a lot there.

Walter said to me one day, "Rosa, there is an old man who is all crippled with arthritis and he just can't get out. He had expressed his regret for not getting to meet you because he had heard from so many about you."

I said, "Oh, Walter, let's go see him." This tall, old man lived in as drab a hut as I had ever seen. He had been one of the early Christians. I think he is the one who gave me an African name, and the name he gave me was Mama Bongenge.

I used to be so sensitive about the title "Mama" when missionaries came back home. I am so glad I got to go to Africa and understand. When they got to calling me Mama I was told that it was a title of respect for a woman. So I asked the Lord to forgive me for all the sensitiveness I had had toward the missionaries.

Recently Walter Cardwell wrote of my visit:

"About thirty years ago Rosa Page Welch arrived at Bolenge, our pioneer mission station in Africa. She was the first black church leader to come from the U.S. church as a visitor.

"The Africans were amazed at her strong soprano voice. They were used to male singers. One day Rosa Page spoke to the student body at Congo Christian Institute. She told them about the strength of black congregations in the U.S.A. and of the strong academic institutions where young black persons received training in the professions. Then she wanted the students to ask questions, which they did for forty minutes. Rosa Page also spoke at the women's meeting in Bolenge church. It was a true celebration of womanhood for the African women, most of whom could not read nor write.

"One of the choruses she decided to teach the students was the Amen chorus. Because she taught it to the primary and secondary school students, they called her, Mama Amen.'"

I had another funny experience in Congo, which is now Zaire. I had been to the church in Coquilhatville and they had had a party for me, a reception at one member's house.

The missionary told me later, "Rosa, after you left, you should have heard all the questions the men asked me about you!"

I said, "Really!"

"When they heard you mention family, they wanted to know if you were married. They also asked if your husband was black. But they were most concerned about you being away for seven months. They didn't believe your husband would take you back. Under the same circumstances *they* wouldn't have!"

After a day or two in the Cameroons I wasn't feeling too well, and I was a guest in the home of a doctor and his wife. She was in charge of nursing in a large hospital. She said, "Rosa, you had better stay in bed, and I'll send one of the nurses over to get a specimen of blood."

I was lying there and pretty soon a young African fellow came in. He couldn't speak English and I couldn't speak French and he just made a motion for me to put my hand out. They finally decided I had a touch of malaria; so I had to stay in bed a few hours and take some medicine.

When I was ready to leave the French Cameroon, I went to Duala. I was a guest in the home of a French official and his wife, who was Jewish. She had a bad experience when the Germans tried to get rid of all the Jews. After hearing me tell about the spirituals and the history of them and all, she told of some of her experiences. It was very teary for both of us.

Eventually we flew to Liberia, landing in Ghana. I had hoped to see the city, but I was not scheduled to do anything in Ghana. However, we had to wait at the airport for about six hours for the flight to continue on to Monrovia. During that six hours it poured rain! That was the monsoon season. I had never seen it rain any harder anywhere. We had to walk in water two or three inches deep, with thunder and lightning all around us. It was the worst electrical storm I had ever seen. We got in the Pan American plane and took off in the storm. I don't believe I was the only one who was frightened. The higher we went, the clearer was that lightning! And the heavens seemed to open. I actually found myself expecting to see someone standing there in the parted sky! When the plane finally landed, and I got off, I felt like falling on my knees and having prayer. I surely started praising the Lord.

There was somebody there to meet us because I was to sing a formal concert for the YWCA in Monrovia. One morning I went out to the university to do a program for the students and the faculty. I also had an audience with the late President Tubman. I was really impressed by that man. When we went to the state house we were ushered into a beautifully furnished lobby. He gave me about twenty minutes to talk with him. I never had the feeling he was hurrying me; he was a very relaxed man.

The Methodist Church was strong there, and I was at the home of the bishop. The concert was a very well attended affair and, of course, all were dressed beautifully.

I shall always thank the heavenly Father for giving me the opportunities and varied experiences with the African people who had truly related to me and made me feel one of them, both in the spirit of Christ and in our common ancestry.

Mission Number Eleven — Europe

We arrived in Lisbon, Portugal, right after midnight and two Presbyterian couples were there to meet me. They took me to the seminary which was a beautiful place. I presented a program for them in the chapel and taught them some spirituals, and then a seminary quartet and the African students sang for me. That evening I did a sacred program for a large, very cordial and appreciative mixed audience at the church. After devotions and packing and a bite of breakfast I again headed for the airport—this time for London, England.

As in most of the places I landed, I didn't know who was to meet me, but this airport was huge and no one seemed to be looking for me. It wasn't difficult to spot me since I was the only black person. After patiently waiting for a long time, I finally asked a policeman what to do. I told him I had expected someone to meet me. He told me that perhaps someone was waiting for me at one of the two train stations in the city. Since I didn't know which would be the right station, I got on the bus to take me to London, planning to stop at Victoria Station first. I enjoyed the trip, for I had never seen such beautiful gardens in all of the homes. It was strange, but when the driver called for the Victoria Station, I felt it was the right stop. Just as I got inside, somebody said, "Mrs. Welch?"

It was like that experience I had in Stanleyville, Africa. I looked around and there was a tall young woman.

I said, "I am Rosa Page Welch."

She said, "Oh, I'm expecting you. I am from the Christian Church, and you are to do a program at our church tonight."

It was late evening by this time and I don't know how she knew what time to meet me. I had a huge suitcase, heavy as it could be because of the gifts given to me in all the places.

I said, "Can't we get a red cap to take us to a taxi?"

"Oh," she said, "It isn't very far. We will go on the underground."

We went on the escalator to the trains. This was a long one, but not quite as long as the one in Moscow, Russia. We got down there, both of us carrying the heavy suitcase. I was so tired I didn't know what to do! I had enough money to pay whatever the taxi was but she insisted on walking. I soon learned how frugal the Europeans are! (British, at least!) So we got on the train and we rode a long time.

When we got off the train, I said, "Now can we get a taxi?" She declared it wasn't very far; but I am sure we walked two to four of the longest blocks I have ever known. We finally got to the church, the two of us still taking turns carrying that suitcase.

It was a nice little church, and the people were there and waiting patiently. I had to go right up on the platform and do a program! On this trip only the grace of God got me through a whole lot of situations.

The thing that surprised me was how small all of our churches in Britain were. There were no large buildings or congregations. I saw very few young people in the churches.

One morning my hosts took me to see Stratford-on-Avon. It was such a beautiful drive to the Shakespearean village. We had lunch at the theater and saw the church and Shakespeare's birthplace. I also visited the Covers in Birmingham who had been to the States.

The following morning I caught the Glasgow train and had a good seat in a compartment with several nice British servicemen, and we soon arrived in Glasgow where Mr. and Mrs. Duncan met me. After a good dinner we rushed to the church for a worship service where I sang two solos and met some very lovely people. It was chilly but again I was delighted to find hot-water bottles in my bed thanks to Mrs. Duncan. The next morning they took me for a gloriously beautiful drive. Scotland is so very beautiful, and I really enjoyed this experience.

In Edinburgh, Scotland, I was met by Chester Sillars who was serving a small church as exchange pastor from America. It was like old home week since we had all been away from home for a while. The family took me to the concert hall to hear the oratorio "Elijah," which was the most exquisite rendition one could hear.

On the Saturday night before Easter Sunday, while we were visiting, Rev. Sillars said to me, "You are to preach tomorrow morning."

And I said, "Tomorrow is Easter! I thought every pastor looked forward to being in his own pulpit on that day!"

And then I was scared; I hadn't expected to preach on Sunday morning. But I was still overflowing with excitement and emotion about the Holy Land. So I decided I had all the resources I really needed, and the response was beautiful.

From Edinburgh, I went to France. The Presbyterian missionaries in Paris could not be there, but they made arrangements for me to live in a hotel near the Eiffel Tower.

A friend in Paris made it possible for me to enjoy two separate sightseeing trips. She took me to the place where Woodrow Wilson helped sign the League of Nations papers. To tell the truth, I was a little disappointed in Paris.

After I left Paris I went by train to Geneva, Switzerland. Robert Tobias met me when I got to Geneva and took me to my hotel. After giving me a chance to freshen up and rest a bit we went out to the World Council Institite. Geneva is a beautiful city. The mountains are partly covered with snow and are magnificent to look at. The Institute is a lovely chateau. In the evening the people who were there from all over the world gathered in the spacious reception room and I sang for and with them. The next day we went to see the offices of the World Council of Churches.

I was taken on a most interesting sightseeing visit and saw the monument erected by the Protestants honoring the Catholics killed during the revolution by Protestants during Calvin's time.

When I arrived back in London my hostess had a stack of mail waiting for me. In all this mail was a letter from Eureka College with Dr. Dickerson's return address. He was then the president of the college, and I opened it after I had read the letters from my family; it said:

"Dear Mrs. Welch:
The Board of Trustees of Eureka College have unanimously voted that you should receive an Honorary Doctorate of Humane Letters from Eureka College in June at commencement on the seventh and I'm writing to ask if you will accept it."

I became weak; I thought they didn't know that I had only finished junior college. They must have made a mistake.

Finally, it was time to fly home. We landed in New York. Mrs. Ross and other good friends were there to meet me. I was excited to see them. After unpacking some of my things I called my family. It was so wonderful to hear their voices, and how grateful I was to God for bringing me safely home. The next morning I met the press and had an interesting time with them.

On Sunday I began by speaking to a large group of women at a breakfast following a very worshipful communion service at the Church of the Master. Then I was rushed to our Park Avenue Christian Church where I sang "How Great Thou Art" at the service.

Monday I made my report of the world tour to the Presbyterian board and representatives of other boards. Don West introduced me as the representative of the Disciples of Christ (Christian Church).

Tuesday morning found me packing again, but for the last time before reaching home. It was a good flight, and when we landed and I looked around, the first person I saw was Mama. She was just beaming. All my family were there and my precious new granddaughter, Brenda Gayle!! What a glorious meeting. I just praised the Lord!

12

Gonna Put On My Robe

UPON my arrival home in April 1953, I had many phone calls welcoming me. I had a wonderful time getting acquainted with Baby Brenda and talking to Mama and Lesly and all my family and friends.

Mama had always been a homebody, but when I was asked to talk about my world trip in an area close to home, Mama would go. She loved to hear me tell about Africa, and she especially liked for me to sing "The Lord's Prayer."

On Sunday our pastor, Elder Sherman, let me speak at our church and tell about my trip. My voice teacher and friend, B. Fred Wise, invited me to speak to his repertoire class. May Fellowship Day found me speaking on the morning program for United Church Women in a church in Chicago. One night I did my program for a large group at First Church of the Brethren.

It was so delightful to be with the "Hungry Five" again. They were intimate friends who gathered occasionally over a period of years to eat and have fellowship. The group consisted of Eleanor Alexander, Ruth Beck, Alberta Lunger, Pauline Osterling and myself. Others were added from time to time. One simply can't underestimate the blessings of friends.

On Mother's Day I was asked to speak for the annual Women's Day service at our church. It was a double honor because during that service Linnie and Jake's baby, Brenda Gayle, was dedicated along with several other babies.

Presentations over the next weeks were given at Newton, Kansas, where I spoke and sang for the student convocation at Bethel College; Indianapolis where I met with Helen Spaulding and her staff prior to my meeting with the Board of Trustees of the United Christian Missionary Society; South Bend, Indiana, where I spoke to the Christian Women's Fellowship on "Glimpses of Our Mission the World Over."

When I had been home from my world tour for one month I had given twenty-six speeches.

I was responsible for such a hectic schedule, but it was difficult for me to say no, especially after such an experience. I had this terrific sense of urgency and I felt compelled to take advantage of every opportunity. I have never had such uplifting fulfillment as the privilege and joy of telling about my experiences and trying to interpret the spirit of the people according to my own observations. Then it became my purpose to challenge all of us to our responsibility of being God's channels through which the needs of the world might be met.

The Presbyterian women were having their assembly in Minneapolis in the spring. At the opening morning session I sang "Amazing Grace," then led the assembly in several songs. From there I rushed to the TV studios where I was the guest speaker for the program "Sanctuary," sponsored by the Conference of Christians and Jews.

My next major appearance was especially gratifying. I went to my Alma Mater. During my visit there, I stayed at the big mansion on the campus. It brought back many memories of happy hours in the mansion with Dr. and Mrs. Lehman when I first entered SCI, so many years earlier.

Barton Hunter gave a wonderful message at the afternoon commencement service.

I had the honor of speaking at the alumni banquet.

Another interesting visit was to Eureka, Illinois. I saw Eureka College campus, and was honored by having Eureka College confer upon me the honorary degree, Doctor of Humane Letters.

I remember thinking, *I wonder if they have made a mistake.*

The next time I saw Mossie Wyker I confided in her. "Maybe I am not supposed to have this, I only went through SCI and that is only a junior college." Well, Mossie assured me that even if I didn't have four years of college I had certainly earned this degree.

I got on the night train and arrived in Chicago the next morning. I was so glad to find my family in good health and spirits. I got so involved telling them about my trip, changing clothes and repacking my bag, that I almost missed the train back to Minneapolis. I visited with Archie Anderson, one of two dining car waiters who were both formerly from Mississippi. He was a graduate of Tougaloo College and knew Annie Page and

Helen Harris. Upon arrival in Minneapolis we went to the Curtis Hotel for rehearsal and then to the auditorium for dress rehearsal.

I was interviewed by a young newspaper reporter, then had such a good visit and lunch with Helen Henderson. We went with Margaret Shannon to the auditorium where we heard such an excellent message by Dr. Leber. Then the program. The testimonies, given by Dr. Hau from Korea, Dr. Oudie from Lebanon, a man from Brazil and Dr. John Hays from China, were very moving. I had the privilege of leading the singing and was able to tell about my being in Hong Kong when Dr. Hays was released from prison by the Communists in China.

In early July, I went to Portland, Oregon, for the state planning commission, and we met at a retreat center. I met James Ballinger, who was serving on our national church program staff. Jim drove me to Portland for the 1953 International Convention of the Christian Church (Disciples of Christ). It was late when we arrived at the hotel near the convention center where I had been registered. Apparently they had not been informed of the fact that I was black, for when I went to check in they would not admit me. Like so many of my white friends in similar situations, Jim was anxious about what to do with me. Luckily he happened to call Oma Lou Myers, whom he knew was supervising the children's program of that great convention. In the telephone conversation, Oma Lou advised that in all probability the downtown Multnomah Hotel would provide lodging for me. Upon arrival we were welcomed by the desk clerk and were both mightily relieved.

John Paul Pack remembers that:

"As vice president of the International Convention in Portland, it was my privilege to introduce Rosa Page for a major address. I remember saying: Ladies and gentlemen, Rosa Page Welch and I have one very important thing in common. We are both products of schools founded and operated by the Christian Women's Board of Missions. I attended their school in Beckley, West Virginia, and have gotten as far as the great Northwest. Rosa attended SCI and has gone to the ends of the earth."

After the convention I went to Southern California to fill three days of engagements at Pasadena for the Council of Church Women and All People's Church in Los Angeles.

The rest of the summer was spent in conferences in Illinois, Minnesota, Alabama, Mississippi, and Virginia. One of my most interesting fall conferences was with Chinese students at Syracuse, Indiana.

It would take a long time to tell about the exciting, thrilling experiences of worship, inspiration, and challenge that fall. Meeting and shaking hands with President Eisenhower and participating on Mary Margaret McBride's broadcast were once-in-a-lifetime experiences.

In November Gale Page arrived home after nearly a year in Korea.

December was a full month, too. One of the nicest surprises was the lovely citation given me by the Chicago area Council of Church Women. Another nice surprise was when the Henrich family published a biography of me in the September issue of their fine little *Sunshine* magazine. My name also appeared in *Who's Who Among American Women*.

Seeing Fifth Avenue and Radio City in New York City in all their Christmas splendor, with Inez Moser and Helen Spaulding was an unforgettable Christmas gift.

I loved to go to an Ashram for I could get my spiritual self "recharged" again being with Brother E. Stanley Jones and Sister Anna Mow and people like that. Whole families were urged to come.

Mama went with us once to Green Lake, Wisconsin. Everyone was so nice to her and just loved her. That was where I met Kathleen Bailey and her children. The children were the same age as mine. Brother Stanley always spoke and Sister Anna did Bible study. We all spent some time every day in a work project. Some helped with dishes after each meal, some tore sheets into bandages. Others sewed them together. Mama helped make layettes for underprivileged mothers. Everyone working brought us all to the same level in the name of Jesus Christ. We couldn't have a complete fellowship unless we all joined together in the whole of life.

As I traveled back and forth across the country, I saw so many marvelous sights and so many historical places. I remember visiting the old Cane Ridge Meeting House a few miles from Paris, Kentucky. This was the site where the Christian Church (Disciples of Christ) had its beginnings. I could almost hear the great voice of Alexander Campbell, founder of this Christian movement, preach as he stood behind the huge pulpit. It pained me as I gazed around the circular balcony to be reminded that it was built as a place for the slaves to sit during worship services.

It had always been Mama's desire to move back home to Mississippi. We never had sold our house that I had purchased the year I taught in Port Gibson. When Mama did move back, her sister, my Aunt Emma, lived with her.

In January, following some surgery, I resumed my work and spent a busy January and February going first to Mansfield, Ohio, and then to Stillman College at Tuscaloosa, Alabama, as speaker for their Religious Emphasis Week.

From there, I went to Florida as one of the leaders of the Florida Chain of Missions Assemblies. They were four wonderful weeks of challenge, inspiration, and fine Christian fellowship

Every year they would always have people from foreign countries, both missionaries and Christian national leaders. This year I met and worked with Dr. Tanamoto. When I first started going in 1949, everyone on the team except black Americans could stay in hotels or eat in public restaurants, but I continued to go because I felt that God would use me to help open doors. The first couple of years I stayed in Negro homes where I got to know some wonderful people and had some great experiences. They came to understand what I had in mind and what my ideas were, to be willing to be a part of God's reconciling force. Then after a couple of years, white homes began to accept me, and in four or five years motels and hotels were opened up. That was the joy of being on a team repeatedly.

The first part of March was spent in Missouri at Culver-Stockton College in Canton, in Hannibal, and Fulton. Then I went to Tougaloo Southern Christian College for a board meeting. While there I had the pleasure of hearing Leontyne Price sing a beautiful concert.

We celebrated Mama's seventy-seventh birthday in May 1955. That morning she didn't get up; she stayed in bed kind of late. I said, "Mama, hurry and get up. This is your birthday and Cousin Josie is coming over to have breakfast with you." And she grimaced, "Aw, I don't feel like being bothered with Josie." She finally got up. For dinner we had some beans, and Aunt Emma had made a cake. The next day as I left on a trip, Mama came out on the porch and I kissed her goodbye. She was smiling and something inside of me said. "Go back and hug her," and I didn't do it because I knew I would cry. I regretted it over and over again.

My cousin called me from Hattiesburg and anxiously told me, "You and Lesly come home as quick as you can, they are not expecting your Mama to live through the night." Oh, the shock! My sister Lesly, my daughter, Linnie, and I decided to go immediately, taking Brenda, almost three, and Jan Elizabeth, two months old, with us. We wanted Mama to see our two darling little girls. Chicago was in a blizzard; we were afraid by plane we would get grounded somewhere, so we took the train, praying hard. We had sent a wire to them saying we were coming on the train. When it came time to eat, I said to Lesly and Linnie, "You go on to the diner and I will watch the baby."

I was sitting, looking out of the window and praying that the Lord would let Mama live until we got there. Suddenly there came a feeling as though a terrifically heavy load was lifted off my shoulders! And I knew that the Lord had answered my prayer and that Mama was better. I started praising God. When Lesly returned, I said, "Oh, I have such a relieved feeling as if a load had been lifted." And she said, "Sister, I feel the same way!" After many weary hours, we finally reached Jackson and when we got off the train, no one was there to meet us. They thought we were flying and had gone to the airport. We called and had them paged. They rushed to the depot and picked us up.

132

When we finally got home, we were stunned to see a wreath on the front door, which meant that Mama had died. They told us how they had all stood around her bed; they knew she was dying. Two of her sisters were there; one on either side of the bed, each one holding her hand. And they said she opened her eyes and she looked at them and chided, "What are you all doing standing around my bed? You act like you think I'm dying!" and she closed her eyes and was gone.

The funeral was in the old church and was beautiful and well attended. People loved my mother.

In all of Mama's struggles, she had always given evidence of a faith that gave strength and endurance to ours. I thought about missionaries whose parents had died while they were out on assignment and couldn't come home for the funeral. I was home.

Welch was retired now and it was good to see him thoroughly enjoying the grandchildren. We were enjoying many blessings.

My call to be on the staff of Jarvis Christian College at Hawkins, Texas, was very exciting. I could combine it with my other jobs, for I was to recruit students and obtain funds for scholarships. Dr. Cleo Blackburn was the president of the college and was written up in the November issue of *Readers' Digest*.

United Church Women chose me for a three-year term as a vice president under the leadership of Mrs. Cynthia Wedel. I had some very interesting and important board meetings and was always happy to do what I could for special days such as World Day of Prayer, May Fellowship Day and World Community Day.

The highlight of 1956 was my two-month spring tour of South America. I was one of a party of thirty persons sent to South America in observance of the fiftieth anniversary of mission work of the Disciples of Christ in Argentina.

After several days of preparation, my family saw me off to Miami where I was to meet the rest of the tour group. We had all been scheduled to stay at a hotel. Apparently, when the first of the tour group checked in, they learned that a Negro would not be allowed to stay there. So, when I arrived, a Dr. Pharr met me and took me to a very lovely home for the night. She was such a lovely thoughtful lady and she made me feel welcome, but I was still deeply hurt that my friends hadn't forced the issue and refused their lodging also.

Our flight out of Miami gave us a chance to get acquainted, and prepared us for our first visit to Puerto Rico. The Disciples were the strongest in the rural areas.

The Puerto Rican Christian Church boasted over six thousand members. The Disciples were the second largest Protestant church on the island. After visiting several of these churches and singing for them, I flew on to Trinidad and then Brazil.

The JMC Mission School, whose students came from all over the interior of Brazil, put on a concert for us, and their conductor asked me to sing a number.

After lunch and a bit of rest, we went sightseeing. Our drive up the mountain and seeing for the first time the statue of Christ the Redeemer was a magnificent, breathtaking experience. God must have worked through the mind of the artist to give us this great piece of art It had been built by Catholics intending it to be a shrine, but Protestant objections made it just a statue, awe-inspiring to all who look upon it.

Before leaving the hotel we formed a friendship circle and I sang for the hotel staff and our group. We prayed and sang "God Be With You Till We Meet Again."

From Brazil we flew to Paraguay. We were very pleased to meet the President of Paraguay. His welcome was very cordial and friendly. While we were at the presidential residence I sang "Bless This House." He seemed to feel the need for spiritual guidance, for those were days of political unrest, student strikes and protests.

I sang at the Cultural Center and taught some spirituals. I also got to meet some state department officials.

Eventually we arrived in Buenos Aires and had a visit with some of our missionaries: the Liggetts, Spahns, and Smedleys.

After a few days of sightseeing and rest, it was time for the big anniversary service. I was asked to sing as a part of the pageant, "Were You There?"

I was so glad all of us had been together long enough to get to know and care for each other. I prayed that our observance of the lack of color consciousness among the Latin American people might help us not to take the easy way out, but to seek God's strength, courage and guidance and that we would give ourselves thoroughly to the cause of Christ.

One of the most memorable experiences I had on this trip was after I had sung a concert in Brazil. It was held at the English-speaking church in Sao Paulo to an overflowing crowd. During the intermission, a very lovely Brazilian woman came backstage to congratulate me and then just stood around before she finally said, "I am the Protestant religious helper at our national prison. My name is Fleming. Tomorrow is Mother's Day and we are having a big program with the prisoners' families as visitors. I wonder if you would be willing to sing a group of songs?" Well, I replied almost immediately, "Yes, I would love to." I had just read an article about the nation's most notorious criminal who was a prisoner there so I said to her: "I have just been reading about Benedito. Would I get a chance to meet him?" She assured me that I certainly would. After my concert I talked to her some more and she related the story of her encounter with him. It seems that all the while he had been there he had never interacted with anyone. He always had his head down and never conversed with anybody. Mrs. Fleming went in and he ignored her too, but she asked him, "What is your name?" No response, so she asked him again. This time he looked up at her and said, "Why do you want to know my name?" She said, "Because you are my brother—and I love you." It shocked him. "No one has ever wanted to know my name, and I do have a name." She had a copy of the Gospel of St. John and she simply handed it to him and left. She did not try to preach to him. He read it and was converted. The article I had been reading showed his picture. He was a handsome man and he was smiling. The article explained that this was the first time anyone could remember Benedito smiling. Mrs. Fleming was led by God to do this work after she had lost her little girl in death.

In Sao Paulo, Mrs. Harper introduced me to a fine looking Brazilian evangelist. She told me how effective his ministry had been, putting out tracts, preaching and converting souls to Christ. An example was when he had helped a very wealthy Roman Catholic who owned three broadcasting stations. He gave hours of time on radio and money to help with a Roman Catholic festival or Eucharist. But when he heard the Roman Catholics charging fifty dollars and more for front seats at the Eucharist he was thoroughly disgusted and was on the verge of quitting the church altogether. Then he noticed a religious tract on his secretary's desk and found it interesting. When he finished reading it he was anxious to know where it came from and who wrote it and how he could get in touch with the writer. His secretary was able to locate the writer in Sao Paulo through the Bible Society and immediately called him long distance and insisted on his flying to Rio at his expense. The author came and the Catholic businessman said, "What you have in this tract is what Brazil needs instead of all this show in their religion." As a result he gave one hour each day on each station. Through this medium plus his special methods and efforts to reach the intelligentsia who never bother about church, this great soul was doing a very fruitful work for our Lord. I am so glad I had this opportunity to meet him.

A very nice couple came to thank me for bringing a letter from their daughter and to ask me to take a package to her. We left for the church. It was still raining, but there was a good congregation. I sang, talked, taught them a spiritual and then I sang, "I Surrender" in Portuguese and had them join in the chorus. A beautiful girl who had heard me the night before, came to me and put her arms around me, kissed me and said, "I've been thinking about accepting Christ and had not been able to decide and now I have." It was a very pleasant surprise and I said, "I'm so glad; we'll both thank God together for his speaking to your heart through me." I always hope he will do just that through my singing and me.

We left in the afternoon and stopped for Mrs. Fleming on our way to the penitentiary. We met the social worker and several others. We went through a long, wide corridor after passing through several heavily locked and guarded gates. In the corridor prisoners had concessions. Finally we got into the large grounds and many prisoners and visitors were listening to a program. Prisoners were all dressed in light suits and T-shirts. They didn't look or act like prisoners and I thanked God for this humane way of treating them. We were told that they decorate their rooms and they learn all kinds of trades. The open air stage was elaborately decorated. Large cakes—one a model of the prison and others of other buildings— all made by prisoners were on display. A tall handsome man, a prisoner, was making a speech honoring the warden of the prison. Beautiful tribute was paid him and the prisoners' applause attested to their appreciation of the director who looks like the fine person they said he was. The philosophy of the prison is that the prisoners are not to think of this as a prison with bad men, but a school where men who have gotten off the right track may learn how to be good citizens and may be rehabilitated. It was an amazing experience to observe the spirit of these men. I had the pleasure of meeting Benedito or "seven fingers," the notorious criminal and murderer. After his conversion he gave up smoking, drinking, and gambling as his first expression of the change in his life. To see him, this fine looking, courteous and happy man, no one would have believed he had lived as he had. This was his first day on his new prison job as "official receptionist." All the prisoners seemed to be proud of him. I asked to meet his parents, sister and brother who were there, and how proudly he rushed me to meet them. I just put my arms around his blessed, apparently burdened mother, and I said, "I know how proud you are and how thankful you must be to God for the conversion of your son, and I thank God too." How I thank God for Mrs. Fleming and this blessed ministry for his use of them. I hope I can do a similar service for prisoners in my country. I sang my program, "Nobody Knows the Trouble I've Seen," "Come Unto Me," a spiritual, and "The Lord's Prayer." The prison officials were all in the front row. They were all gracious and appreciative.

In summarizing these two months, I would make two observations. First, there was no segregation of people along color lines. Discrimination exists on economic, social, and intellectual levels, but *never* because of color differences. Second, the deeply spiritual quality of the ministers and missionaries in South America made me wish that it were possible to bring back to the States some of the spirit of humble and consecrated service which they manifested, and motivate some of our Christian leaders here.

Not long after returning to the States, I was sent as one of four persons on a deputation team to Missouri and Kentucky, representing the social welfare department of the United Christian Missionary Society.

Each member of the team was certain that the power and grace through Christ could manifest itself just as dynamically in our own USA as anywhere.

One Sunday in St. Louis each of the team spoke in a different Disciples' church in the morning and in other churches in the evening. We also took part in a mass meeting at Centennial Christian Church in the afternoon. It was known that St. Louis had done one of the better jobs in public school integration, but apparently the individual churches, for the most part, had not kept pace. This was not peculiar to St. Louis.

About a year before the World Conference of Christian Education was to be held in Tokyo, Japan, I received a letter from Dr. Chepell who was the chairman, stating that the program committee had unanimously voted to ask me to direct the music for the 14th World Conference and would I accept this invitation? I was very surprised and thrilled to receive such an invitation. I wrote back saying immediately, "Of course, I would be happy to do it."

On this, my second trip to Japan, I flew by way of San Francisco and Hawaii, arriving in Tokyo in the middle of July.

I met first with all the music leaders, the choir directors and musicians. I was the only woman in that field at the time, and I know they were wondering about me.

The Japanese musicians had written the theme song for the convention. It was written in Japanese, and I had to learn it. Japanese Christians were celebrating the 100th anniversary of Christianity in Japan, and in conjunction with the Christian Education Conference, they called one day Children's Day. I had never seen so many children. They came from Christian institutions all over Japan. One daily newspaper that was printed in English had wonderful editorials about the celebration. It read, "In spite of the fact that only one percent of Japanese are Christian, the impact and the influence of Christianity upon Japan is immeasurable."

When the World Conference was over I went to South Korea for five days and did some work for Church World Service. I spoke and sang my heart out even at the 38th Parallel, as arranged by Harold Shorrock.

I returned to Japan to do a concert tour benefitting the Naomi Kikuta Home Foundation. One of my concerts was in Hiroshima. I sang in the big auditorium and afterwards was taken to the peace park. In the park is a tall burned-out building that was left standing as a monument to the burned children. On it is a plaque stating: "We Japanese accept part of the blame which brought about part of the suffering of the war. But we the Japanese promise never to be part of war again."

Dr. Tanamoto, who lived in Hiroshima, and my interpreter, told me about that fatal day the atom bomb fell. The school in which he was principal was destroyed. He had taken his family up in the mountains on a picnic and they were not injured. I was told that those who were seriously burned, jumped into a lake and then begged to be pulled out. When people would reach out for them their skin would peel right off in their hands. Listening to the horrible stories about what happened was sickening. I went to the hospital and told them that I would sing for as many as could come.

This area also was the home of the Eta people. They were discriminated against because of the kind of work they did. Dr. Tanamoto explained to me that they were the slaughter house workers and the leather tanners. I always feel badly when people are put down, so I identified with them because of the way my people had been treated years ago. I stood up and told them, "My husband works for one of the largest packing houses in America . . .. It is really very useful work. If you didn't kill these animals, even the people that look down on you wouldn't have meat to eat and if you didn't tan the leather they probably wouldn't have shoes to wear. So you are doing a wonderful work. You are doing a noble work. You do not have to hang your head any more. God loves you as much as he loves anybody and if God loves you, you are all right. That's the way I feel about you." Well, bless their hearts, I could just feel the depression ebbing. I had hoped that God would give me something to say that would lift their spirits.

I sang "No Man Is an Island, No Man Stands Alone," "Sweet Little Jesus Boy," "Swing Low, Sweet Chariot," and concluded with "We need One Another."

The Japan tour had been a rewarding experience, yet it left me with the feeling that the mission of the church was never-ending, and we needed more Christian leaders, both at home and in foreign lands.

Going back into the various states and renewing acquaintances were always highlights of my ministry. Returning to Nebraska was no exception, for it was in Lincoln, Nebraska, that I had my first assignment back in the early thirties! Oma Lou Myers was another of those state executives of Christian education who invited me to come time after time to lead singing, speak or lead discussion groups on human rights and race relations. Oma Lou provided a unique experience in April 1961 during a youth convention held in Scottsbluff at the First Christian Church where Charles Livingston was pastor.

Lawrence Williams, who assisted Oma Lou in all of the state activities, arranged with the Burlington train officials for the same train which I took out of Chicago to stop in Omaha and put on several extra cars that would carry the youth and their sponsors across the state to the convention. It was after midnight when Oma Lou came to my roomette and awakened me to tell me that some 185 youth and their sponsors were now on the same train.

When I looked out of my window early the next morning as we pulled into the station, Blessed Redeemer, Nebraska was having a late blizzard. As the train stopped, Charles Livingston whisked into the waiting coach singing. "Oh, What a Beautiful Morning," as the snow flew furiously around him. After this hearty greeting he advised us that church people were waiting in their cars to take us bag and baggage to the First Christian Church. Several of the faithful women of the congregation had braved the storm early that morning and had prepared breakfast for everyone. Mildred Livingston, the minister's wife, was in the midst of it all, making hot chocolate for the whole crew. Such hospitality!

I was never one to turn down the chance to serve Christ and his church. Protestant women in Mexico were planning a meeting and a woman from the Chicago area made it known that she would welcome someone to go with her and she would share expenses. It was suggested that I accompany her, and so we went as delegates, representing the American Church Women United.

As always, when leaving a foreign land and new friends, I found myself hating to leave. I remember a missionary from our station or mission in Aguascalientes drove me over to see the hospital, which was badly in need of repairs.

As the busy summer progressed the upcoming Christian Women's Fellowship Quadrennial made me think of the first Quadrennial I had attended in 1957. Because I had served in so many youth camps and conferences over the years and had been involved in so many local churches across our land as well as most of the International Conventions, I had met many of the women of our denomination who were attending that first Christian Women's Fellowship Quadrennial conference at Purdue. Among those women was my good friend Adele Pack. She, too, remembers:

"Rosa Page and I shared a room and as we walked from the dorm to the dining room, we never took more than two or three steps that we were not stopped by friends from all over the land who hugged and kissed her."

Our International Convention meeting in Kansas City with Perry Gresham was one of the largest in our history. Seeing so many of my friends inspired me to sing my heart out for them. The whole issue of human rights in the 1960s was no longer something that was talked about because of my presence at white gatherings. The Supreme Court decision striking down the "separate but equal" laws made everyone think about his or her actions and attitudes. United Church Women had always stood for inclusiveness, and as they struggled with steps they could take I found myself more and more involved in workshops and visitations to local communities.

Mrs. Wedel, national president of UCW reports:

"United Church Women were trying to carry out their deep convictions that UCW must be—from the beginning—an inclusive organization. We had many problems—separate black and white church womens' groups in many places. I was in so many meetings where we agonized over the racial problem. Through all of this Rosa Page was always there. She gave a great deal of good sense and wisdom to our discussions and when things became really tense we could always ask Rosa for a song, and the tension dissolved. She gave more than she can ever know to white church women who were trying to find the right way through a very thorny issue."

Howard Royer shares the insights concerning human relations and the churches responsibility:

"Throughout her travels in the past decades, Mrs. Welch was pressed hard concerning race relations in the United States. It was the first question put to her wherever she went. In Africa, the second question was: Do Negroes and whites in America go to the same church?

"She spoke candidly about race. 'The racial unrest and tensions in other countries are the direct result of the awakening brought about through the teaching of the Gospel. These teachings acquaint a man with the fact that he is equal to any other man anywhere in the world.'

"Christians ought to work aggressively for integration, she believes. At a national missionary convention at which she was a leader she deplored the absence of any statements on racial justice. It would have been most appropriate, she declared, for the convention to commend the progress made in human rights and to indicate willingness 'to give ourselves, even suffer, to make further progress.'

"Mrs. Welch is no Johnny-come-lately in the battle against segregation. In the late forties the Mississippi native declared: 'Something is wrong with any intelligent Christian who says that such a way of life (segregation) is satisfactory to both Negroes and whites and who attempts to justify such a system. When I see doors marked *colored* and *white*. I ask myself. Why, oh why, does this need to continue? Aren't there enough courageous, right-thinking Christians to make this impossible? What about the ministers. the elders, and members of the churches?

"Through the years her response to prejudice has been one of forgiveness, prayer and hope. 'As much as it hurts, as much as it imprisons my body and sometimes my mind, I am determined that it will not imprison my soul,' she testified. But she does not deny the struggle she has had through the years to keep her soul and heart free. She finds it taxing to hear persons disparage the mentality or morals of Negroes when she feels the doors to growth have not been open to them. 'I pray forgiveness for myself and for those who condone the system of segregation by their failure to speak out against the practice,' she said."

One of the exciting experiences I had was in a work camp in western Nebraska near Hemingford. Dorothea Stahr, who was then serving as Director of Education for the Nebraska Council of Churches, had invited me to come and help in this new venture. The state directors of each denomination were asked to select young people who would participate in the work camp. So, it was interdenominational and interracial.

Jack Swartz, a Congregational Christian minister, headed up planning for the local communities. We all worked together and no one sat around being an "official." The local people had picked a site and were preparing a campground for the migrants who worked in the local sugar-beet fields.

When we first went out to see the place where these migrant people were encamped, I couldn't describe the feeling that came over me. It was on the edge of town near huge quonset granaries that were built during World War II. A little stream ran on one side. There were no laundry facilities. There were two outside toilets, one for men and one for women. One of the white churches in town had built a new church and had torn down their old one. Thinking they were doing us a favor, the lumber left from the old church was hauled out to the campsite and dumped. There were nails sticking out and broken boards all heaped together.

Every morning very early the migrant workers would go to work in the sugar-beet fields. We tried very hard to clean up the area and make a nice safe play area for the children. We took old tires and put sand in them for sandpiles.

One of the biggest and hardest projects was digging a trench six-feet deep in which to lay drainage pipe. I helped by shoveling dirt back in the ditch after the pipe was laid. That was hard work.

We would all take turns and help with all the tasks. Everyone would stop for lunch which we all helped to make and serve. Every afternoon a group of women from the different churches would come out with cookies and cool drinks.

In the evenings we would have worship services at the site, hoping some of the migrants would join us, but they never came. They couldn't understand what we were doing, and of course, their suspicion was aroused. We decided to invite everyone to a party, both migrant workers and townspeople, on the last night. Dorothea Stahn told the workers how much we enjoyed being there, and some of the townspeople brought toys. One of the migrant women was able to tell us how grateful they all were for what had been done.

That experience helped me realize that a work camp can be a very fulfilling experience. We would be so tired at the end of a long hard day's work, but it was a glorious tiredness.

One of our youth workers, Judy (Reinhardt) Groeling, recounts that fulfilling spirit so well in a letter:

"Rosa Page Welch had a voice of velvet. She would sing and lead us in singing as we walked from the migrant work camp to the fairgrounds (our camp headquarters). One of her favorite songs was 'My Feet Are Tired, but My Soul Is Happy.'"

Unknowingly, my experiences in this work camp were preparing me, both physically and emotionally, for opportunities yet unfulfilled.

13

Kum Ba Yah

ONCE a seed is sown, it may lie dormant for many years before taking root and coming to life. That can and did happen for me while attending a late summer Ashram with my friend, Anna Mow, of the Church of the Brethren. We were walking arm in arm one afternoon during a free-time rest period when something prompted me to share with her my lifelong dream of being a missionary to Africa. I had entertained the idea ever since I had heard the visiting missionaries who came to Southern Christian Institute some forty years before. I could still hear the Emory Rosses as they told of their experiences in the Congo. My daydreaming was surprisingly interrupted when Dr. Mow asked, "Rosa, how would you like to go to Nigeria under our Brethren Board of Missions?"

I stopped dead in my tracks, for I couldn't believe my ears. "Oh, you know me. It wouldn't make any difference to me who sent me; I'd be glad to go." Then, realizing what she had said, I exclaimed, "Oh, my Lord, Anna, you know how old I am." She said, "You could go for a short term—two or three years." I told Sister Anna that I would love to be associated with the quality of programs and people in the Church of the Brethren, then dropped the matter.

Weeks later when I happened to be home, the phone rang and when I answered it, the voice on the other end said, "Rosa Page Welch?"

I said, "Yes."

He said, "I am J. Henry Long, Foreign Missions Secretary for the Church of the Brethren, and I have a letter received this morning from Anna Mow. She says that you would be interested in going with Brethren

Volunteer Service as a short-term missionary to Nigeria. Are you really interested?"

I said, "Oh, my. I have always wanted to go to Africa as a missionary, but I never dreamed that, at my age, any church would be interested in sending me."

He said, "I'll tell you what. When can you come to Elgin so we can talk about it in person?"

Well, we agreed on a date and I said I would be there.

When I hung up, I was afraid to say anything to my family because I had not been discussing this with them. I went to Elgin with both fear and apprehension. Mr. Long met me and showed me around the Brethren headquarters where I met some of the staff. In his office he said, "So you really would like to go to Africa?"

I guess I sorta grinned.

He asked, "What can you do?"

I said, "Lord have mercy, child! I don't know. Maybe you got the wrong impression. I tell you what. I don't have any special skills. All I would try to do would be to go out there, love the people and, with the help of God, do the best I can. That is all I have to offer."

He asked, "How soon do you think you could be ready to go?"

Then I really became weak. I said, "Well, I will need some time, because I'll have to go back home and talk this over with my family."

I went back to Chicago and that night I shared this idea with Welch and the children. I approached the subject by asking, "Do you all know why I went down to Elgin? They knew Sister Anna well, so they were not really surprised when I told them what had happened. They just looked at me. I hurriedly asked Welch if he would like to go to Africa with me. He replied definitely, "I wouldn't think of going out there where all those snakes are!" The rest of the family showed more excitement about it, but I think they had yet to realize how long I would be gone.

One question I kept hearing, over and over, on my world travels was, "Why aren't Negroes sent out as missionaries? Why don't you come and help us?" Now I was going to have the opportunity to be an answer to that question.

The list of things to be accomplished before departure time seemed endless. The days and nights passed so rapidly that there just wasn't time to get everything done.

Two weeks before I was to leave for Nigeria the Beatrice Caffrey Youth Service honored me at its Third Annual Merit Dinner in Chicago. It was a gala occasion held in the VIP Room at McCormick Place. All were so generous in their comments.

Linnie did a beautiful job singing "My Task" as a solo and Mrs. Douglas spoke on "Why a Merit Dinner." I was given the opportunity to respond and was able to tell them of the letters I had been receiving from Nigeria asking me to bring "homey" pictures of Negro Americans, their families, homes and activities. The Youth Service agreed to help send such pictures. Then I sang a Nigerian song and invited them to sing it with me.

The last frantic hours of preparation ended when we dashed for the train. I was so glad Gale Page could be there, along with the rest of the family and so many of my good friends.

The following morning the train pulled into New York City, and I was overjoyed to have several hours to visit in the home of my friends, Emory and Myrta Ross.

The next morning we went down to the pier at Hoboken, New Jersey. My roommate was a lovely German girl.

On Sunday I sang, as promised, at the morning Protestant service. Afterward the Roman Catholic priest shyly and hesitantly asked if I would sing at their noon mass. "Of course, I'll be happy to," I replied.

We arrived at the port of Rotterdam ahead of schedule, went through customs, then took a taxi to the hotel. I got to the railway station next day just in time to catch the train to Amsterdam. My luggage was heavy, but there was no redcap in sight to help with it. The trip was an hour long and the scenery and the cities were beautiful all the way.

We flew out of Amsterdam, and my seatmate was a fine Dutchman with whom I had a pleasant visit. The flight was smooth and comfortable, but when we arrived in Kano we had a very hard time going through customs. It was thrilling to see the Nigerians in the top places of responsibility, so dignified and so efficient. I thanked God for the kindly, courteous way they treated the British and all white people in spite of colonialism.

After we boarded the plane for Jos, we were served a refreshing glass of orange juice, and I discovered there were several Americans on board. One asked me if I were from America, then asked, "Would you be Rosa Page Welch?" She had heard me sing at a United Church Women meeting in Cleveland. The flight to Jos was beautiful and interesting. We arrived safely and were met by a group that took me to the Church of the Brethren guest house.

I awoke refreshed on a glorious Sunday morning, remembering the Church Universal and my home church, praying for all. When I was asked by the missionaries how I slept, I was frank to tell them how lonely I had suddenly felt. They told me that this was the case with all of them when they had first come to the foreign field.

I shall never forget that first Sunday in Nigeria. I was the first American black woman the Nigerians had ever seen. I went to Roger Ingold and said, "Please tell me how to greet them in their own language." Thank goodness it was a very short greeting. "Usa; all you have to say, Rosa, is Usa'," he explained, "You really ought to say 'Usa Giri'."

The worship service was a great spiritual experience. To see the women carrying their bundles of grain for their offering was a true sharing of their daily labor and their deep devotion to Christ. Even though I did not understand the language, I was inspired. The children sat on the front rows of seats and the huge congregation filled the rest of the building to capacity.

It was interesting to hear the different women report on their local church activities. Their dedication and devotion were humbling. I think every single woman who gave a report had a plot of land on which she grew nuts for grinding or guinea corn or something else to harvest and sell. The money was used to help those in need, the sick and others in their own village. The women reported on how often they had gone to visit the sick and how they had sometimes gone in groups to do particular things in helping those who might be handicapped or sick. They did not have a lot of money, but they gave themselves. I think this whole business of giving ourselves, our skills, our strength and our minds to tasks is far more beneficial than just giving money.

We left the next morning to go to Uba, about seventy-five miles away, closer to the mountains and not very far from the French Cameroons. We were going to attend a goondala, which was like a district conference. When we arrived I was surprised to find hundreds of people. Many of these people walked as far as twenty or twenty-five miles, some of the women with their babies on their backs and bringing their sleeping mats and food with them.

The next day I was taken to our mission at Garkida. As my experience was later printed in the *Horizons* magazine:

"Mr. Ingold, Dr. Blough and one of the teachers at Hillcrest drove me the 430 miles to Garkida. They were acquainted with the surroundings and we had a lot of fun driving along.

"We finally arrived at Garkida at 2:30 in the morning. I was taken to this nice little round guest house. It was the first time I had ever slept in a house all by myself. I had not met even a single one of my new African friends here. Well, the little house had a grass roof. You know all the things you hear about a place before you get there. I finally got to bed, but I couldn't go to sleep because I could not see how there could be grass on that roof without lizards or snakes in it. I lay awake a long time. I never had a lonelier feeling in all my life.

"It was similar to how I felt as a little girl when I had gone to Vicksburg to visit Aunt Emma and had gotten so homesick, I actually cried. It was a sort of fear mixed with a peculiar loneliness. Then I prayed, asking God to take away my fears, to make me strong and to help me remember the purpose for which I was there. I asked for the assurance of his constant presence and sleep. He heard my prayer as he always does when it is said with faith and surrender."

Back at Garkida one afternoon, some missionaries went with me to make some calls in Nigerian homes. We first went to see Lenius, a well-educated Christian who taught the Bura language to the missionaries. He had arrested tuberculosis, so he did not leave his compound. It delighted Lenius to have me sing several songs for him.

On the morning before Christmas I awoke early and arrived at Rev. Good's. After breakfast we left for the worship service at the large beautiful sanitarium for lepers. The church was filled, and it was a great service.

We then had to rush back to the Garkida church in time for that service. The Christian preparation for Christmas was very moving. The rostrum was laden with gifts of produce. What a blessed way to give! Their gifts consisted of guinea corn, stacked in a great mound, many baskets of ground nuts, grain, and black-eyed peas. The congregation sold some of it for the church treasury and shared the rest with the poor, sick, and needy of the village.

These were interesting, busy days, but there was still no news from my family, and it left me deeply despondent. I just couldn't understand it. In reading the new *Time* magazine, I saw that our nation was considering more bomb testing, and there was an article about African students and their attitudes regarding American Negroes. I was greatly disturbed by it all. Lord, have mercy on all our souls.

There were only two days for mail delivery that week, and I had received numerous greetings from many friends. Many of the missionaries at other stations remembered me, too. I had been feeling lonesome and blue for my family and not a single greeting from any of them, so these letters helped put me back in the spirit of Christmas. I had been learning to adjust to all situations. God bless my family members. I prayed they would be happy and really get a new and more significant awareness of Christmas.

I awoke Christmas morning wondering about my family, and had to fight back the tears, for I was lonely for them. As I pictured my precious little grandbabies, I prayed that their Christmas would be filled with excitement and joy.

Jennie Ingold, who had been under the weather, but now felt much better, helped me with my hair. We used all kinds of things and she put most of it up on her small curlers. Then I sat in the sun to dry it and read some more in my book *Love Is Something You Do*, by Speakman. It was a wonderful book, given to me by Lesly. I thanked God for her and for our precious mother. I was grateful for our daddy, too. I thought of them and my immediate family that I still had not heard from. I told myself, "I must be strong. My Lord is always at hand, a friend, a Father and a great consoler. We have no heartache or suffering that God has not had, and his promises are always true. I pray that I may learn all there is to learn for my own soul from all these experiences."

I moved into my little house and managed to write a letter to Lesly the same day.

I was home but a short time when two Nigerian ladies came to see me. We did not know each other's language, but they came into my little house and we visited anyway.

At my next Bura study time, I wrote the names of the days and the numbers from one to twenty. I hoped I could improve my memorizing. Just as I was leaving my little house everyone was trying to find a snake that Jenny had seen. The boys had tried to kill it but it got away.

I had a visit with one of the fine theological students I met. He said, "For a long time we wondered why no Negroes came as missionaries, and we wished for them, so now you have come and we are so glad. Thank you for coming." I assured him that I was glad to be there, and that my plans were to visit the theological schools and spend some time in conversation.

After my Bura lessons I prayed and sang with Lenius and said hello to his children.

One day I packed my bags and polished my oxfords in preparation for a trip to Waka. We had a full car and the scenery was beautiful. We drove up higher so we could look back over the gorgeous valley.

We later went to the Royer's house for tea. Fern, Roger and I met Mrs. Royer and her two lovely little girls. After a while three European missionaries came in. Roger rose and introduced himself, "I'm *Mr.* Roger Ingold; this is Rosa Page Welch and this is *Mrs.* Fern Baldwin." This really distressed me. This was what made it difficult for Negroes to believe a white person was ever completely authentic. According to the experiences I had in Europe and other countries, the culture and refinement of men would not allow them to forget to be courteous. I was furious, and becoming hostile inside, and since the conversation was not including me, I went out and took a walk and prayed that God would help me to forgive, to be less sensitive and to be strong to take whatever happened. The purpose for which I was there was greater than Roger or me. Perhaps this was a part of the crucible through which I must pass for my own soul's salvation. I asked God to help me.

At dinner we met some missionaries and Nigerians. Mr. Smith, the secretary of the Tarayya, introduced himself and welcomed all of us as guests. At the evening service I was asked to bring greetings and to sing. Roger introduced me, and in doing so said "this woman," but Mr. Smith, a European, who interpreted into Hausa, used "Mrs. Welch" instead of repeating "this woman." I was grateful for this courteous gesture of his and the next day when I saw him again with Mrs. Smith, Miss Nissen and Fern, I expressed appreciation to him for it. Fern responded somewhat defensively:

"Well, that's the familiar term used by the African men."

I replied, "I know it, but I'm here as a missionary and I expect the same respect, no more, no less than one."

Both women responded almost simultaneously. "That's right, you are a missionary, just like the rest of us."

I was glad they had said this before Fern, because I was shocked by her quick response. I was still really surprised and disappointed with Roger and I intended to talk to him about it when I got back to Garkida. Perhaps one of the reasons the African men (Christians) had not done better in respect for women was because most, or some of the missionaries, had shown no concern either.

One thing that I could not equate with what we were to do and be as Christians was that during the holidays, none of the missionary homes to which I was invited ever included a Nigerian person. After this revelation, I decided to invite Nigerians into my home for meals and fellowship.

I was to begin teaching soon. I knew it was going to take plenty of time to understand the British school system, how to pronounce the students' names, and to learn the Housa language.

I had my first meeting with the teacher-training school on Valentine's Day. It was a large class, but I really enjoyed my first session with the participants. From the very first, I determined that I would have a short devotional at the start of each class session.

One morning as I was going to class I heard singing of a familiar hymn, and I was surprised and pleased to discover that a group of guilders had stopped to have devotions. As I drew nearer I joined them in singing the lovely old hymn, "Take the Name of Jesus with You."

We got up early one morning and walked two miles to a village where a meeting had been scheduled. Twenty-eight villagers, including women and children, came. After a time of singing, someone gave a prayer and message, and I brought greetings. The leaders said that no one had been there to tell them about Jesus.

One day Roger brought me letters from J. Henry Long and Mr. Tulley of the Brethren national headquarters in Elgin, Illinois. I was surprised at the invitation from the young people to be their speaker at the National Youth Conference in August at Estes Park, Colorado. The next day Roger and Dallas talked to me about the letters I had received and I didn't like their attitude. They seemed to resent the fact that I had been asked, and that all that money would be spent on me. They pointed out that that amount could well cover the fees of twenty boys in the school there. I reasoned that perhaps if I were allowed to go, the youth might contribute enough for forty boys. Their response was: "We're expecting you to begin the concert tour to colleges and universities in September and to be at Kulp Bible School in July and August."

I explained to them that it took time and much correspondence to plan a concert tour and that colleges and universities usually planned their cultural events a year in advance, usually beginning in September or October. It was quite apparent that they had not received definite commitments from anyone. I mentioned that I would be glad to work through June and use my vacation time for the trip back to the states. Roger replied, "No, you must have your vacation in June and you must do language study in May."

Now, this struck me as not being very consistent. I had been there all this time with nothing definite to do and I felt that I didn't deserve a vacation so soon. Well, I finally told them that they could decide if I went back for the conference or not. As I explained, "I will gladly abide by your decision. I came for two years and I would be perfectly happy to stay on right here through the end of my term."

Roger said that Dallas would make the final decision and would talk further with me. That afternoon I packed all my things and moved to Waka along with Dallas, Gladys Royer, and Mrs. Hare. I stayed at the guest house high up on the hill and took my meals with the Shanksters who were a nice family. My new house was certainly a much-welcomed improvement over my abode hut.

As Gladys Royer recalls:

"At Waka she still lived alone but in a stone house with a proper door and windows. The maintenance man asked her what color she wanted the walls of her house, and to his amazement she chose for her living room to have two walls painted bright red and the other two black. Surprisingly enough that room looked very attractive with all the decorations she put up, but, oh, how they absorbed the light at night!!! When the next teacher moved into the house and wanted light walls it took three coats of paint to cover those dark walls."

I still had a hard time sleeping. If I had just learned to turn matters over to God and let him take care of everything, in due time, he would answer my prayers. I realized that this was one of my great weaknesses.

Dallas came by to talk again about my trip to Estes Park. He opened the conversation by commenting, "It will be difficult for us to explain to the students why so much money is spent to send you back home when you have been here such a short time."

I did not understand why the students needed an explanation for the way the missions used their funds. In my own mind, I was also convinced that the committee that decided to invite me had seriously considered all of the factors involved. I'm sure J. Henry Long and Mr. Tulley knew what they were doing or they would not have permitted the youth to invite me.

Another Sunday morning I was up at 5:30 to go to a village at the foot of the largest extinct volcano in the area. The fertile valley was beautiful and it was a gorgeous morning. We stopped first at the teacher's home. He and his wife were the only Christians in the village. We then started for the chief's compound to greet him, but we met one of his wives who told us he had gone to see his sick sister. We continued to the assistant chief's compound and learned that he had left even earlier than the chief. The third leader was also away, but we finally met and greeted another lesser leader who was very cordial. There were many people around and they began to ask about me. I asked the teacher to tell them who I was and they seemed very interested.

We returned home and went to the garden and brought in collard greens, green peppers, turnips, and radishes. I made cornbread to go with the vegetables.

I was awakened by the noise of the lorry which brought my barrels from home at last. It had taken four months for them to arrive. It was like Christmas since I'd practically forgotten what I had packed.

One particular Sunday I sang at a morning service, after which a group of church members and Christian students invited me to go with them to a village about forty miles away to attend a wedding. Once we got there, we gathered under a large tree and waited for a long time, for they had not been able to find the chief to get permission for the ceremony. That village was all Moslem. The groom was Christian and had expressed the desire for a Christian wedding. The chief was finally found at the market. When he and his elders came back they started a palaver in his compound. After some time the groom's friends came out to collect coins and Kola nuts for a "gift" for the chief. But, the palaver continued and not until they collected the third time was the chief satisfied and gave consent for the marriage.

The bride looked to be about thirteen or fourteen years old and was so nervous and shy it was pitiful. She was nicely dressed in a new western-style cotton dress. An offering was taken for the bride and groom. Afterwards they served us rice and sukwa. We left, and the bride and groom returned to the Waka village.

I had been dreading the possible physical effects of a camping experience I was now undertaking, but an inner voice had quietly urged me to come. How I thanked him! Blessed Redeemer, the very students who had come out of curiosity and criticism apparently were the ones who had been most significantly inspired and impressed and who did some of the most effective witnessing. The village congregation had us share their service by asking the students to dramatize the Bible story of Joseph. The whole camp sang "It's Me, O Lord" and "Give Us Oil for Our Lamps."

Upon returning to Waka I met with the choir for a good rehearsal. They quickly learned a new spiritual, "Couldn't Hear Nobody Pray." How I wished they knew something about harmonizing!

My house boy, Ata Kuala, helped me prepare for the curry dinner I was giving one night for a class of married students and their wives. I had to leave long enough to go over to the women's class where I talked to them about caring for their hair. I pressed the hair of two of the girls and talked to them about how to test the heat of the comb. It was a joy to see the light on their faces when they saw the difference it made when it was pressed. I had hoped I would get to press all of their hair. I got home in time to finish the preparations for dinner and promptly at six o'clock here came the men by themselves. I greeted them with, "Well, where are your wives?" They replied, "They're coming, madam." I said, "Listen, when you come to my house with your wives, you let your wives come beside you, not behind you. Now you go and get your wives."

They laughed and I did too and I said, "I know this is not your custom, but we are Christians; so will you go back and get your wives and let your wives walk beside you to my house?"

They went back, but the wives were so shy that the husbands had difficulty getting them to walk beside them! Later we talked about these things—how God made woman also and that she was to be more to her husband than someone just to bear children and to work and take care of him.

We also talked about the Christian home and family life. I tried to help them understand how we could have happy homes when the husband and the wife prayed together.

The next night nine more couples came, and we had lots of fun and more time to talk. My goodness, all the questions they asked—about climate, whether American Negroes marry Europeans, etc. If I stay here long enough, won't I get as black as them? I gave them a little talk on black skin being just as beautiful and important as white skin. I told them of accomplishments and achievements of Negroes in America, as well as in Nigeria and that black people could do what others do if they had the opportunities and if they were willing to study and work hard.

Over Easter weekend there was to be a Tirayya, which was the annual meeting of the Fellowship of Churches of Christ in Nigeria. Some of us drove all night to get there, but the trip was beautiful.

Soon after that I started on a concert tour to Zaire and Samarru where we met several U. S. Government, business, and Peace Corps people. We went to church in Wausasa and saw the Anglican school where Faye a missionary, once taught. Then it was on to Bakuru to the Northern Nigeria Theological Seminary and to Kaduna and St. Peters College, the site for another church conference where we saw many old friends and many, many new ones.

It was good to get back to Waka and my little house. On one particular morning I was up at 5:00. After prayers it looked so cool and quiet and peaceful outside that I decided to go for a walk. I had a glorious experience of worship and meditation as I walked along and I looked into the vast spaciousness of God's wonderful world, the sun broke through the clouds in glorious splendor. I sang "How Great Thou Art" and "My God and I." I thought how, if we trust God, if our faith is real enough, His love and help, the light of Love and wisdom and His power to protect, heal and to bring joy breaks through the clouds of doubt, anxiety, disappointment, heartache and sorrow. What a blessed experience it was and I came back to my little home walking on tiptoe, on the clouds of joy and refreshingly free from any cares.

I had a talk with the mission coordinator about an invitation I'd received to return to the States for a Brethren youth conference. It was unfortunate that the invitation to Estes Park had caused such a furor intitally because of the distance and expense. But, I had felt secure in my decision to go, for the national office in Elgin, Illinois, had approved it.

We decided I would leave on July 28 from Kulp Bible School.

In preparation for my trip, I had started to pack books and clean out my desk when I heard someone at the door. It was an old lady from the village who had come to greet me. I asked her about going to church, and she answered, "I'm all dirty and what I have on wouldn't be good enough for church." Pointing upward, I said, "You may go as you are; you are going to worship God."

Then she told me that she used to come to church when she had a cloth, but when her sister died she used the cloth to bury her in and she hadn't been able to get another. I decided to give her my colorful new Zhebie. As I gave it to her, I suggested that she could go and wash herself and be back in time for church. She couldn't thank me enough, bless her heart, but I told her to thank God and then we would thank him together.

A lovely couple came to my house to have me name their baby. I gave it the Bible name Lydia and my name as a middle name. We had a brief dedication service. Mallam Didu offered a prayer. I talked to the mother and father, reminding them of their obligations and responsibility, then I named her Lydia Rosa Kwatamdiya and prayed and kissed the precious little one.

I had learned about a baby born on campus the previous night and how three hours later the mother had gotten up and gone to her kitchen to prepare food for her family. During class I talked to the women about how they should help each other in such situations. One of the women said that at one time they had been organized and had done things like that. I told them that as Christians we should go to see what we could do to help. After class I went to the home, and there was the mother sitting in the kitchen in pain, holding her baby. One of the girls was already there helping. I told the woman's husband, who was cleaning and doing the best he could, that his wife should stay in bed at least two days. I looked at the baby, and the cute little thing was not really clean so I told him I would go to my house and get hot water and come back and bathe the baby. I came back with water, soap, and a big piece of old cloth, and a bandage to put around the baby to cover the navel. The father had gotten out a big basin and had a sufficient supply of cold water ready. I enjoyed bathing the baby, and it brought back pleasant memories of my own babies long ago.

It came time for me to go back to Waka to begin my trip to the States for the Church of the Brethren young people's conference in Estes Park. After stopping in Waka I went to Jos and then on to Kano.

As we left Lassa we had to cross a wide river, which was very rocky. Mrs. Burke put our bags on the jeep. We all had to get out and walk across, because it was too rocky for the jeep. The African women didn't have shoes, so they stepped on the rocks to get across. Right before the distant shore the water was deep and it was a long step between rocks. The Nigerian women just hopped across, but I knew I didn't dare step in the water because there was a disease that resulted from coming in contact with snails. Several young missionaries had gotten it, including the couple for whom I had been substituting.

I was standing on a rock and trying to make that last step but, Blessed Redeemer, I just couldn't force myself to put my foot in the water. Finally, one woman put her baby down and came to my rescue and bent over in front of me. Even though I couldn't understand the language I knew what she meant. I just couldn't do that. All the women on the jeep were motioning for me to get on her back and come on. Since I didn't know what else to do I finally did and she stepped right over and as soon as we got across I slid off her back and repeated the only word of thanks I knew.

"Usa," I gratefully said, "Usa." I thought, "Lord, I've got to do more than this."

I was wearing my nicest earrings, so I pulled them off and handed them to her. She paused a moment, then reluctantly accepted them.

It was so exciting to be invited by the Church of the Brethren young people to attend their first national youth conference to be held in the YMCA camp at Estes Park. I had served in many of the UCYM activities, and many of the young people knew me from our being together at Camp Mack for summer youth conferences. I had served several summers at that Brethren Camp.

I was asked to share with them my experience in Nigeria and to challenge them. Some of what I said was:

"I'm here to tell you young people that you are never too young to learn and to understand, to seek and to ask for and receive the gift of the Holy Spirit. It is the Spirit of Jesus within us. The Bible says you are not a real Christian unless you have this spirit. I know what it means to have it because it can relieve you of your burden. It can give you hope and it can teach you how to seek God and actually surrender all your problems, all of the things which disturb you, and all of the questions you have in your mind to him, and a new joy and a happiness will possess you that you've never known before.

"I want to ask you to do one thing for me before this conference is over. I want you really to listen. I have discovered in Nigeria and in other parts of the world that young people have identically the same kinds of problems. Deep down in your heart you have questions. You want to know more about life and you want to know about God.

"Nobody can ask you questions which make you really wonder and which really put you on the spot like my Nigerian students. For instance, one day in my class a student asked, 'Madam, has anybody ever seen God? How can we talk about him if nobody has ever seen him?'

"I quoted scripture and I said, 'No one has seen God except Jesus, but we can feel him. We can know when we have his Spirit within us.'

"I wish somehow that you young people would be willing to give up some of your comforts. One of the tragedies about us in America is that, as we study, the greatest thing in our mind is to get out of school and to get a big job so we can have all of the fine things and be comfortable. And one of the other things about us Americans is all of this talk about security. Everybody's getting ready to have security. For what and why? How can we have security when the rest of the world is hungry for food, for an education and for health?

"Do you know the life span in Nigeria is 35 to 38 years? When I told some of the students about my family and my grandchildren they looked at me very strangely. They asked how old I was. When I told them 62 one student said, 'Oh, madam, you couldn't be that old. When a woman gets 40 years old, she is very very old!'

"I said, 'My dear child, in America 40 years is still very young.'

"When I was talking with some of the married men students about their customs, they mentioned the 40 years again. I asked them if they knew why their women looked so old at 40 and they said no. I said 'It's because you ought to help them out a little more than you do carrying loads like they do' and they said, 'But madam, this is our custom.'

"When you become a Christian, you leave off that part of your custom which is not good, I told them.

"I would like to say this, as I look at you and I think of your potential, I think if just a fraction of you would decide to really give yourselves wholly to God in his service you could turn the world upside down. And the world needs turning upside down, not by nuclear weapons, but by the gospel of Jesus Christ. There are people hungry for it, not only in Nigeria and in Ecuador and other parts of the world, but also in the United States. Many of them don't know what they are hungering for. But you are not to come here and receive what we are receiving this week and go home and just keep it. Because you have been here, you are to be a better Christian than you've ever been before.

"You ought to know more about how to witness for Jesus Christ in your homes, in your church, in your school and wherever you go. You can witness as you are on your way back home from this place. You can witness for Jesus Christ right here on these grounds. May God help you do it. We don't have much time left to do it and I'm convinced that unless we are busy about witnessing for Jesus Christ, those to whom we have been sending the gospel of Jesus Christ, will have to come back to America, to the Western world, and evangelize us and Christianize us.

"May God help you not only to have a desire to prepare yourselves, to go yourselves, but may God help you to be willing to share of the material possessions right now. I hope in your offering tonight that you will give because God has been good to you, not grudgingly, but that you will express thoroughly your giving in your thanksgiving to God. That's the only way to give. For what we have, all of it, is a gift from God, and he's always waiting to give us more if we are willing to trust him by sharing generously what we have of his gifts to us."

It was now late August, in fact, the twenty-third, which was my birthday. It had been such a happy and eventful day at the conference, and that evening some of the adults were talking to me and I was getting anxious, for I knew that everyone else had gone into the auditorium. They finally let me mosey over, and as I entered everybody stood and sang "Happy Birthday" to me.

The conference was wonderful, but I enjoyed going home at last. My family was very proud of me. Welch was thoroughly enjoying his retirement. He continued to sing in the choir and helped mind the grandchildren. He was head chef for the whole family. Linnie had been busy with her teaching, directing her church choir, and accompanying the many solos and concerts on special days. Lesly too, had been a big help with Linnie's young son, Mark, and the rest of the grandchildren.

While I was in Chicago, I was pleased that the J. Henry Longs from Elgin came to our home for dinner, and we sat around the table visiting. He seemed quite pleased at what I had accomplished and shared my enthusiasm.

When I returned to Nigeria I was happy to turn over the generous love offering of the Brethren youth from Estes to help in the completion of the new chapel at Kulp Bible School.

I was sent out to visit as many as I could of the eleven mission stations, twenty-four congregations, and nearly fifty schools of the Church of the Brethren.

A new young missionary couple came for me and we went to the leprosarium at Mkar. The group filled the house to overflowing. I spoke and sang for them with a fine young Nigerian as an interpreter. I taught them "Amen." The chief, who was a fine gentleman and a leprosy victim, arose, greeted and thanked me. The interpreter had promised to write down what he said. Afterwards I got to meet him and some others. It was a humbling experience to observe those people, some happy and so patient like the chief, so deeply spiritual and smiling, with praise and thanksgiving in his whole being. The doctor was a wonderfully educated Englishman. We went to her house and I recorded two songs for her to have to play to the patients, "There Is a Balm in Gilead" and "I Got Shoes." Later I received the following note of what the chief had said:

"We are very glad to hear your teaching and songs. We too are very happy that we know Jesus even though we have no hands and feet. We are thankful we know Jesus.
By Chief Agour of Benue Leprosy Settlement"

One day in a village I became aware that not many of the people knew who I was or where I was from. I took time to tell them about myself and America, and the response in all my classes thereafter was better. In the final classes we had some heartwarming testimonials. God was with me wonderfully as he had always proved to be. After a much needed rest for my tired, weary body, I awoke refreshed and met with several different groups of students. Many came for counseling because of personal problems, some refused to pay their school fees and some wanted scriptures explained. One wondered which would come first, eternal life or judgment day. My answer to that was: If one truly believes in God through Jesus Christ and if one really lives as best he can the Christian life, then he can be sure of the kind of judgment which will guarantee him eternal life.

One young boy was filled with doubts, and I tried to assure him that it was human to doubt and that all of us doubted at one time or another, but if you stopped and talked to God about it he would take away your fears and doubts. Afterwards we packed up and left for Garkida.

We stopped enroute and picked up a big bundle of mail. What a nice surprise to get a long letter from Linnie. I was at the Baptist College in Minna by the time I observed my first anniversary of service in Nigeria.

It was so good to see Rahila again. We had a long talk about the possibility of her going to the U.S. to study. I cautioned her about getting too excited too soon and suggested that she talk to Dr. Blough and others. I went to greet her mother and sister. Several others came by and we had a nice visit. None of the people I talked to about Rahila gave any encouragement. I couldn't understand their attitude.

One of the missionaries brought me a letter written by young people in East Germany to young pople in West Germany I gave him a copy of an article someone had sent me on "Dialogue on Race Prejudice of Missionaries in Africa." He came back the next day and returned the paper and began to talk about the weakness, superstition, and self-centeredness of the spirituals. He also criticized the imperfect theology of the Sudan Interior Mission people. After he left I prayed for him, but I was thoroughly disappointed and disillusioned.

Among my letters was an exciting one from Bob Nelson of the United Christian Missionary Society. He had been commissioned to come to Africa and had invited me to meet the group at Lagos in March. I just couldn't believe my eyes; so I read it twice. I rushed a letter back to him at Coquilhatville, Congo, and also sent one to my local coordinator requesting permission.

On a Monday morning I was taken to the airport for the flight to Lagos.

One of the people on the commission, W. A. Welsh, recalls our meeting at the airport:

"I suppose the most memorable contact I ever had with Rosa was in Lagos, Nigeria, in the spring of 1963. The Commission to Africa of the United Christian Missionary Society had just finished a month-long visit to various places in what is now Zaire where Disciples did overseas work; we had flown out and were spending a couple of days in Lagos to rest a bit and to consolidate our various findings. When we arrived at the airport, the first person to greet us was none other than Rosa. She was doing some voluntary missionary work in the outlands of Nigeria. She knew we were coming, and made a special trip to spend time with us. I am sure she was as glad to see us as we were to see her!"

Elizabeth Rowe, the only woman on the Commission, shares two very exciting and hair-raising experiences:

"We had a more exciting experience than anticipated. The ride to the hotel was something! To see cars driven to the left side of the road is a frightening experience until you get adjusted. You're sure that you'll collide with oncoming traffic. All along the 14 miles were tiny stands with merchandise of all sorts, and candles burning for light— no street lights—and with all the long robes and head coverings, this makes a fascinating scene.

"The Federal Palace Hotel with its spacious lobby looks like nothing we have seen in Africa. We unloaded and registered for our rooms well past midnight. Bob, (Nelson) Pat, (Ira Paternoster), Rosa Page and I got on one elevator with other guests, and started up to the fifth floor. It was soon evident that this was not an elevator that whisked you on your way, and finally it came to a dead halt about four feet below the third floor. No amount of pushing or pounding would make it budge—even the door wouldn't open—and here we were, all of us, crammed in the cubicle, with no air conditioning and no apparent help. The heat become almost sickening, and finally Bob managed to push open the vent in the ceiling which helped a bit—and no one outside seemed aware of our predicament. Finally we yelled and pounded enough that someone came and said he'd have to get some help. But Africans don't move swiftly, and we had visions of ending our days right there. Everyone was a good sport about it exept one African who looked very grim through it all. We learned later that Beauford (Norris) had realized our elevator must be stuck when we were so long in coming, and he finally was able to round up some help. When we finally saw the outside door move and were able to crawl out, we felt like prisoners must feel who have just been granted a reprieve. I went to my room and washed every soaked thing I had on! I never enter a crowded elevator but that I think about that episode and Rosa Page.

"Because of the pressure of work to be done in a brief period of time, our further meetings with her in Lagos were limited. We did see her again when we visited the university at Ibadan. I have a very clear mental picture of standing at the top of a long flight of steps on the campus, and seeing her in the distance as she walked toward us with her arm extended high in the air, and smiling, bespeaking her warm gesture of recognition, a symbol as she always was for me, of confidence and hope."

I got up early the first morning and had breakfast with the group and then they went into conference, working on their report, and I enjoyed a bit of vacation. In the afternoon they invited me to share my experiences as a missionary and they also asked me some questions. I had a chance to visit with John Compton and Bob Nelson and to exchange observations of missions in Africa. I was so glad to have had this opportunity to talk with them alone for a few minutes and to express some of the thoughts I'd had about Africa for a long time. Bob's problems and anxieties were comparable to J. Henry Long's.

We all took a side tip to Ibadan to visit the university. After touring some of the buildings we went to the Protestant chapel, which was one of the most beautiful and worshipful sanctuaries I had ever entered. We also saw the unique Muslim mosque and went to the bookstore and the student union. I shall always be grateful to the Brethren for sending me to Nigeria. I hoped that what I had tried to do through the years and what I would try to do in the future would help me to be worthy even in a small way.

The reports of the racial troubles in America sickened me. I just could not keep back the tears as I read about the bombing in Birmingham, Alabama, which killed four little girls. I was so glad I could pray "Father forgive them," I also read of the young white mother at Little Rock, who had dared to take her son to the all-Negro school near her. I prayed for those of her own who were molesting, tormenting, and threatening her and that God would bless, strengthen, and keep her strong and courageous in him.

It became increasingly busy with a lot of visitors toward the end of the day. Thankfully, Kermon and Margaret Thomasson came over to help.

The Royers came for me and we left for Garkida. We stopped to greet a lady whose husband had died the day before. Then to the mission office and to the Goods' home. There Pastor Mei Sule, his wife, plus Rahila and six church leaders came for tea and held a short service in my honor. I was so grateful for this farewell and impressive expression of love and appreciation by my Nigerian Brethren.

Unfortunately, the pleasantness of my last few days in Nigeria was to be disrupted by a terrible event. The wife of the new governor of Nigeria

160

was having a conference of United Church Women. She had invited me to be her guest and we attended those meetings together.

We had been in a meeting all afternoon. The chauffeur was bringing us home, and just before we got to the house, she looked out the window and asked, "Oh, I wonder who the European is." (It was the Canadian Minister.)

The car stopped and she greeted him. He said that no one had answered the door. She replied, "Oh, they should be here," and she started in and we all followed. The Canadian Minister sadly said, "I came to give you the bad news."

Just then, Governor Ibiam came running through the doors, shouting, "Oh, my God, President Kennedy has been shot! If this is the way America feels about him . . .."

He was almost in a rage. He felt that Kennedy had been shot because he had gone so far for the black people.

I was just standing there, grief-stricken because of Kennedy's death but also because of what the governor was saying. Before I knew it, I exclaimed: "Oh, Governor, all white people in America are not like that."

He had been listening to television. I rushed up to my room and I was so concerned about what was going through the governor's mind. I fell on my knees and prayed. I didn't know what to do. I had learned on my travels that in every country Abraham Lincoln was most revered because he had stood up for the disadvantaged.

As time approached to leave Nigeria and go back home, I had mixed feelings. My long term of service was coming to an end. The thought of being with my family again was counterbalanced by what I know still needed to be done here.

The day I left Nigeria I went to a United Church Women's tea with Lady Ibiam. She had a lady from Trinidad and me sit on the platform with her. We introduced ourselves and talked for a little while. At the closing part of the session, Lady Ibiam spoke briefly and called on me to speak. I tried to challenge the women to recognize their responsibility, their potential, and the need for developing a deep prayer life. I closed with singing, "If I Can Help Somebody." When I left, Lady Ibiam took me to the airport in her chauffered car. Finally I arrived by plane in Beirut.

I was to participate in a church service and met the fine Lebanese minister, organist and choir. It was a worshipful service although it was done in Arabic and I couldn't understand.

I loved those Lebanese people who were warm, hospitable, and appreciative. I was involved in so many different groups and sang with and for such a mixture that I just thanked God for all that had happened.

I later wrote in my diary:

"We had a beautiful trip over the snow covered pass and on into Amman and from there into Jerusalem. I went immediately to the Garden Tomb which is my favorite spot. I had more time and saw so much more of the Holy Land on this trip. We went to Bethlehem and saw the Church of the Nativity. Went to Jerico, gazed at the Mt. of Temptation, then on to the River Jordan where Christ was baptized. I grieved at the sight of a large refugee camp of over 40,000. Went to the Dead Sea and saw the large mountain where the Dead Sea Scrolls had been found. Came back to Jerusalem and then went to Bethany and down the twenty-five steps to Lazarus' tomb. We stayed in the guest house on the Mount of Olives. We walked today seeing the Tombs of the Prophets. I was deeply impressed at seeing the church with the Lord's Prayer printed in every written language, the Garden of Gethsemane and through St. Stephen's Gate into the Old City. Looked into the Pool of Bethesda where excavation was being done. We actually went into the prison where Jesus was kept between trials, and further down we saw the dungeon prison where the thieves were kept. Walked the Dolorosa Road and back to the Garden Tomb again for a blessed experience. We went to Damascus through the St. Thomas gate down a straight street and to the Church of St. Paul, where he had been let down the wall in a basket to escape. Visited the Church of Annanias, where he went to heal Paul and where Saul was converted. Went inside the large Mosque to see John the Baptist's tomb. Walked wearily through the old ruins in Jaresh, and then Zekiah and I took a cab back to Beirut to the Haddads. it all made a wonderful climax to two unforgettable, rewarding years in Nigeria."

A lifelong dream had been fulfilled.

14

Amazing Grace

I HAD hardly arrived home in time to spend Christmas with my family when I was off again reporting to as many of the Brethren congregations and gatherings as would ask me. I felt a kinship with them.

I was also delighted to receive an invitation from Helen Davis, who was then the director of the Florida Chain of Missions, to go on tour. As she remembers:

"Rosa joined Emily Curry and me in Daytona Beach that year; the Chain had been going for a few days in Jackson and when she spoke at the First Presbyterian Church that night she told them she had been on the Chain many times. But she had been met by a group of young adults at the bus station the night before, taken to a Howard Johnson's for something to eat, then to a motel on beautiful Daytona Beach to stay with the rest of the "Chain Gang" (which we so often jokingly referred to this unique bunch). She was received so graciously by the motel operator, she dropped on her knees when she was alone in the room and thanked God for the changes that had been wrought, for always before she was carefully housed in a private home—sometimes white, but more often in one of the fine black homes. Then she sang without any announcement or anything prearranged, 'How Great Thou Art.' Everywhere we went throughout the state this news went ahead and folks requested her singing this after her message on Nigeria. She had just come back as a missionary to Nigeria and had a real mission message that all wanted to hear. She would have the audience sing parts of the song with her. The music director of First Christian Church in Tampa that Sunday morning had special music by a youth and adult choir, and he and Rosa sang 'How Great Thou Art' as a duet. One of my cherished slides of the Chain is a picture of the two after the service—Rosa never looked so beautiful in her blue lace dress and wearing a huge orchid, standing by Chris Napoli.

"The Chain never took a program into any church in Florida that did not accept all races. It did more to set the good climate that Florida had in the fight for human rights and the other organizations such as CWU, Florida Council of Churches, Florida Christian Migrant Ministry and Council on Human Relations, working together, meeting behind the closed doors with the governor, school principals, etc. That year everything continued to be just great until we got to a city where so far everything had gone fine. It was our last day in that city. A new restaurant was next door to our motel and the motel operator called our room and said, 'The restaurant just opened this morning; why don't you take your people over there and eat breakfast?' We asked her if all our people would be graciously accepted and she assured us. Emily and I had much business to take care of before we started off for the day's programs. Emily carried a frying pan, coffee perculator, etc., so we could eat in the room if we needed to check on programs, make phone calls, etc., so we could be completely with the speakers and do what was needed for them during the day. We called each room and told them about the invitation to eat. Hardly had we started to work and the phone rang—the one who had called said, 'I am sorry, some of your people have been turned away.' We rushed over. An Episcopal from South Africa (an Englishman) had just been served his breakfast when Rosa and others walked in and they refused to serve Rosa. The minister told them then he could not eat his either and paid for it and they all walked out. We all went to a Howard Johnson's instead. The real part of this story that I am telling is—the next day we were to leave and go to another city right after breakfast. Emily suggested we fix breakfast for everyone in our room. We asked the motel operator, who was still distressed about the day before, and she gave her consent gladly. Some of our folk would be leaving us and we always liked to give them a fond farewell. We had a lovely breakfast, the Episcopal priest from South Africa, Dr. Alexander Reid, Methodist Missionary from India, Mr. Hutcheson with Church World Service, Claire Randall, now Executive Director of The National Council of Churches, Rosa, Emily and me, and maybe one or two others whom I cannot recall. After we were finished with our meal I thanked them and said we always say goodbye to those leaving us by joining hands and having each one say a prayer. I would begin

164

and asked Rosa to conclude. The prayers were short, but sincere and then it was Rosa's turn and without a word of introduction that voice sweeter than ever sang 'Sweet Little Jesus Boy—They Treat You Mean, They Treat Me Mean Too—They Didn't Know Who You Were.' We left in silence. I'll never forget that moment."

Sometimes after Easter, I was showing slides and telling of my Nigeria trip in the churches of the surrounding Chicago area. I found myself thinking about Rahila, my little Nigerian nurse friend. She had wanted so badly to come to the States for further training, but I had not received any word from her. Then, one morning the postman delivered an airmail letter which read:

"I'll be arriving in Chicago in two weeks. I would love to accept your invitation to stay in your home. So anxious to see you. Love, Rahila."

She stayed with us a great deal of the time while she was taking her advanced nurse's training. She was the same sweet girl, and the whole family loved her.

Summertime took me to Nebraska again. Among my accumulated mail I found a letter from Oma Lou Myers, state Minister of Christian Education, inviting me to attend the 'Crossview' summer youth conference at Peru State Teachers College. Louella (Bonnell) Christy was serving as an associate in Christian education, and she remembered her experience in the conference when she wrote:

"In the summer of 1964, we were on the Peru State College Campus in Nebraska for the Crossview CYF conference with about 185 youth and counselors. This time Mrs. Welch was serving as a co-counselor for part of the week before her busy schedule took her to yet another commitment. I was a self-conscious, inexperienced, newly-graduated Phillips University alum and had a million mixed feelings about what I could contribute to the event!! My most memorable occasion was when Rosa Page first taught us the noted Negro spiritual 'Amen.' That evening before she left, the whole group gathered in the lovely parlor of the student union building. Mrs. Welch's interpretation, leading, and singing of so many spirituals and songs inspired us to sing our hearts out! A monumental moment I experienced was when Rosa Page asked *me* to teach the group and her the different versions of singing together the 'Battle Hymn of the Republic'—I'm an alto! Who was I to lead a song in her presence? How did she even know I knew that song? I couldn't believe it! I'm sure it was her confidence in me that gave me the courage to continue leading the singing times during the rest of the week. After being with Rosa Page for just a few days, one counselor remarked, 'It's like being on Cloud Nine—then after she's gone, it takes two or three days to get your feet on the ground again!'"

But, I'll never forget that night of singing. Not only were their voices beautiful, but the spiritual part and the whole atmosphere just kept developing and growing. We simply couldn't pull ourselves away.

The annual Conference for The Church of the Brethren was held the same summer in Lincoln, Nebraska. My assignment was to report on my missionary tour to Nigeria. I was the featured speaker at the foreign missions dinner. The high point of the conference for me and for many was the presence of condemned killer Nathan Leopold. He and Loeb had killed in Chicago and both of them had come from socially prominent Jewish families. After several years in prison, Leopold was paroled to W. Harold Row and the Church of the Brethren. They were able to get him a job in Puerto Rico, and he got so involved in his work as a lab technician in a hospital that he almost lost his life.

I was told later that many of the townspeople, as well as some of the Brethren, had been apprehensive about bringing Nathan Leopold to the convention, but after they heard him speak, the tension lessened and he was graciously welcomed.

Near the end of the Brethren convention, Oma Lou Myers came down to the Cornhusker where we had breakfast together. Afterwards, we walked into the lobby, and just as we made our way up the stairs, I noticed that Mr. Leopold was standing alone and apart from the throng across the room from us. I drew Oma Lou's attention to him by asking, "Have you met Mr. Leopold?"

"No," she replied, "but I would surely like to."

We had to push our way through the crowd, but we finally managed to get over to greet him. I introduced myself, saying that I had lived several years in South Chicago. He and I were surprised to find that we had lived only a few blocks from each other during his early years. As I turned and introduced my friend, Oma Lou, and her hand had clasped that of a former murderer, I put my hand on her shoulder and without a spoken word we all seemed to know that God was right there. No matter whether Christian or Jew, black or white, we were assured that we were all God's children.

As I think of all the varied concerts that I've given during my years of service, one benefit concert stands out vividly in my mind. It was the one held at Palm Beach, Florida.

I had been staying in the home of Maine Fredericks, a social worker. She had shared her concern for the young Negro boys who had been unjustly arrested and thrown in jail with hardened criminals. She had been housing some of these delinquents in a small house just back of her beautiful home. She also shared the dream of building a home for these Negro children. So, before I left for home, I found myself offering, "I'm interested in what you are doing and I would like to make a contribution. Could you sponsor a benefit concert? All I'd need would be my expenses."

Mrs. Fredricks exclaimed, "Would you do that?" "Sure," I enthusiastically agreed.

Some of the wealthy women in the area agreed to help and set up an invitation-only concert at the Everglades Club in Palm Beach.

The night of the concert approached and when we went to the club to look things over, the attendant at the gate refused my entrance saying, "No black people allowed to come in here."

It only took one phone call from these women to get action. I wasn't frightened when I saw couples like the Pierponts and the Dodges, for I knew it was for such a good cause. My singing must have touched their hearts because the checks they wrote in response totaled over four thousand dollars. I thanked God for the opportunity of helping those poor young boys to have a better chance in life.

My busy schedule took me in and out of Chicago, but somehow Rahila had grabbed every opportunity for talks and prayers together. I was so fond of her I hated to see her go, but she had done so well in her training that she needed to get back to Nigeria, where she would be supervisor of the big hospital at Kano.

Our International Convention met in Detroit that fall. W. A. Welsh was the President and the theme was "God Reconciling the World." I had so many friends to greet and to tell about my experiences in Nigeria for two years, but Charles Livingston remembers something else about that convention:

"I remember Rosa Page Welch as one who always seemed to be in control, except once. At the International Convention in Detroit we fooled around one evening after the closing service until they ran us out of the book display area, and as we started to leave the building, here came Rosa Page at a half-trot, wringing her hands saying, 'I missed the last bus—what am I going to do?'"

"For one brief moment I was the man of the hour for I said, 'Mildred and I will take you home.'"

"Despair vanished and she again was Rosa Page Welch, beautiful, charming, and ready to face the future with complete confidence."

During that Detroit convention, Spencer Austin, who was in charge of Unified Promotion for UCMS at that time asked if he could interview me about a job.

Some of the black Disciple leaders had approached Mr. Austin and suggested that he hire a black to be on his staff, and they recommended me to represent them. Mrs. Thelma Hastings had already been hired to serve in the same capacity. Mr. Austin started off by telling me what a very beautiful woman and a very fine person Mrs. Thelma Hastings was. I told him that "Tippy" Hastings and I had been counselors in summer youth conferences many times, and I knew and respected her very much. I also said, "But I don't want to be like Thelma Hastings. I am Rosa Page Welch and that is all I want to be."

I was hired to serve on the staff of Unified Promotion, but acceptance was slow. The headquarters for the United Society was in Irvington, which was a suburb of Indianapolis and was not integrated. I could not stay in that area unless I was in a private home. Some of the staff did ask me to stay with them from time to time, but for no prolonged period.

Mrs. Ed Mosely was very upset that they never made any arrangements for my housing, and didn't think I should have to spend so much time traveling into the city where I could stay with Rosa Brown at the Rev. Robert Peoples' home. Finally, one day Edith Eberly came into the office and said, "Listen Rosa, I have an extra room and you can stay in my house. I have to go visit my niece and when I get back you can move in."

Well, I had a trip out of the city, too, so I was looking forward to it. I was so relieved. But, while Edith was visiting her niece she had a heart attack and died. So, I continued to stay with the Peoples. Bless their hearts, I will never forget them. The Roland Huffs, Spencer Austins and Helen Spaulding were also especially hospitable.

I enjoyed working with Thelma Hastings. She was very helpful to me. They never found an office space for me and I had to make space to work where I could find it. Thelma let me use her office when she was out of town.

I was to work part-time, which meant through the months from February through April and September through December.

Our task was to acquaint our churches with the involvement of our denomination in mission across America and around the world.

My experiences in many parts of the world were a great source of help in my attempts to make clear and understandable the reasons for the services we sought to render. One of the disappointing things was that the black churches were slow in making requests for my time.

One day I was told that since I had reached retirement age my services would be terminated.

I was told that I could come to the board meeting of the United Christian Missionary Society and that my retirement would be announced and I would be given two minutes to make any comments I would care to make.

At the board meeting when my retirement was announced they thanked me for the good job I had done. When it was time for me to speak I said, "I need a little more than two minutes; could you give me at least five minutes?

"First of all I want to express my deep appreciation to my black brethren for asking for representation and for choosing me.

"I hope God has used me in a meaningful way, that is my hope in everything I do. But I think I will give you a few pointers. The new slide series showing your new program for missions is excellent except for one thing. The only representation you have of any black person is that slide of a baptism service in the Congo. I want you to know that we black Americans like our heritage, but Africans are different from us. I know that among our black Disciples here we have some genuine Christian families whose pictures could have been used. You want to send those slides out, and how do you think the black churches are going to feel when they see those slides representing everybody but us? We are sensitive about it."

A cable came from my two dear young friends, Rahila and Marly, in Nigeria. They had gotten together and had set their wedding date. How I wished I could have been there. But, I knew I couldn't, so I simply sent an airmail card of congratulations.

Racial tension in our nation had been building higher and higher, ever since Mrs. Rosa Parks had refused to give up her seat on the bus in Montgomery, Alabama, some ten years earlier.

During the height of the Civil Rights Movement I went to work in Mississippi for two weeks. I remember arriving in Memphis at the airport and being so pleased and yet surprised to find so many from the United Christian Missionary Society joining in the work. We all changed planes and flew into Jackson. From there we were assigned to different places around the state of Mississippi. Mae Yoho Ward and I happened to be assigned to Hattiesburg. We were at the SCI campus at Edwards north of Jackson where an Episcopal rector was in charge. We received training on how to act under attack. We were taught how to protect ourselves if we were attacked or beaten. By the time I learned all of that I wondered if I was doing the right thing by being there!

Mae and I went together to the bus station. It was crowded and there were policemen all around. The seats in the white waiting room had been removed; so neither white nor black could try to sit down. We stood outside and were glad when the bus came and picked us up.

Young adults, who had been working there for weeks and who understood the situation, explained the kinds of things we were up against; we changed our whole plan. There was wonderful cooperation.

I had relatives in Hattiesburg, but did not stay with them. My cousin was a teacher, and she dared not show any support for fear of losing her job.

Mae Yoho Ward tried to talk to the white minister of the Christian Church, but he would not acknowledge her attempts. She was a vice president of the United Christian Missionary Society. She attended the Sunday worship service and was avoided by the members and not recognized by the pastor. On her way down the steps as she left, a young white girl asked if she could drive her to where she was staying. As they turned on to Mobile Street, the young lady told Mae that it was the very first time she had been on that street even though she had been born and reared there. As a child her parents had told her never to go on that street. When they approached the home where Mae was staying, she drove into the driveway to let Mae out. Someone on the porch called to her, came down and extended an invitation for her to come in for a while and meet some of the folk. She got out of her car and went into the black home, and it was the very first time she had even been in one. She was treated so nicely that she didn't want to leave.

While we were in Hattiesburg, the bodies of three young civil right workers were found in a swamp nearby. They had been buried with a bulldozer. Memorial services were held in every city where Civil Rights workers had gathered. I was asked to sing for the service in Hattiesburg, and I prayed hard for God to give me the right songs. It was an emotional sight to see both black and white young pople, all wearing black armbands and weeping together. Most of them had known the three young people who had been killed. I sang "They Crucified My Lord," and "He Never Said a Mumblin' Word," followed with "Were You There When They Crucified My Lord?" I finally finished with "Sweet Little Jesus Boy," with tears streaming down my face.

In Hattiesburg there were several white families who were concerned, but they had to be very careful. They invited a group of us to come over for the evening after the service. We drove up quietly; the shades were all drawn and as soon as we got to the side door it was opened for us. The house was in disarray for the family was packing to move. As we sat, wherever we could find a place, the white couple poured out their hearts. The man had been on the faculty of the college in Hattiesburg, and because he had dared to teach his students the meaning behind the Civil Rights Movement and the injustices in Mississippi, his teaching contract had not been renewed. The couple had been born, reared, and educated in Mississippi.

Many black people don't know what some white people had to go through and the sacrifices some of them made for their cause. I met a newspaper person who was reared in the Mississippi Delta, and he told me that he was eighteen years of age before he knew it was wrong to kill a black person. He told me how he had been shot in the leg because he had written favorably about civil rights.

The white young people were not responsible for what happened, but the responsibility falls on those who could do something about it.

We all have the power to forgive. In the Lord's Prayer that little word *as* makes all the difference when we pray, "Forgive us *as* we forgive."

I firmly believe, as did the woman who penned: "Black people alone can free whites from the unbearable guilt of the unspeakable sins of racism." I agree with her that we can do it by loving instead of constantly reminding ourselves and everybody else of the evil and ugliness of it. We have to forget it, too, and repay it with forgiveness and love.

After this stressful and emotional experience, I was happy to receive a letter from Louise Woodford, associated with the Florida Chain of Missions, who was inviting me to St. Petersburg for a vacation with her and another churchwoman from Columbus Ohio, before Louise and I were to attend an important planning meeting in Washington, D.C.

Each night we listened to the news, for the tension was very high. One night Martin Luther King, Jr. was on the air and he was pleading for people to come and join the last few miles of the march from Selma to Montgomery. It was so moving that I became emotional. When it was over, I had decided.

"I can't go to Washington. I've got to go to Montgomery."

Louise said, "But Rosa, you have your ticket to Washington."

They immediately understood what I was saying, and the next morning they went with me and I got my ticket refunded and purchased one to Montgomery instead.

When I got to Montgomery I was told to take a cab to the home of the head of the Agricultural Department of the State College in Montgomery. There were many people there, and one group was making sandwiches for the marchers.

We were taken by truck to join the marchers, and as we drove through town we saw them building a platform for the speakers. They were using casket boxes that black undertakers had given them.

When we got there we saw that Catholic nuns and priests, Jewish rabbis, ministers of all denominations, movie stars, and people from all over the nation, even from abroad, had come to show their concern and support.

Reverend Martin Luther King, Jr., his wife, Coretta, and Andrew Young and his wife marched in the front line. The rest of us were lined up about eight deep, marching and singing such songs as "Don't You Let Nobody Turn You Around" and "Keep in the Middle of the Road." On each side of the lines were peace marchers who were holding signs saying "Keep Smiling." There was a little black woman marching beside me. She was jolly but she got so tired. She never gave up, but someone finally pulled her out. When we got to Montgomery all the blinds on the office buildings were closed. The streets were lined with all kinds of human beings. On one side were black handicapped people and old people waving to us. Some were laughing and some were in tears. On the other side were young white men who called us names of all kinds, but we did not answer them. When we got to the capitol grounds and the speaker's stand we gathered around to listen. I didn't know I was so tired until we had stopped, but it was a glorious tiredness and none of us minded.

If anyone had ever told me that I would march those six miles at my age I never would have believed it. But, when you're caught up in an emotional and spiritual experience such as this, somehow you can.

It was such a thrill to see such noted blacks as Sammy Davis, Jr., Andrew Young, and Julian Bond representing our people.

I shall never forget when Dr. King walked on that platform and gave his convincing and eloquent speech. Then to hear the voices of hundreds of people start singing almost instantaneously as the giant Christian leader lifted his hand to lead us in singing, victoriously and triumphantly, "We Shall Overcome."

As soon as the march was over, we went directly to the railroad station to go back to Chicago. When we reached home one of the Civil Rights people was there to tell us that a woman from Detroit had been killed.

My cousin in Mississippi had an interesting experience with voting. He always went to the polls and tried to vote every election. They would let him mark his ballot but would challenge him at the ballot box each time. The first question had to do with belief in the laws of the great state of Mississippi, supporting segregation. Of course, my cousin did not believe in that system so he would say so. The second question had to do with fair employment.

They would get a white lawyer to come and question him, but my cousin could not in good conscience give the answers they wanted, so he never had the opportunity to vote in any election, even though he was a war veteran.

I went to the 1966 International Convention of our churches in Dallas. Dr. Stephen J. England was convention president that year. The city was still feeling the effects of President Kennedy's assassination. I had been manning the booth for Unified Promotion, and I wanted to change clothes before going to dinner and the evening program. I thought the morning session had been dismissed since not many people were around. I asked someone about it and was told that they were still debating the resolution on interracial marriage and that I ought to go in. Well, as I slipped into the balcony, I heard someone say that interracial marriages were increasing and that it would hurt the cause of Christianity if the resolution was passed. I was not going to let that go unchallenged; so I headed for the nearest microphone. The person in charge of it was ignoring me and did not let me have my turn. I finally yelled out, "Mr. President," and dear Dr. England heard the pleas of "Let her speak" and recognized me; so the man with the mike had to let me use it. I said, "White poeple think the Negro has nothing to say on this. I'd like to point out that there are very few pure Negroes in America today. In skin color the Negro comes in all shades from pure white to nearly pure black and this is not all our fault. It is a symbol of the aggression of white men on Negroes, not of Negroes on the white race. The whites have no objection to intermixture. They object only to legalizing it. This is an insult to the Negro race.

"But don't think I am bitter toward you because of this. I decided long ago to put aside bitterness. No one is going to make a sinner out of me! You are my brothers, and I love you all whether you like it or not! I am not concerned with what you are doing to me, but with what you are doing to the church of Jesus Christ in America and all over the world."

I soon left the assembly to go to my room. When I got on the elevator, one of our black ministers was there and he thanked me for saying what I had said. I replied to him, "Why in the dickens didn't one of you get up and say something?"

It was relaxing to join other folks attending the convention at a chuckwagon supper in nearby Fort Worth. I'd been there but a short while when a tall, serious-looking black gentleman came toward me with outstretched arms, saying "Thank you . . . thank you, Rosa, for saying what you did today. You told us what everyone needed to hear."

His voice broke and with tears streaming down his face he continued, "You were able to say, as a black woman, what we black men could never say and be heard."

It meant more because I knew him as a fine Christian gentlemen and the father of my young minister friend, Enoch Henry, Jr. I thanked him, for he had revealed to me the deep feeling that the black man had carried as a burden all those years.

Ethel Rallins also remembers that speech:

"It was a most spiritually uplifting experience as my family and I sat viewing the late news on TV, when word came from Dallas, Texas, that Rosa had confronted an entire General Assembly in their struggle to respond to a resolution dealing with the question; What should be or should there be a position taken by the church on interracial marriages and adoptions? Then came the many newspaper reports of Rosa's message to the Assembly. Her plea that no person or body of persons have the right to pass judgment on what should be the status of anyone's relationships. This gave me immeasurable courage to take a stand for freedom of choice for everyone."

Dr. Martin Luther King, Jr., spoke at the convention and the auditorium was packed. He gave a stirring speech, bravely attending without bodyguards. After the speech was a panel, and I was asked to be on it.

The subject of the forced intermixture of races came up again that November when I was invited to speak at a special Thanksgiving dinner at the Lincoln Avenue Christian Church, in Fremont, Nebraska, where Gerald L. Peters was pastor. It was such a fine new congregation. Jerry shares his remembrance of my visit at the Peter's home:

"Rosa spent the night in our home. It was then that she spoke of something that has stuck out in my memory. She talked about the feeling of shame regarding the way the white men had violated the black girls during days of slavery and even since and therefore caused her race to be impure. This was a matter that I had never considered before, but since then have often recalled the pride she was expressing in being black and the shame that she felt because of what these men had done."

Upon reaching home, the most important piece of mail I picked up was a special greeting announcing the birth of a baby girl to Rahila and Marly in Nigeria. I could scarcely believe my eyes when I read that they had named her "Rosa" for me. Blessed Jesus, what an honor.

I found more and more requests from Women's Day services and retreats. I was in fourteen different states for six different denominations besides ecumenical groups like Church Women United, Operation Good News, American Leprosy Missions, and Ashrams. I also had my first experience with 4-H clubs in Missouri and spoke for several grade and high schools. Many of my requests came as a result of contacts I had make all over the world.

A few months later, I once again experienced the frustration of being unable to find lodging at a hotel. This time, however, it was not racism to blame, but baseball. It was the 1967 Convention of the Disciples of Christ in St. Louis. The St. Louis baseball team was in the World Series and as a result there was not a room to be had in the whole town. A good friend, Maudie Wilson, from Lincoln, Nebraska, recollects that several Nebraska friends once again came to my rescue.

One of the most enthusiastic and vibrant Christian Church preachers and evangelists was Rev. L. O. White. His spirit of evangelism was contagious. Some of my happiest memories were of several preaching missions we did together. But one of those missions was also linked with one of my saddest memories, the tragic assassination of Dr. Martin Luther King, Jr.

We were in the midst of a preaching mission at Centralia, Washington, when the shattering news reached us. I was completely devastated.

Rev. L. O. White recalls the tragic day in March 1968:

"The sanctuary had been filled each night and sixty-one people responded to the invitation on that last Sunday of the two-week mission, largely because of Rosa and her witness.

"It was during this mission that word came of the murder of Martin Luther King, Jr. We were all shocked and grieved. Rosa was crushed. However, she rose to the occasion, and the church was moved by the vile act as they never would have been without Rosa to witness.

"Because of the tragedy, the sanctuary seemed to overflow with the healing power of the gospel as the people joined together in their heartfelt outpourings to God."

15

I Walked Today
Where Jesus Walked

I NEVER visited Washington State without visiting my good friends Dorsey and Goldie Cunningham. It was always a joy to be with them. Goldie writes enthusiastically about one trip:

"I called Rosa and said, 'When are you coming to see us?' and she said, 'In two weeks I will be in Seattle to attend a ministerial conference of all denominations.' She said that on Sunday she would speak at 4:00 p.m. to the young people—high school and college groups—and that at 7:30 p.m. she would lead the singing in that great civic auditorium for the conference.

"I suggested to her that she come on Saturday and stay with us and speak at our 11:00 a.m. service on Sunday morning. Then, Dorsey and I would take her to Seattle for the 4:00 p.m. appointment. Our congregation loves to hear Rosa's inspiring messages, and no one goes to sleep when Rosa Page Welch speaks!

"On our way to South Tacoma, the weather was perfect and Rosa was enjoying the scenery, something she had never seen before because she usually comes to Seattle by plane.

"We did a lot of visiting on this trip enroute to the Viking where we had reservations to eat. We had already worked up an appetite when all at once—BANG! a terrible noise! Dorsey said, 'That's a blowout!' This was something new for us, and of all times to be delayed because we were running on short time anyhow.

"Dorsey said, 'Now, what will we do? We will have to cancel our lunch at the Viking and get this tire fixed.' I knew he didn't know much about fixing a tire when he had on his good clothes. All at once I noticed a gas station about a block up the street and thank the Lord, it was open and doing business!

"There was a small restaurant across the street from the gas station. Dorsey said, 'You ladies go over there and have some lunch, and I will stay with the car. The attendant will work faster if I am here, and that's what we need—speed to fix the tire.' So Rosa and I did as our chauffeur suggested.

"The cafe was neat and clean. We found a nice place to sit and I asked for a menu. The waitress didn't offer us one and she acted as if she didn't want to wait on two good-looking and well-dressed ladies like us. 'Oh,' I said, 'we only have time to eat a sandwich.' The waitress still didn't take our order, and I explained that my friend was to be on a program at 4:00 p.m. at the civic auditorium and again at 7:30 p.m.—and that we were delayed because our car had a blowout.

"While the waitress was talking to the cook, I looked up and saw a sign on the wall that said, 'No colored folks allowed.' I was hoping that Rosa had not seen the sign. I bowed my head and said, 'Dear Lord, help us out of this situation.' About that time here came the cook. He had heard me tell the waitress why we had to be in Seattle for the ministerial conference of all denominations. He asked many questions and Rosa had all the good answers. He couldn't believe that Rosa was asked to come from Chicago to Seattle and be on this most important program twice in one day.

"After talking to Rosa, he asked if anyone could go to the meeting in the evening at 7:30 p.m. Rosa said 'yes.' He looked very happy and said, 'You might see me there tonight.' I thought he was joking. Then he walked over to the sign and took it down and replaced it with a sign that read Cox Restaurant.'

"Dorsey and I went to the auditorium early. I wanted to see if Mr. Cox was really in the audience. About 7:20 p.m., Mr. Cox came in—all dressed up.

"After the meeting was over, he waited for Rosa. Many people were going to the platform where eight prominent ministers took part in the evening's program. They were standing with Rosa. Dorsey and I thought, 'How nice to see all those speakers all together on the stage.' Mr. Cox came over to see us and to tell us how happy he was to be at the meeting and hear Rosa lead that huge crowd in singing the beautiful gospel songs. He said, 'Mrs. Cunningham, I am going to attend church more often'."

One of the highlights of 1968 was my co-directing a tour of twenty-one days to Rome, Lebanon, the Holy Lands, Turkey, Bulgaria, Russia (Moscow and Leningrad), Finland, Sweden, and Denmark.

Our tour group consisted of a mixed group of fine, congenial and friendly people representing four or five Christian bodies and a number of professions, ranging in age from eighteen to eighty-four years. We had many revealing, inspiring, and challenging experiences.

It was always a pleasure to return to the countries that I had visited, for I always saw more the second time. However, the country that intrigued me most on this particular tour was Russia, for its vastness and mysterious nature were alien to me.

In Moscow they said the hotel where we had been assigned was full, and we had to go to another place of lesser quality. One morning I was in my room all by myself and the maid came in. She commented with sign language on what I was wearing. She was kind and the only way we could express our love and concern was with the use of our hands, eyes and shoulders.

The guides on the tours were women and they spoke impeccable English.

We were there on a Sunday, and I had heard about a Baptist church. We asked at least six taxi drivers and none of them knew where the church was located. We finally got there, and a guide told us that at one time there had been 700 churches in Moscow and now there were only four. They were limited to certain hours so there were funerals and weddings and worship services all going on in different areas of the church.

In Leningrad there was a park where you could stand and look over into Finland. We went to Finland and back to Copenhagen, where we stayed two days and two nights. We also went to Athens, Greece.

Later that summer, I had an experience with the Bart and Jeanette Wilson family. Their little son, John, had come to a Nebraska family camp near Lexington. He was a brown-eyed boy who challenged me from the time I met the Wilson family. Jeanette, the camp nurse, observed our little drama and described it perfectly:

"Rosa Page was not the first black lady John had ever seen, but she was the first one he had ever been close enough to talk to and touch. He was about five years old and really shied away from Rosa Page. I asked him what was wrong because John was always so friendly with everyone. He said he was afraid of black people. Rosa Page was way ahead of me because she had sensed something wasn't right between her and John. Rosa Page talked to John from a safe distance the first night. The next morning she sat at our table for breakfast and shared some fascinating stories about her travels in other countries. John still kept his distance and in mid-morning Rosa Page walked into the room where John was playing and played ball with him, which was his favorite pastime. I had to go see Rosa Page to make arrangements for the evening program and asked John if he would like to go with me. Well, John always wanted to go someplace, so away we went.

"Rosa Page was resting on her bed when we got to her room. The door was open and when she saw John standing there watching her, she invited him to come in. She did not stand up but sat on the edge of the bed and looked John square in the eye and said, 'What can I do for you, John Wilson?' and reached a hand toward him. I could see the wheels turning in John's head—whether or not he would go to Rosa Page or stand his ground. He finally decided he would take a chance and went over to Rosa Page but stopped and without touching her, just looked. I could see great love and compassion in Rosa Page's eyes. She wanted to give John a big hug in the worst way, but she recognized John wasn't ready for her hug.

"We had several other encounters with Rosa Page but never contact in the next two days. Then suddenly John had something to show her. He sought her out and grabbed her by the hand, leading her across the camp grounds to a wooded area and there he had left his friend Philip Piper to guard their fabulous treasure. Philip was down on his hands and knees looking at something. Rosa Page had to bend down real low to peek through the tall grass to see the beautiful black and orange caterpillar that the boys had found. John was so excited, he said, 'Look! Rosa Page, he is black like you and pretty too!' That's all it took and from that minute on John and Rosa Page were best of friends. John got a lot of hugs and kisses from his 'very own' black lady. John always looked forward to family camp and was especially happy when Rosa Page was there to give him a big hug."

The program planners for the annual meetings of the National Council of Churches of Christ dared to hold their annual conference in Chicago, practically 'on the heels' of the fiery eruptions that had surrounded the 1968 Democratic Convention there.

Although they realized the risk they were taking, delegates were housed in the same hotel that had served as the Democratic Convention Headquarters.

The challenge of all this, along with the fact that it was to be the last meeting of the many sections of the Department of Christian Education of the NCCC, brought one of the largest assemblies of Christian educators from all over the nation that we had ever met.

I was thrilled to be asked by Dr. Olivia Pearl Stokes, staff associate of Urban Education, to help in the planning and the carrying out of the worship programs for the entire week.

The theme of the week was "Man in the City" and it was a joy, not only to work with Olivia but my good friend, Dr. Ross Snyder, professor of Christian education at the Chicago Theological Seminary.

The atmosphere was filled with a sense of pride and renewal as the fast-spreading new philosophy, "Black Is Beautiful," permeated the whole assembly and cast a new spirit of cooperation and support. As Olivia Stokes later wrote in her letter of appreciation to me, "The sensitivity with which you sang, 'I Listened to the Agony of God' moved us all. I suppose the people discovered this agony even more as they moved out and found it among God's created human beings."

That spring and summer were filled with concerts, summer conferences, retreats, and sharing with local churches across the land.

I had to move to Denver; I really liked that area of the country. The people seemed so friendly and receptive and it was easy to get to most any place in the country from there by air, rail, or bus. I had looked around for housing each time I was in the city. To my great surprise the Park Hill Christian Church had even extended me an invitation to become their resident pastor which I considered seriously, but I didn't feel God was calling me to that type of ministry. My Colorado friends kept me busy with various church events. Mrs. T. Earl wrote her appreciation after one of their Church Women United sessions in the Rocky Mountain area, "Rosa was the speaker at a Church Women United area meeting. We had an unusally large crowd and she gave such an inspirational message and we'd never had such a large offering. One older woman said to me, God has never been so near to me as he was this afternoon."

The big assembly of Christian Churches, which was scheduled to meet in Mid-August of 1969, afforded me another opportunity to visit the great Northwest in Seattle, Washington.

The tense and heated discussions during the business meeting of that great assembly had been particularly provocative. Many had voiced their opinions and convictions, leaving some with doubt and mistrust concerning the resolutions that were to be passed. Nellie Kratz relates a highlight of that meeting at least for us:

"The black caucus was meeting at the same early morning hours as the Disciples for Mission and Renewal and sent a delegation to the later meeting to say that they were planning to ask for the microphone and present a gift to the black organization and wanted it to be done publicly. Rosa Page Welch had consented to receive the gift and they wanted to ask me to request the mike and present it. The issue had come before the assembly as an emergency resolution and had been voted down. The morning paper had carried the banner headline, *Another Denomination Says No to Civil Rights Group.* That headline was what drove our black caucus to plan the action.

"I knew that it would not meet with approval by those in positions of responsibility, but I conferred with my regional minister and the president of the Women's Fellowship of my region and went ahead.

"My dear friend, Al Pennybacker, was presiding. I went up to the edge of the platform and asked if I could make a statement from the platform. Whether he knew what it was about or whether he just trusted me, I don't know; I made the presentation of money and pledges,—over $1000—and beautiful Rosa Page made a lovely appreciative acceptance speech. There was a very big cheer, but then who wouldn't cheer Rosa Page Welch!

"On the way out of the convention hall, I was stopped and rebuked by one of our greatest leaders and one of my dear friends, and Rosa was scolded by his wife. I simply said, 'You have been supportive and approving so often—if you differ with me this time, I have to accept it.' I was sorry that at the business session the next morning the moderator saw fit to publicly rebuke Al Pennybacker for allowing the interruption."

Although disagreeable and unpleasant things may happen in church groups or conventions, we have to acknowledge that God's reconciling love and forgiveness are always available if we but seek it.

When Oma Myers invited me back to Nebraska to serve as guest leader for an annual family camp to be held at Halsey over the Labor Day weekend, I was filled with anticipation, because it would be a new experience.

Oma Lou and I had purposely selected as the basis for the weekend discussion excerpts from "The Black Manifesto." All that hot summer, there had been civil riots and racial disruptions throughout the United States. Some of the worst riots took place in Omaha, as well as in the Watts area of Los Angeles, and in Detroit. Each adult in the group that encircled the table was given a copy of the material. One of the participants, Dick Rhinehart, when he noticed the subject for discussion, left his copy on the table, withdrew from the circle and sat a distance apart. As Bill Campbell remembers:

"I'll never forget how one of the young husbands quite strenuously opposed the discussion and I was amazed how Rosa, in her sweet way, was able to handle the situation. By the end of the first session you could feel a softening in his attitude and before the camp was over she had miraculously changed his thinking. She had completely won him over and he was loving her like anyone else. It was this kind of response on Rosa's part that brought Dick to the decision that maybe he'd better take another look at this."

At this camp I told the people that when my grandparents had been sharecroppers they were subjected to cruel injustices from the landlord, never being allowed to keep their fair share of the crops. I also told them that my father often had gone to vote and had stood in line for hours, along with so many other blacks, only to be turned away without being able to exercise his hard-earned privileges of voting as an American citizen. And how, when traveling with a couple through Mississippi, we were all denied the use of the restrooms, as well as being refused service in restaurants. Many in the group showed their surprise.

The camp ended with a high note of loving enthusiasm and total acceptance. As we formed the final friendship circle I was overjoyed to see that my life-discovered theory was working. You can *love* hate out of people. Another of my most deeply spiritual experiences was a week spent with the Augustana Lutheran Church at Minneapolis, Minnesota, and their illustrious minister, Dr. William Berg, whom I recognized as one of our modern saints. We served with a team of Christian leaders, Dr. E. Stanley Jones, who, in spite of his eighty some years was still that dynamic servant of Christ.

I had a thank-you letter from Brother Bill in which he wrote:

"Thanks for your letter expressing gratitude for your visit here. But we are the ones who are deeply indebted to you for your presence and radiant witness for Christ in our midst in the Mission.

"God has given you the wonderful gift of communicating Christian love and concern and understanding in a beautiful non-verbal witness—through the glow of your personality, and through your giving yourself in friendship and goodwill and in joyful mood to others.

"In addition, you have the gift of music in which you so effectively communicate your sense of the presence and glory of God to others. God bless you and keep you going in this ministry!"

Having friends remember you is one of my richest joys. To have the following account take place is among my greatest pleasures:

"We, [the A. T. Degroots] took up residence regularly in Estes Park. We learned that Rosa Page Welch was to speak in her church, an integrated one, on Woman's Day. We decided to surprise her with a visit, so we went there on that day. We enjoyed not only the worship and her address, but also the dinner which we shared following the service. She always brought uplift and advancement to all the people, including the inspiration and joy of her splendid singing. It is always a joy to say, yes we know Rosa Page Welch."

Sometime later I traveled to New York City, for unbelievably, I had been chosen as one of the recipients of the Ministerial Interfaith Association's Reconciliation Awards.

Their intent was to make our religious beliefs a practical asset to our world. As the Awards booklet stated:

"We first preach and teach reconciliation to God and we do this by 'binding up the broken hearted' setting at liberty the captive (both of mind and body) and bringing good news to the poor.

"An idea came to us that we should recognize those who had been in the forefront in this business of reconciliation through the years. Therefore, we attempted to bridge the generation gap by showing our young people what great men and women have done in the past. We are also attempting to stem the tide of polarization between races and faiths in our communities, by showing what great souls are now doing in these fields. The scandal of the Christian Church has been the schisms and the manifestations of the brokenness of man through the brokenness of the church. All along there have been those who have given themselves to the healing of wounds in the body of Christ. Some of these we honor."

Thirty-five persons, ten women and twenty-five men, were honored. All the women were black. Among the other recipients were Marian Anderson, Jane Bolin, Terrance James Cooke, Lawrence L. Durgin, Harry Emerson Fosdick, Thurgood Marshall, Norman Vincent Peale, A. Philip Randolph, Ralph W. Sockman, Olivia P. Stokes, Franklin Clark Fry, and, posthumously, Robert F. Kennedy, Martin Luther King, Jr., and Dr. Samuel H. Sweeney. I just couldn't believe, as I recognized these esteemed leaders, that I, Rosa Page Welch, was being honored along with them.

In the spring I had the exciting experience of going to Waynesboro, Viriginia, for a week to rest a bit and then to tape my first stereo LP record. We entitled it "Rosa Page Welch Sings of God's World and His Wondrous Love." It was a glorious experience! My voice naturally wasn't as flawless as in my younger years, but I'm sure I had within me more of the Spirit of the One who had blessed me with a good voice. I shall always be grateful to the dear couple who anonymously chose to finance the project.

I was so pleasantly surprised to learn that I was listed in the first edition of *Who's Who Among American Women.*

But equally pleasing was a letter from S. Loren Bowman, the General Secretary of the Church of the Brethren, stating that I had been elected to their General Board. I was the first person outside of the denomination to become a board member under the new provisions that allowed them to name one person each year on the basis of expertise in denominational and ecumenical affairs.

16

Equal Opportunity Demands Equal Responsibility

THE Protestant Women of the Chapel are the wives of servicemen. My good friend, Mossie Wyker, had gone to Europe and worked with the Women of the Chapel so I had gotten quite interested in such a program. I had heard her report at a United Church Women meeting and realized what a tremendous service it was but found myself thinking, *Oh, they probably wouldn't invite a black woman.*

I was privileged to meet Ruth Youngdahl Nelson at a Lutheran Women's Conference where I led the singing and she reported on her experience with the Protestant Women of the Chapel in Europe. She was the second church leader of my acquaintance to be invited to serve in that capacity. She was a powerful speaker and a marvelous Christian. This tremendous experience began a lasting and rewarding friendship between us. Dr. Nelson, Ruth's husband, had been recognized as one of the twelve outstanding Protestant ministers in the nation. One of Ruth's brothers served as the governor of Minnesota and later on the Supreme Court.

In about a year, after Ruth returned from serving the PWoC, lo and behold! I received an invitation to go on a similar mission. While she had been there, Ruth had suggested my name.

I was faced with another terrific decision, for I had long declared myself a pacifist. I recognized this as a marvelous opportunity to witness for Christ among these women in a military situation, yet my strong belief that war was wrong led to many prayerful moments before I decided to render this service. After I had spent three weeks in Northern Europe, Ruth's cousin, Chaplain Stevens, who was in charge of all the PWoC assignments, invited me to go to the military bases in Alaska. Then because the Southern European group had heard of my service in Northern Europe, they too invited me.

Almost every evening throughout the tour we had a lovely dinner and usually the Commanding Officer and his wife were guests. The chaplains were also nice to me, and as I moved from one base to the next I just knew the Good Lord meant for me to be there. It was really the church at work.

I had gone under the auspices of the Air Force. One day an Army chaplain asked me if I could spend a few days in England on his base; so he got permission from the Air Force for me to spend several days with them.

I was anxious to get acquainted with these young women of the PWoC. My heart never went out to any group of young wives as it did to those I found on those bases. It was almost as if I were in the mission field again. The way they honored me and the joy they expressed at having me with them was very gratifying. Some of them would come to me in their loneliness and pour out their hearts.

I came to understand the worry they all were going through, the deep concerns they shared about their husbands' safe return. I always took time to lead them in singing, for it did more to lift their spirits than talking to them.

We flew down to Madrid near the big naval base in Rota, Spain. The chaplain asked me if I would be willing to go across and meet the servicemen on board a big ship. Many of the sailors were black. We got on board and went to the chapel and the men came in. Some looked lonely, some disinterested, and I felt so sorry for them.

On the Southern European trip I was in Germany, Turkey, Italy, Spain, and Greece and Crete. I'll never forget the experience in the chaplain's home on the Isle of Crete. We had flown from Athens to Crete. While in Turkey I had met the president of the Crete PWoC chapter. She was a beautiful black girl who was deeply spiritual.

I was invited to the Crete chaplain's home for dinner to meet his wife and two teenage children. They were anxious to hear about the Civil Rights Movement and what had happened. The chaplain told me of his son's being a champion of the racial cause. The father said, "Mrs. Welch, tell us about conditions, now." I told what had happened to many white people who went south to help. Some of the white Civil Rights workers had been able to get into the homes of the white residents. All of us kept a record of our conversations at that time.

I told of the white people from the North who went down representing all white people. Seventy white Methodist ministers had to leave the State of Mississippi, some of them because it was too hard for them to refrain from preaching the truth and others because they were asked by their congregations to leave because they had spoken favorably about the Civil Rights Movement.

By the time I'd finished the story the chaplain, with teary eyes shared, "Mrs. Welch, I was one of the seventy. That's why I am now serving as a chaplain in the military."

I had to fly home on a big military plane and it was a miserable trip. The seats were straight up and did not recline and every seat was taken. The cargo was in the middle and the seats were in front and behind. I don't know when I was ever so glad to get home.

After a few days' rest in my quiet Denver home I reflected on my trip, and somehow the marvelous experiences with those young service families had given me the assurance that, whether in war or in peace, God could still use me to tell of his goodness.

The Regional Assembly of the Central Rocky Mountains of the Disciples of Christ was held at the South Broadway Church in Denver. The national leaders present were Kenneth L. Teegarden, President of the Christian Church, and Dr. A. Dale Fiers, Executive Secretary of the UCMS. Walt Lantz was the regional minister and I was again humbly appreciative when Mr. Lantz presented me with my Retired Ministers' Pin.

I was thrilled when my old camp buddy, Dennis Savage, who was pastor of the First Christian Church in Whittier, California, invited me there for a few days since he knew I was coming there for the annual meeting of Church Women United. It was so great to see my friend again. We had such fun reminiscing until late at night about the times we'd shared at summer youth conferences.

When I registered for the Greater Pittsburgh Conference, I had the following reply from the secretary to the registrar.

"It is always an exciting time when the mail arrives, but there was a special excitement and joy when I saw the name on one envelope, Mrs. Rosa Page Welch. That name brought instantly to mind a flood of memories of the great auditorium on the campus at Purdue University when 6000 women of the Presbyterian Church gathered for their national quadrennial meeting (my dear mother and I among them) and Rosa Page was on the platform each morning, leading us all in a deep worship experience as she sang 'Spirit of the Living God, Fall Afresh on Me.' That was the first time I had ever heard that beautiful song which has been so much a part of my life ever since."

I then dashed off to speak at the North Heights Christian Church in Wichita and this newspaper story followed the event:

"The 12th Century prayer of St. Francis of Assisi might well be the very now prayer of Rosa Page Welch as she brings her own special brand of peace, hope, light and joy to members of North Heights Christian Church and everybody else with whom she comes in contact.

"She is a quiet woman, but when she recounts her experiences working for the church—her voice has a ring of excitement.

"When speaking about her work with the Protestant Women of the Chapel she says 'I don't think I have done anything that has meant more to me spiritually than this. I met so many wonderful people. I'm a pacifist, and when I was first asked I did a lot of thinking and praying about whether I should take part. Spiritual hunger is very prevalent and the women were precious. I was so impressed with them. They have all the problems we have plus living away from home.'

"Mrs. Welch is also disturbed by the hatred arising on all sides in our own country, and the troubles around the world are heavy on her heart. When she addresses groups she doesn't often look at her notes. 'I depend on the guidance of the Holy Spirit and go on the response of the people. I'd like to help people understand that the whole of life must be related to God because he is the giver of life. I'd like for them to understand the love and joy of the Christian life. Faith instead of doubt, hope in the place of despair, joy rather than sadness, love replacing hate; this is what Christianity is all about. If you still have the same ugly attitudes toward people after you have accepted Christianity, nothing has happened to you. You can dislike the ways of people, but you've got to love the person because he is God's creation. People are afraid; they don't understand that everyone needs love. So many people do the things they do—drugs, crime, suicide—because they think nobody cares. And it is so simple to smile at a person, to speak to someone.'

"Mrs. Welch feels that the reason religion means so little to so many people is that they are not willing to put anything into it. People get so caught up in materialism or they go to church out of habit, or they use church for their personal benefit. She doesn't promise that religion is going to make everything come up roses in a person's life. But it can make a significant difference. It's not so much what happens to us, but how we are using what happens."

Since I had moved to Denver, I had filled the pulpit many times for my little church and had spoken for Scout Sunday when First Christian invited our small Park Hill congregation to attend that service.

I just can't believe all the invitations I've gotten over the years to sing at weddings and anniversaries. Busy as I was, I always tried to attend, especially those of my close friends. One such special occasion was the Golden Wedding Anniversary of my dear friends Dorsey and Goldie Cunningham.

Two more local church requests came in from Nebraska. I spoke at East Lincoln Christian Church at their annual Thanksgiving Dinner. The following Sunday I was to speak for the Women's Day service at the First Christian Church in Nebraska City. Both occasions were well attended and I always appreciated the friendliness of the people in Nebraska.

I was always surprised and pleased when I was invited to serve in some capacity at community conventions. The Mayor's Conference on Women, held at Temple Buell College, asked me to serve on a panel of women in organized religion. I appreciated the opportunity to meet with church friends, both black and white, and share in the responsibility of discussing and solving the most difficult problems we faced. I firmly believed that in all things, "Equal opportunity demands equal responsibility."

I've been blessed by taking many tours and each one seems to have been better than the last. A Christmas letter I received from my good friend, Mr. Wade Rubick, a legal consultant for the United Christian Missionary Society, reports on our 1975 tour:

"This is just to say again how wonderful it was to have traveled with you and our other twenty-five friends on Holy Crescent Tour. I still can't believe that we did all those things, saw all those people, and visited all those places. It's just too incredible."

Mr. Rubick and Kathleen Bailey Austin served as co-directors of the tour, and their fine leadership made it one of the most significant of any of the tours I was privileged to take.

In Egypt at Cairo we met the top Christian officials. We had an audience in a tiny chapel with Mary, a woman who had been brought to the States by Church Women United, and being aware of our coming she had made the arrangements for us to meet the highest Christian official in Egypt, His Holiness Pope Shenuda, of the Coptic Orthodox Church.

We met him at a huge compound with a big school and church. He told us about the school and the young people there. The Christians in that area had suffered a lot of persecution. It wasn't easy, for in all of these countries, Christians usually clustered all together as a sort of protection where Christianity was not the predominant religion.

In Kuwait there were very few Christians. We were there on a Sunday; so Wade asked the proprietor of our hotel if we could have a service there. They let us meet in one of the lunchrooms. There were no Protestant churches, but there were missionaries there.

We went from Kuwait to Rome, where the highlight of our visit was walking through St. Peter's Square.

In Teheran, Iran, we attended a worship service. We had to be very careful about holding services. We understood that freedom of religion was as we had never understood it before. We realized what it meant for Christians to be persecuted and afraid. Later when we went on to Iraq, we crossed over into Russian territory, where there were a few open churches. After a few more days of travel we arrived in Turkey. All the travel made me realize again the vastness of God's world.

Even with the limitations, we were so grateful to share communion with fellow Christians in Algeria, Kuwait, and Hungary. The one at Kuwait was perhaps the most limited. We had to use water instead of wine or grape juice, for the government of Kuwait prohibited the sale, or even the use of alcoholic beverages, which even included grape juice.

These worship services gave me a chance to sing my most used spiritual "Were You There?" and the beloved hymn "How Great Thou Art." We all appreciated the spiritual knowledge we had gained on this meaningful tour, but we unanimously agreed that it was so good to be home. Wade Rubick expressed it best when he wrote; ". . . Maybe you would say along with me that there was nothing quite like coming home." Sam Dixon added "It sure m akes you appreciate the USA," and I certainly do agree.

Blessed Jesus, I was so weary that I decided, for the moment, at least, that I would never go on another overseas tour.

The Christian Churches of the Denver Metropolitan District presented a Silver and Gold Concert at the Central Christian Church. I was asked to be a guest artist with Arland Johnston. Actually this concert had its beginnings twenty-eight years earlier when I had been an adult leader and Arland was a youth delegate at a CYF Commission in Champaign, Illinois. I represented the Golden Age and Rev. Johnson the Silver.

We talked about doing a concert for over a year before we got down to rehearsing. Arland did things like "Ol' Man River," "I Got Plenty of Nuttin'" and we sang together "Mighty Like a Rose" and "How Great Thou Art," just to mention a few. The chapel was full and we really had a good time. In fact, two years later we did another one and we enjoyed that one too.

I was asked to lead the singing for the first Conference for Women in Ministry for the Christian Church (Disciples of Christ) at the St. Paul Theological Seminary which preceded the General Assembly held in Kansas City, Missouri. It was so exciting for me, for my good friend Winnie Smith was one of the worship leaders. We all attended the General Assembly and heard Mr. Bokeleale, the head of the Churches of Christ in Zaire speak at dinner. Helen Davis writes about an incident following that dinner:

"As we left the room to go to the main convention hall, Rosa, seeing me for the first time, grabbed my arm and for the next fifteen minutes or so, we were oblivious to all the people around as she told me about 'The Greatest Mission of Our Time.' Those were her exact words and for the first time I heard about Habitat for Humanity. As we reached the hall, there was a string of Rosa's friends waiting to greet her, and my dear husband had managed to keep up with us. Rosa said, 'Go right into the book room and buy the book *Bokotola* and read it; it will set you on fire.' My sight was bad and the Christian Board of Publication book room is a big thing at our Assemblies and I felt helpless as I walked in, but a miracle happened, I walked right to it and it's the only book I have been able to read all the way through in a long time. This was just before I lost the sight in one eye, but it did set me on fire, and Rosa and I are both very much involved in Habitat for Humanity."

Once again I was invited to Lincoln, Nebraska, to share in a Church Women United World Day of Prayer dinner and service. During that same weekend in Lincoln, I was able to renew a meaningful relationship when The Church of the Brethren people had a gathering of many of my friends and acquaintances. During the evening many people present told something about the event in which they first met me. I was struck by the many events there had been across the country . In fact, there were even some Nigerian students present whom I remember meeting but Rev. Emmett G. Haas writes of a result of the evening:

"Rosa Page Welch has been a blessing to our personal lives and to East Lincoln Christian Church across the years. Whenever she spoke from the pulpit of our church, it was a memorable event, and our people were inspired by her spirit and the insightfulness of her message.

"The force of her Christian personality came back to us in additional ways. On one occasion Rosa Page was speaking in a sister church in our city. A Nigerian student was present in the audience to hear her speak. One of the families from our church was present and after the service fell into conversation with this Nigerian student. He was very much impressed with Rosa Page. They told him that she was a member of the Christian Church (Disciples of Christ) and invited the student to attend East Lincoln Christian Church. His wife came from Nigeria to join him and they both united with East Lincoln Christian Church. They have had two children during the time they have been in the city, and these children have been dedicated in the Christian life. The whole family has added an important dimension in the life of East Lincoln Christian and it all began with the inspiration that followed out of the life of Rosa Page Welch."

Just as in Chicago and Nigeria, I always loved to have friends in my home. I had learned that in these homey visits, just having a cup of tea brought out the deepest concern as well as the chance to really get to know each other. Patricia Towns Caldwell writes about just such a visit:

"We sat at her little white kitchen table, drinking herbal tea and sharing histories. I munched on a warm slice of her now-famous zucchini bread, wishing aloud that I could cook and bake as well as she. 'Oh, nothing to it!' she offered in reply. Just use what the Good Lord gave you and have a good go at it!'

"Looking around her sunshine-yellow kitchen, I observed that healthy, green foliage grew everywhere. There were fern covered white-framed windows; philadendron crawled down the corner plant-stand and encircled nearby vases; other greenery of various types burst out of glass jars and sprouted their ways toward ceilinged heaven. I've never seen such plants, Aunt Rosa, growing hither and yon. Do you have a special plant food? What is your secret?'

"'Goodness gracious, no, Girl.' She smiled, amused at my naivete. 'You just love 'em. Why, I just give them the basics and love them to life!'

"My rare times with Aunt Rosa on her housecleaning days were both a pleasant and a painful experience for me. Donning old pants, a kerchief and low-heeled shoes, Aunt Rosa's take off like a house-o-fire, with me in tow. Exhaustion would overtake us many hours later, but the entire place would sparkle like a shiny, new penny. 'Whew! Aunt Rosa! How did we get through all this in just one day?'

"'You just take things one step at a time, Child,' she told me, 'and be persistent!'

"I realized then as I do now, that Aunt Rosa's recipe for a good Christian life had been given me in a simple day of domesticity:

"Nobody is perfect and we all have to learn in life. Yet, all we need to do is, 'use what the Good Lord gave us and have a good go at it.'

"We all know that relationships with family and friends can be difficult at times. However, all we need to do is love them. 'Give them the basics,' she said, 'and love them to life.'

"Finally, life itself can be very, very hard at times. Often, we seem to face one challenge after another after another. But, as Aunt Rosa said with a sweet smile I'll remember to eternity, 'Take things one step at a time, Child, and be persistent!'

"Thank you, Aunt Rosa, for sharing with me this Bread of Life."

Lynnette Rhay Biggers, whom I knew from the Yakima Indian Christain Mission, shares her observation from a Western trek:

"At each of the two one-day retreats it was always a time of tears and laughter to watch Rosa Page Welch greet long-time friends. Some drove from neighboring states and communities just to give her a hug and return some of the love she had shared with them over the years.

"At the weekend retreat at Aldersgate Christian Church the whole time could have been spent in 'memory lane' but she would not allow this. She challenged, shamed, inspired and drove us to face the place of our faith and the message of Christ in the world *today*. Women of all ages responded.

"In the midst of all this Loretta McQuary appeared. I had heard her sing when I was a child in Lewiston, Idaho, and had loved her all these years. The thrill of having Rosa call her to the platform and tell how they had sung together through the years was tremendous. When the crowd urged them to sing again there were many wet eyes as the voices from these two great souls filled the hall in 'I Would Be Like Jesus,' and 'I'd Rather Have Jesus Than Silver or Gold'—because they lived what they sang."

During that retreat, I met a pretty and vivacious young minister's wife, Penny Paxton Shorow. Before the week was over she was ambitiously planning for me to come back the following April to lead them in a series of spiritual enrichment experiences, where I would both sing and speak. Penny and her husband were pastors of First Christian Church in Salem, Oregon. I was thrilled that her plans worked out and I found myself going back to Oregon. I was a guest in the Shorow's home for the four days I was there. As Penny relates enthusiastically:

"I had scheduled Rosa so tightly while she was in Salem because she had shown boundless energy when she had been at the women's retreats. And besides I wanted everyone to have a chance to be touched by her. We went to the Oregon State penitentiary first. My husband and I had conducted services there for over eight years. Two months prior to Rosa's visit, however, an inmate had held me as a hostage. It was a harrowing experience and neither my husband nor I had been back to the penitentiary since that episode and I must confess that I was very nervous about returning, especially with so precious a person as Rosa. Many of the inmates had written letters to me apologizing for what had happened, to say that the incident reflected on them and that they hoped we would not stop coming. When Rosa read the letters with me, she encouraged me to return. 'Don't put yourself in a dangerous situation, but Jesus calls us to go to all people. Don't be afraid. He'll take care of you.' It was a shame that our service was limited to one hour because when Rosa began to speak to the prisoners, they were spellbound. She told stories of other inmates she had known and how they had coped with incarceration. She was the grandmother some of the men hadn't seen in years. She loved them and they responded to her so beautifully and many still today ask about her and say that when times get hard, they remember what Rosa had said to them that day.

"Rosa visited our Sunshine Class at First Christian. This is a group of mentally retarded adults who have recently been released from Fairview Institution. She spoke at the worship service to a packed house who responded to her with all the love and affection which she so freely gave that day. She met with the elders. She spoke at the evening service and sandwiched in between all this was an open house in her honor at which she visited with many, many people personally. This was day one, and most of the days were similar. It's a wonder she didn't drop, but she kept going and although tired, she would never let anyone down.

"One day she spent at the Oregon State Hospital, the site of the filming of 'One Flew Over the Cuckoo's Nest.' Her dear friends, Ulista and Dean Brooks, OSH Superintendent, took her all over the facility and spent hours talking about the patients and the kinds of problems they have. Rosa was especially concerned about the patients who had suffered incest abuse and the scars they had as a result.

"She visited the Willamette Lutheran Home, spent one day at the CWF spring fellowship, and spent unforgettable times in the homes of people who were like me—they never thought they would know Rosa personally although they had loved her from afar for a long time. Little kids were taken with her and high schoolers responded to her."

In 1980 I was asked to co-host a tour to five of the Hawaiian Islands,
preceding and including the World Convention of Churches of Christ
meeting at Waikiki in July. Twenty-seven persons were on the tour. We
visited many interesting places, including the Lyman Missionary House
and Museum; Volcano National Park, driving around the Crater Rim
and walking through the Thurston Lava Tube; Hulihee Palace and
Hawaii's oldest church, Mokuaikaua Church; Father Damien's mission to
lepers at Kalaupapa; the famed Fern Grotto; Polynesian Cultural Center;
Pearl Harbor; a Buddhist Temple and the towering precipice of Nuuanu
Paii, with its breathtaking view of Oahu. It was a very educational and
inspiring tour.

Most of our time was centered on the World Convention, the main
reason for our being there.

One of the main speakers at the convention was my dear friend and
traveling companion through Japan almost forty years ago, Hana Kawai.
I was so thrilled with her presentation and her manner of speaking. I was

talking to Kiyo Kamikawa and she told me that Hana had done special work in speaking to prepare for this convention. I was so proud of her and so delighted to count her among my dearest friends.

The 1980 Honolulu convention will long be remembered by me, but the words of Allan W. Lee describe that event:

"I guess the most exciting experience with Rosa Page took place at the 1980 World Convention in Honolulu. As General Secretary, I was presiding at the evening session in Blaisdell Arena before some 6,000 people. It was a happy pleasure to announce and present the Special World Convention Citations which are awarded to only five people each time the Convention meets. I had already presented four Citations and was ready for the final one. Rosa Page was the final award winner, and when I finally announced her name, the entire convention crowd rose to its feet in acclamation and loud applause. Rosa Page was sitting clear in the rear of the arena. It must have seemed like a long walk for her to the front platform and up the dozen steps to where I was standing with the citation. She walked up, hugged me and cried. It was one of the most moving moments of my life. That was the one time I didn't mind getting hugged in front of a crowd! These experiences still remain in my heart and keep me mindful of a beautiful Christian lady who has thrilled and inspired me since my youth."

17

Back To The Quarry

I WAS invited to my hometown, Port Gibson, Mississippi, to lead a Spiritual Life Retreat for my church, Christian Chapel Church. Elias Harris was the pastor and he took me on a sight-seeing tour of the town and I was surprised to see how much it had grown and expanded. We saw a new church and I asked about it. It was a charismatic church and was open to blacks. We drove down by the old railroad station; it was all painted a bright yellow and looked so nice. It had a big parking lot where I remembered several buildings had stood. When I asked about it, Rev. Harris said, "Oh, this is a first-class restaurant now."

"What!" I exclaimed, "Can blacks eat here?" and he replied, "Yes, they can."

He took me to lunch there and as we arrived, I was remembering that the parking lot side of the depot was where the white passengers entered. Blacks had to go around to the back. A white couple was just leaving as we climbed the few steps to the door so we stepped aside. In the doorway stood another young white man. I stood back thinking he was coming out too, but he asked, "How many?" Elder Harris said, "Two." He asked where we wanted to sit. I looked around, and seeing some nice tables near the window, I replied, "I would like to sit by a window." I knew many memories would flood my mind as I looked out on that side of the building where the railroad tracks were and formerly the "Colored Entrance."

When we reached the table the young man courteously pulled back the chair for me to be seated. Well, I nearly dropped, for I had never seen that happen in Mississippi before! I looked around and liked the way it had been renovated. A white man and a black man were sitting at another table. Elder Harris explained that the black man was the executive secretary of the YMCA in Vicksburg.

I looked out the window, recalling the many times we had come here as young people to see the five o'clock Illinois Central Train come in on a Sunday evening. It was our only recreation. I also remembered, as a little girl, the time Booker T. Washington was coming to town and was to give a speech at the station. The schools had been dismissed and Mama and Aunt Sissie and all of us went. Before the train came I got such a terrible stomachache. We could not use the toilet facilities in the station, so we had to return home and by the time we got back, Mr. Washington had finished speaking.

I was called out of my reverie when I heard someone say, "Mrs. Welch!" I looked up to see a very distinguished white woman, who had addressed me as Mrs., a title I had not expected to hear.

"I am Elizabeth McClenden. You may not remember me. I recently retired from the post office where I had worked for many years. I saw the article in the newspaper with your picture and that you would be leading this Spiritual Life Conference at the Christian Chapel Church. I just wanted to come over and greet you."

I replied, "That's very kind of you and I am so glad to meet you."

I sat there thinking: *Am I in Port Gibson where I was born and reared? Is this my hometown and a white man holds my chair for me and a charming white woman leaves her table and comes over to speak to me and addresses me as Mrs. Welch?* Elder Harris was enjoying my surprise and pleasure. Seeing Mrs. McClenden, who was a choir member at the Episcopal Church, promoted him to tell me that he had invited the Episcopal vicar to preach at Christian Chapel on Race Relations Sunday and two or three of his members had come with him. The next year he had him preach at our church again and more of the Episcopal members came, and there were black and white members in the choir as well as both black and white elders presiding at the communion table. Brother Harris was so pleased to tell me about it.

After a wonderful experience participating in the retreat, I was to go to Cleveland to sing at the retirement celebration for Herald Monroe who was State Executive Secretary for Ohio, and for whom I had done various programs through the years, both when he was a local pastor and after he was in state work. Since my only living aunt, my mother's baby sister, Jessie Robinson was living in Cleveland along with both her son and her daughter and their families, I was delighted for an excuse to spend some time visiting all of them. I was staying with the daughter and her husband

and on the day before I was to leave for Denver, just before supper I got a dizzy spell and had to go lie down. I kept feeling worse, and kept praying that everything would be all right, if I could just get my bags packed and get home! They told me to leave my door ajar so they would hear me if I called out. I continued to get more ill, and by the time I realized it, I was too weak to go open the door. Before leaving for work the next morning, my cousin decided she had better look in on me and when she opened the door and saw me she screamed, "Oh Rosa, why didn't you call us?" She called the paramedics and I ended up in the intensive care unit of the hospital for two days, with five pints of blood and all kinds of tests. On the fifth day, the diagnosis was diverticulosis. I had never heard of it before. When I became better I went to be with my family in Chicago for a week. After I got back to Denver, I kept thinking, *That could have happened to me here and I would have been in this house alone*, and I thought, *I've got to make a move*. I did not want to live in the city of Chicago again. I had always loved Port Gibson and had dreamed of going back someday. My children liked to visit there and my sister, Lesly did, too, and even offered to sell her house in Chicago and move down there. Then, when I discovered just how much the racial situation had improved I just decided that that was the place for me now.

My friend, Oma Lou Myers, had been writing my life story and when she learned that I was moving away from the Denver area and going back to Port Gibson, she insisted on spending some time with me to get some information. The only time she and Marj Manglitz could come was the week before I was to move. I dreaded to have company at that time and already I was suffering pains in my hands, but I finally told them to come along. Oma Lou was constantly interviewing me every possible moment that first afternoon and evening. Both of these gals, bless them, proved within a few hours that their being there was helping trememdously in my getting ready to move. So, while Marj packed, Oma Lou and I made seven more tapes.

When I got to Port Gibson, the contractor who was to remodel my house had refused to begin work. I finally had to find another contractor. I had no idea things would be so bad trying to live in the house while it was being worked on. The summer was hot and humid, the remodeling was dusty, drawn out, and very inconvenient.

I was so glad to leave it all behind when I left in July 1981, to attend the General Assembly of the Christian Church in Anaheim, California. I really shouldn't have gone, but getting to see so many old friends made it worth the effort.

In October I went to Mission, Texas, and spent some time in various churches and served as resource leader for a prayer retreat in the valley.

On the Sunday afternoon before Christmas, members of my church, Christian Chapel, the First Baptist, St. James Episcopal, and St. Peter's

AME Church presented a community worship service at the Baptist church. I was asked to read "The Black Madonna" by Margaret Applegarth and I sang "I Wonder as I Wander," "Sweet Little Jesus Boy," and "O Mary, What You Goin' to Name That Pretty Little Baby?"

I was delighted to see an integrated congregation in my hometown, with a goodly number of participants from the various churches.

Sometime in early January, my cousins from the Mississippi Delta were visiting me. My house was still in a mess with the remodeling; Rev. Harris was there too. I heard a knock on the back door and went to answer it and there stood Elizabeth McClenden, the former post office employee and a member of the white Episcopal church. She greeted me: "How do you do, Dr. Welch?" I invited her in and she explained, "I just came by for a minute. I have friends in Florida who send me fruit at Christmas and I want to share it with my friends." She gave me four of the biggest, most beautiful grapefuit and oranges I had ever seen. I introduced her to everyone but she still lingered. Finally, she turned to me and said, "Dr. Welch, my church has asked me to come and ask you if you would direct our choir."

I must have looked shocked and I exclaimed, "What?"

"Yes, we want you to direct our choir."

I said, ' Are you sure?"

"Yes, several of us from our church were at the Christmas worship service, and we saw and heard what you did. We do not have a director for our choir, as the one we had got married and moved to another city. We would like you to be our choir director."

"Oh Mrs. McClenden, are you sure? Do you really mean that?"

"Yes, we do," she assured me.

"Well, I couldn't give up my church."

"You won't have to. Our service is from 9:30 to 10:30 and yours doesn't begin until 11 a.m. and one of us will be glad to see to it that you get to your church on time."

"Can you believe it?" I asked my guests. Their eyes were all big, and they were so excited and exclaimed almost simultaneously, "That is really something!"

"Lawd, have mercy," I exclaimed! This was really the Lord's doing, but I was glad that I was leaving town for a few days to visit in Denver and to see my family in Chicago. That would give them more time to think about it, and it would give me time to see if I was dreaming or not.

Well, I went on to Denver and told my friends. My white friends showed more shock at this news than my black friends did, but they were all very surprised too.

200

When Church Women United held an Assembly at Glen Eyrie, near Colorado Springs, Charlotte Cox Haynes led the singing and Ruth Ann Steele was the pianist. I did not know that Charlotte had such a marvelous singing voice and I said to her.

"Charlotte, why don't you do a concert?" She was shy. Ruth Ann was standing there and I said, "Why don't we all do one together?"

Charlotte writes about that dream:

"The concert really happened on February 14, 1982, when the three of us presented 'Rainbows and Other Promises' at South Broadway Christian Church in Denver for the benefit of the Mother-to-Mother program in Colorado. Doretta Philpot, Colorado chairperson for that ministry, did a fine job of arranging publicity, programs, and refreshments following the concert. We had to plan our part in the concert by mail and had only a couple days after Rosa's arrival to rehearse. What a warm audience it was!! Besides their applause, they gave about one thousand dollars for the work Christian Church women do to help mothers encourage change through their involvement."

Rosa working on a benefit concert with Doretta Philpot of South Broadway Christian Church in Denver and coordinator for the Mother-to-Mother program, and Charlotte Haynes of First Christian Church in Boulder.

We were each presented a certificate of appreciation by Doretta and we really had a good time.

Several of the mothers of the Mother-to-Mother program were present and Doretta had made it a special point to bring a beautiful young Indian woman, with her two lovely children, to meet me and said, "Rosa, I want you to meet this wonderful lady, because you were constantly reminding us of our need to include all minority peoples and now we have this lovely Indian lady."

Soon after the concert I did in Denver, I tried to fly to Lincoln, but we had terribly heavy fog. I left Denver and we could not land at either Omaha or Lincoln; so we were flown back to Denver again. On the next attempt we were able to land at Omaha, and Oma Lou and Marj had to drive through that fog to get me.

After two days of work on the book—reading, revising, and taping— that dense fog finally lifted just in time for them to take me to the airport in Omaha once again.

I went on to Chicago. Welch had had surgery for gallstones but was getting along just fine. Linnie's second daughter Jan was making plans for a July wedding, and her son Mark would be graduating from high school that spring. Lesly was still trying to sell her home there so she could join me in Port Gibson.

I was still wondering if the Episcopal folk had changed their minds; so while I was still in Chicago I called Mrs. McClenden. "I'm calling to ask you if you all still want me to direct your choir."

"We surely do. We are waiting for you."
"When is the rehearsal?"
"We have rehearsals every Wednesday evening."
"I will be back in town on Tuesday."

The first time went very well. I led them in prayer before we began, and our directions for what to sing on any given Sunday came from the vicar. So, we only used the hymns and the responses. I really had to work, for their hymn tunes are so different from ours.

I liked the way the whole congregation sang together and participated in the liturgy and responses. The Episcopal church seemed to enjoy observing all the special days.

My first observance of a special day with this congregation was when my choir and I were asked to participate in the Easter sunrise service. It was held outside and it was quite cool. I was overjoyed to see all of the ministers, both black and white, with their congregations in that assembly as worshipers together.

202

I sat with my choir, and on the first hymn the choir was to lead with the solo on the verse part of "Up from the Grave He Arose" and the congregation was to join in. The words were all printed but the people were not singing. Well, you know me. I stopped them and said, "I really hate to stop you on a morning like this, but do you realize that we are here on Easter Sunday morning? We have gone through this week thinking about the sadness of the suffering and death of our Lord, but this is Easter, the day that he rose from the dead, and we ought to be joyous and happy and sing like we are."

So, they started really singing and by the time we got through the second verse it dawned on me where I was. I felt the Lord was using me. Finally, just before the last hymn I felt compelled to say, "I hope you will forgive me but this is one of the most marvelous experiences of my whole life. I remember that I was born and reared in this town many years ago and here we are worshiping together like this. I never dreamed that I would live long enough to see it happen."

The heavens were suddenly aglow with the approaching sunrise just as I started singing, "Were You There When They Crucified My Lord?" With tears slipping down my face, I led the whole group in the last verse, building to a high crescendo as we triumphantly sang, "Were You There When He Rose from the Grave?"

I have never had a more genuinely beautiful response and acceptance in all my career than at the St. James Episcopal Church. To have been asked to serve as the choir director of this all-white church has proved to be one of the highest honors of all of the many honors that I have received. It has made me realize how many changes have occurred and how many of my dreams have come true between the time I grew up here and my return. Lord have mercy, what a day!

Postscript

"Precious Lord, Take My Hand"

IF ALL the persons we were unable to contact for one reason or another, were added to these approximately two hundred who did contribute to the writing of my life and ministry, like the Book of Hebrews, the pages of this volume would not hold all we have to tell.

Since I readily admit that I am not a writer, I have been so thrilled that others have made the writing of the story of my life a labor of love. As I think about how God has so richly blessed me, I am amazed to realize how much he has used my talents in affecting the lives of others. When one answers the call of God it demands many sacrifices. The cost of discipleship is without limit, but the rewards are deeply satisfying and fulfilling. It afforded me the opportunity of knowing and serving many religious and secular groups all around the world.

I felt deeply that it was a reconciling ministry; almost every group I met began to show an interest in furthering better understanding and acceptance of my people. I struggled constantly with the feeling of guilt. The urgency of my task was in direct opposition to my desire to be with my family and take care of my children. I spent much time in prayer, and finally God answered. Mama was able to come and assist Lesly and Welch in the rearing of the children.

One of the things that helped me continue to reconcile my mission and my family responsibilities was the reading of Dietrich Bonhoeffer's book *The Cost of Discipleship*. Many times I saw the similarity in the way Mary supported her son, Jesus, in his ministry to the way Mama always supported me in mine.

As I used my musical talent to express God's love for all people, I felt that the overwhelming response everywhere I went was evidence of God's sustaining power working in and through me.

The older I become, the more I am concerned with the attitude of many of our black people in keeping alive the memory of the injustices and cruelty imposed upon us in the days of slavery. I use every opportunity to challenge young black people to realize their present day potential in all aspects of life. We need to forget our differences and work together as God's children to improve world conditions for everyone, and to bring about peace and goodwill among all nations.

Somehow we must convince everybody that we are all God's children with common needs of God's love and reconciling grace.

I marvel at the response of those asked to send a short message relating their observance of the effect of my presence, my leadership in song and speaking or conversation with the groups, for I could not do that for myself. Many of these are included in preceding pages. I could only know what God through Christ was doing for me through the sharing of these experiences.

This book is not to glorify Rosa Page Welch but to glorify our Lord, and to help encourage and challenge others to discover the joy which comes when one determines to keep loving, trusting and serving God as long as life lasts, even in tribulation, disappointment or whatever life brings.

There just isn't any way adequately to express my deep gratitude to Oma Lou Myers for penning this book. She did a good job of being me. I am also grateful for her many beautiful friends who helped compose, edit, type, read, or in numerous other ways have given many hours of loving service. I am extremely grateful to everyone, and especially Marjorie Manglitz who read my many diaries, letters and programs, which greatly helped Oma Lou.

My journey of faith is not finished, for I am still on the go. People are still requesting me to speak and sing—not as often as those exciting, rewarding event-filled years, nor of the acclaimed quality, but still with the same sincere desire to portray a wondrous God in the message of song and word, which to me is more important than the melody. I still get a real joy and deep satisfaction with every opportunity afforded me.

My deep desire is that others, in reading my life story, will experience the reality of God's love and in turn be themselves inspired to share it with everyone He has created, wherever they find themselves, and in spite of whatever happens to them—to glorify God.

—*Rosa Page Welch*

Epilogue

ROSA PAGE WELCH had come back to the quarry from which she was mined. The quarry that had shared with the world a precious gem, shaped and polished by the dedicated commitment of one who had chosen to follow Jesus Christ as her Lord and Savior.

Walking in Rosa's shoes has not been easy for the more than three years that I have devoted time and thought to writing her life and ministry. Yet, I firmly believe that it is only when one has fully experienced feelings and similar circumstances that one can truly say, "I understand" or "I know how you feel!"

For this reason, I attempted to step into Rosa's shoes, to feel as she felt; walk where she walked; rejoice with her in all of her happy moments; cry with her as she wept; identify with her as honors and achievements marked her pathway of life and ministry.

My task was made easier, for I found, when all was said and done, that our life principles and goals, our philosophy of life as well as our theological beliefs and practices were almost identical.

My own faith has been strengthened, for this unusual experience has caused me to reflect upon my own life and ministry.

Many times, while penning these pages, I laid the pen down and decided it to be an impossible task, but somehow God would remind me that what I had undertaken needed to be done and that he would be with me all the way.

So, as Rosa would say, I kept struggling with a dream on one hand and present reality on the other, that constantly prodded me to keep on writing.

I am first to say that it was only by the grace of God and the persistent and marvelous help of so many that the story continued to unfold.

My life, my Christian convictions and my deepest feelings have been affirmed as I have spent endless hours "listening" to the dozens of tapes accumulated by personal interviews with Rosa. It has taken seven years of frequently sitting down together either in her Denver home or at mine in Lincoln, Nebraska.

Together both Rosa and I want to express our deepest gratitude to all persons who have contributed in any way in the accomplishment of this, what appeared to be, an impossible endeavor.

Thanks go to Marj Manglitz, who has given countless hours, days, and months these past years to researching Rosa's old diaries, program booklets and newspaper clippings, as well as helping tremendously by putting the chronological facts in order, including the hundreds of letters received from old friends and church leaders the world over; to Wilma Stevens, who worked diligently editing the first draft; to Ruth Cromer, as well as other good friends: Viola Bullock, Elsie Lou Erickson, Loma Jones Chalfant and George Manglitz, for early proofreading.

Thanks go also to the several folk who gave volunteer time to typing; Helen Bogott, who transcribed numerous tapes, Darlene Herriott, for typing multitudinous tributes, names and addresses, and to Marie Schmer, who gave several hours to the transcribing and utilization of taped material. Special thanks should be given to Marilynn Williams, the overall typist of the manuscript.

Last but not least, we want to express our appreciation to David Myers, who has given unlimited time to checking spelling, dates and historical accuracy as well as assisting in the composition of these final chapters. Finally, we express our deep gratitude to my newly found friend and Rosa's life-long comrade in the faith, Mrs. Mossie Wyker, who has written, as requested by Rosa, the Introduction.

Yes, stepping into Rosa's shoes and literally living through her beautiful life these many fruitful years has proved to be one of the greatest and most rewarding projects of my career.

Thus, I thank God for giving us Rosa, the primary content, and for giving me the courage and guidance to preserve what might otherwise have been lost for posterity and to provide for both young and old the inspiration to follow in the footsteps of our Master and Lord.

—*Oma Lou Myers*

Tributes

"If it had not been for Rosa, my first friend of another race, I doubt if I would have become a member of the Chuirch of the Master in Harlem, an association that has lasted almost 40 years. I am indebted to her for my love of the spirituals, my attitudes about worship, and the deep conviction that Christ has broken down the partition and made us one."

Margaret Flory

"We all have to choose how we can best be used to have an influence on the great problems of our day. Rosa Page Welch chose to dedicate her gifts (joy, music and her ability in public speaking) to change us all, and make us better people as we worked with her to open wide the doors to disadvantaged and hurting people everywhere. Rosa Page Welch will continue to disturb and change people as she goes on loving and forgiving wherever she is."

Mossie Allman Wyker

"She stood before us
    in her slim dark beauty
And sang her heart away.
Ballads of far-off places,
Haunting lyrics of our day,
Deep stirring spirituals
    of her choice,
Light, lovely, prayerful things,
And God was in her voice."

Margaret Bradt Southmayd,
OUTREACH, May, 1951
(Presbyterian USA Women's Publication)

"Just ask, 'Have you met Rosa Page Welch?' and people begin to share how she has blessed their lives. God has blessed all of us by letting us know this messenger of Christ."

James H. Tilsley

"Rosa Page is one of the Disciples from this generation who deserves to be remembered. We remember always a warm and gracious lady whose demeanor combined dignity with unpretentiousness and charm—who was always easy to meet and unfailingly friendly, whose singing touched the heart, and who always conveyed a sense of spirituality and inspiration."

Ronald and Naomi Osborn

"I hope this letter finds Rosa praising the Lord as I am sure she is. I never told Rosa this before; but most of my inspiration I received from her and Welch. I taught my choir to sing the songs I heard in Chicago. She also taught me to do the best I could. Rosa was the first to tell me to give God the glory and praise. I love her."

Ruby Henry

"Recently Mrs. Welch had dinner with my mother and me. In this one brief evening, I saw flashbacks of a lifetime of Christian service as I listened to her talk about 'her God'. In a couple of hours, I witnessed a truly contagious Christian personality and ecumenical spirit. Mrs. Welch is a royal servant in whom God is well pleased."

Samuel Graves

"God granted her a voice. He nurtured in her a faith. He planted within her the capacity to love, sincerely, many people. He sprinkled her personality with the dew of contagion. Hers is a contagious spirit! To him be the glory, and to my dearest of dear friends, Rosa Page Welch, goes the thanks for making this life a lot more worth living."

Russell F. Harrison

"Rosa Page was at her best, most persuasive and powerful, when she was able to reflect the Suffering Servanthood reality of her spiritual commitment. Her audiences recognized this for what it was, a genuine reflection of the real Christian strategy in human relations."

John Harms

"Members of the Church of the Brethren have been most fortunate to have had Rosa enhance their annual conferences and Camp Mack mass meetings with her presence and her vocal music through the years. Thousands have heard her and wept as she sang 'Let Us Break Bread Together', and 'Were You There?'

To my parents Rosa Page Welch held a special place in their hearts . . . to those of us who have known her personally, our lives have been better and enriched."

Mrs. James (Carole) Shultz-Davis

"I was first attracted by her singing, then by her beautiful creative philosophy of life, her ringing laughter and her life long loving attitude toward segregation and discrimination in the South or wherever she was confronted with negative attitudes.

"Having been born also in the deep South, many incidents occurred in my life—but she gave me courage. Her beautiful prayer life, and her non-violent direct action were the only way to go. She spoke out. She sang out. She prayed out. She loved out."

Carmella Jamison Barnes

"Rosa Page Welch is truly one of God's chosen people. Her life is a song. The music encompasses all walks of life, just as her activities do—all Christ-centered. We all have grasped for her hand, recalling when we last visited. Yet she makes her friends feel as if *they* are the important ones!

"How many hundred thousands of miles she has logged as God's Ambassador! People are Rosa's business—people from every walk in life; people of every color and creed. People are precious to Rosa, precious because we are all God's people. Praise the Lord!"

Mrs. Robert (Eleanor R. Pope)

"I believe the thing that has amazed me the most about Rosa Page Welch is her memory. No matter where I have seen her over the last twenty years, she has always remembered my name, and remembered me and remembered other times when we were together.

"Considering the fact that she has relationships with people all over the world, it amazes me that she has the ability to remember. To me this reveals that which is most precious about her; namely that she truly cares for people."

Robert Hayes Peoples

"When Rosa Page Welch graduated from the Southern Christian Institute, my father, Walter M. White, gave the commencement address. When he returned to our home in Memphis he said to his family, in telling us of the occasion, 'I heard a young woman sing who had a quality of soul in her voice that I have never heard before; her name is Rosa Page; and I am going to do all that I can to further her musical career.' He did do what he was able to do, and enlisted the interest of others in her, among them Mrs. Mae Potts of Chattanooga, who helped her financially as long as she lived.

"I saw that quality of soul, which my father described, grow and grow as she witnessed to her radiant faith and sang to the glory of God! As we have shared in depth our joys and sorrows, she has taught me of the enabling power of our Lord and how growth in the Spirit is possible."

Adele White Pack

"It must have been in the summer of 1935 that I attended young people's conference in Bethany Park, Indiana. Rosa Page was the interracial representative. It was the first young people's conference in which she had ever worked. She captivated me as she did the entire conference. Years later I attended an International Christian Youth Fellowship retreat in Bethany Hills, Tennessee, as the adult youth adviser for the youth of Oklahoma. Following lunch one afternoon the youth gathered in front of the diningroom to sing. They soon began singing, 'Were You There When They Crucified my Lord?' When they came to the verse, almost by silent conspiracy, all remained silent with the exception of one beautiful voice. It was a moving experience for me, and after it was over I went up to the one with the beautiful solo voice and said, 'I have never heard anyone sing that spiritual as beautifully, other than Rosa Page Welch.' Then she replied, 'I am her daughter.'

"Rosa Page Welch's music and Christian spirit not only lives on in her daughter, but in the lives of literally thousands in our own country and beyond."

Roland K. Huff

"Rosa Page Welch has been our true, golden friend. In September, 1952, Rosa made a trip to Japan, alone. Her visit in the early life of Japan's recovery from World War II with rehabilitation and much reconstruction in progress, made a great contribution. She sang her heart to the Japanese youth; many heard a Negro singer for the first time. She was an ambassador of Christ, a missionary at heart."

Drs. Aigi and Kiyo Kamikawa

"As I thought of writing a suitable tribute to Rosa Page, I could see her, face uplifted, eyes closed, singing 'The Lord's Prayer' or maybe she was leading us all in singing 'He's Got the Whole World in His Hands.'

"Long before most people thought that color blindness was a necessary ingredient in true friendship, Rosa had it. I don't think she ever saw any color differences in any people. Black, white, brown, yellow or red were all alike to her.

"Rosa crossed national barriers too, just as easily as she crossed color lines. I, a white Canadian, know this from experience. She shared a room with me, she invited me to her home, she visited my Canadian family for several days and all of this was before great public demonstrations on race relations.

"Knowing that she, herself, is a child of God, Rosa views everyone else as part of her family and therefore part of her love and concern, regardless of nationality, race, color or creed."

Jessie M. Trout

"We count Rosa Page Welch as one of our dearest friends. Through the years we welcomed opportunities to see and visit with her at Disciple gatherings—the International Conventions, the General Assembly of the Christian Church, the Florida Chain of Missions, the World Convention of the Churches of Christ, at various special meetings and ecumenical occasions, and in our home in Manila and our home in Indianapolis. Her friendship has meant much to our family. Her warm, outgoing personality, her rich, beautiful voice, her Christian witness will be long remembered. She is a courageous woman of conviction and her contribution is beyond calculation."

George Earle and Margaret Owen

"Rosa Page Welch taught me that I had something to learn from black leaders and friendships to be gained with black persons. When I grew up in Little Rock, Arkansas, black and white persons lived in separate worlds. My parents taught me always to honor each person—without regard to race and color. Although we believe in equality, we had little opportunity to know persons of other races.

"Paul D. Kennedy, staff minister for the Christian Church in Arkansas arranged for Rosa Page Welch to be a guest leader at the summer conference for high school youth held at Ferncliff, Arkansas, in about 1940. As a teenager, I became an admirer of this beautiful black woman, who talked of religion simply and powerfully, and who sang with a rich lilting voice.

"In the forty-three years that have passed since then, Rosa Page Welch and I have remained friends, and it has been an important and symbolic friendship. I think there is much greater possibility of genuine friendship across racial lines for Disciples, because of her life and work."

Charles Harvey Lord

"We first met and heard Rosa at an International CYF Commission meeting in the late 1940s.

"After that she came to Washington State one summer and worked several weeks with us in junior high camps and CYF conferences. Her beautiful singing, her warm pleasant personality, and her deep Christian faith has had a profound effect on the life of the Christian Church.

"In 1980, we were privileged to enjoy all her contributions all over again as we were with her on a tour to Greece. Rosa Page Welch is truly one of the great saints of the church today."

Jim and Evamarie Ballinger

"Rosa Page Welch is one of the few friends with whom I've stayed in happy contact through a long and extraordinarily 'peopled' Christian life. I have *tried* to keep up with Rosa because I couldn't help myself. It is Rosa's and the Lord's holy humor that she, an eighty-three year old black musician, conducts music for a white church in Mississippi. I'll wager that her fellow church members don't remember often that Rosa is a somewhat different color. I know I haven't thought of it in years; nor does she seem to notice my whiteness. She's simply God's child Rosa."

Eugenia Price